VALERIY POLEKH

French Hornist Laureate of All Russia

AN AUTOBIOGRAPHY

DAVID GLADEN

WORKBOOK PRESS LLC
187 E Warm Springs Rd,
Suite B285, Las Vegas, NV 89119, USA

Website: https://workbookpress.com/
Hotline: 1-888-818-4856
Email: admin@workbookpress.com

Ordering Information:
Quantity sales. Special discounts are available on quantity purchases by corporations, associations, and others.
For details, contact the publisher at the address above.

Library of Congress Control Number:
ISBN-13:   978-1-960752-57-4 (Paperback Version)
              978-1-960752-58-1 (Digital Version)

REV. DATE: 10/14/2022

CONTENTS

YOUR VALERIY POLEKH

Aknowlegements:

For participation in the preparation of the materials of the book, I express sincere thanks to my son-in-law Andrey Kuznetsov, Zakhar Lozinskiy, and the publisher "Glavnaya Kniga."

Moskow, December, 2005

V. Polekh

ONE

Childhood

I was born July 5, 1918, in Moscow, in Zamorskvorech. Big Kaluzhskaya Street, where we lived, was plowed up for gardens. In the winter Kaluzhskaya Street was covered by the cleanest of snows and sleighs drawn by chestnut horses crawled along icy trails. At Easter, there was a crimson bell and the faithful went to early mass. My parents took my brother and me to church with them. It was interesting to watch the procession of the cross, and after the church service, joyfully go home with lighted candles.

Lyalya Dima age 14, Lyalya age 8

(See footnote)*

We really loved the Christmas holiday. The decorated fir tree, candles, colored lights, and, of course, Christmas presents. In the time of my childhood, the holiday of Christmas was forbidden. It was almost impossible to buy a fir tree, but my Papa, by hook or by crook, got a fir tree. Sometimes, he drove to the forest and cut down a little fir tree, or on Christmas Eve went to the fire-wood yard where late at night, they secretly hauled in fir trees and sold them for a high price. Papa brought the tree to our place—it was usually two meters tall—and hid it in the barn. Not until Christmas Eve came did he bring it into the house. Out of the closet Papa would pull a big box of Christmas decorations. First, a beautiful star was established at the top. After this, balls of various colors were hung, and there was a lot of them.

There were icicles! They were so realistic and made so that it seemed as though drops of water would drip from them. Here, the snowman with a carrot for a nose. Here, the Snow maiden–hanging near her would be little snowy stars. Here, a jolly little cook carried hot pies on a tray. There appeared gold and silver fishies, horsies, and various little animals, puppets and dollies and with them Punch from the show. There stretched a line of beads and Christmas cookies. They were varied—small and large. Around it, on the lower branches hung a golden paper chain. On the heavy branches were fastened candle-holders and candles were standing in them.

Beneath the tree were bon bons with nuts and chocolate-coated raisins. In the middle hung the "Magic Lantern." It had a multi-faceted lens, and in its middle stood a big candle that lighted everything around with rosy flames. That was the Christmas tree and its decorations.

But we had to closely hide all this beauty. You know, it was

---

* Lyalya is a diminutive nickname for Valeriy. Dima is a diminutive nickname for Vladimir forbidden to observe the Christian holidays. The Christmas tree also was under the ban. So, in order to hide our beautiful tree from other people's eyes, we set it up in a large space that had been curtained off earlier.

Christmas arrived, and in the morning my brother and I, having awakened when it was just barely light out, ran to the tree. There awaited us two sacks with Christmas gifts from Grandfather Frost. We wanted to touch everything—every toy, every bead and Christmas cookie. Having looked our fill at the abundance, we ran to the bedroom to brag about the presents to our parents. In the bag marked for me were two beautiful books with pictures, and many colored blocks. My brother got a little collapsible house and a book of stories by Pero. We also received as gifts two tickets to the theater. That is how our beloved Christmas Holiday went.

I remember what Mama did very early in the morning. Often, when I awakened, and opened my eyes, she was already looking at me—my sweet mama with her sweet smile. I would begin to feel so good!

"Mama, sing my favorite song." And she would begin to sing.

Before my eyes would come forth a picture of flowering summer; as though Mama, my brother—Volodya, and I were in the forest. Mama sang with inspiration, in such a gentle voice, that her singing somehow flowed together with shaggy fir trees and birches, with the blossoms of bluebells and dandelions, with wondrous silky grass-spiderwebs. The sounds of Mama's song were mixed with the songs of birds, and the cuckoo was counting out someone's years.

Parents: Vera Alekseevna and Vladimir Vasilevich Polekh

Mama had a phenomenal memory, and remembered a great deal. Whatever I would ask, she had a ready answer. Her memory for music was also amazing. Just let Mama hear some musical performance once, and she remembered it forever. I would go to her with questions about art or music and always received an exhaustive answer. Our Mama did not work: she was occupied with our upbringing and taking care of the household. Weekdays, we were occupied with lessons. Mama read to us or told us about something. Sundays, we went to the movie theater "Velikan," that was located on Serpukhovskiy Square. Mama carefully chose films that would be interesting and useful. We also frequented the dramatic theaters. The first show I saw at MKhAT was *Blue Bird* by Meterlink, and at the Bolshoi Theater we saw the ballet by Punya, *Hunchback's Hobby Horse*. This was the first musical show I had seen in my life and it left a very strong impression on me. Years later, after I had joined the Bolshoi Theater Orchestra, one lovely day I was assigned to the show *Hunchback's Hobby Horse*, and it seemed I remembered the musical ballet from beginning to end.

The school I attended often gave out tickets for shows at the Bolshoi Theater. At that time, the shows were presented at the Lensovet Theater that is on Ordynka and now is affiliated with the

Maly Theater. We heard the operas *Eugene Onegin, Deamon, Barber of Seville, Rigoletto, Carmen, Lakme*, and others.

Attending shows at the Bolshoi Theater was a real holiday for me. I prepared myself for each show. It was essential to go to the barber. I asked Mama to get a white shirt ready, and wore a necktie. Mama told us about the show, about the composer, and what he had written. At the Bolshoi Theater the singers were always brilliant. In my time these were Barsova, Stepanova, Maksakova, Obukhova, Katulskaya, Dzerzhinskaya, Pirogov, Reyzen, Mikhailov, Nortsov, Politkovskiy, Migai, Lemeshev, Kozlovskiy, Alekseev, and Yudin. Mama told about the artists, took us to the Tretyakovskiy Gallery and the Museum of Fine Arts (now called the A. S. Pushkin Museum). Mama tried to expand the range of our knowledge as much as possible, and she succeeded in this to a great extent. We always were grateful to her for this.

Mama monitored our acquaintances very carefully, and asked us to bring each of our new friends home with us. She got to know him, visited with him, found out about his inclinations and interests. If the boy was OK, she gave permission to be friends with him. However, Mama did not do all this as though giving orders, but very quietly, correctly and intelligently. We always were in view. Mama helped the two of us and also our good friends set up interesting evenings, where we drew, sang, told each other short stories, or recited poetry. Mama read very well, and the guys listened to her with bated breath. Sometimes she would invite everyone to tea with home-made biscuits or traditional pirogies with apple jam.

We always gladly helped Mama straighten up the apartment. We called this our voluntary overtime work.

I remember the large, friendly Petrov family—the family of my aunt by birth. Aunt Nastya had six girls and three boys—all of them my first cousins. The head of the family was Nikolai Petrovich Petrov. The Petrovs lived not far from us on Donskoy Street in a small house. In the house, was a large Russian oven with a sleeping platform atop it. Often we youngsters climbed up on the oven bed.

Several long sheepskin coats lay scattered about on it. The bed was both warm and soft and had some kind of special smell—the smell of a Russian oven. Another time, the older children also climbed up on the oven and told us stories that were interesting, but at times, strange. I remember, as I climbed up the oven with difficulty, how the older ones helped me up to sit beside them.

At one o'clock in the afternoon, Nikolai Petrovich came home from work. Everyone sat at the big table. Nikolai Petrovich took oven tongs in his hand and out of the Russian oven pulled an enormous cast-iron kettle of cabbage soup. Aunt Nastya ladled out the soup into bowls. The eldest girl, Lyubochka, sliced dark bread—fragrant and still warm from having just finished baking in the Russian oven. Nikolai Petrovich read a prayer, after which everyone began to eat. The second course was buckwheat porridge with cracklings. This is hog fat cut in tiny pieces, browned to high color, crushed, and mixed with porridge—it was my most favorite course. Nikolai Petrovich knew about my predilection and always told me, "Lyalyon, for you a little extra is given. Eat in health."

The Petrovs really loved puting on a variety of theatrical presentations: plays, vaudeville, and excerpts of musical shows. I remember the grown children put on a play in which boyars had a part. The oldest brother, Seraphim, played the part of Ivan the Terrible. The preparation for the show took about two months.

They made themselves costumes, wigs, and decorated head-dresses. The opening performance drew near. I liked the costume of a boyar very much. To be more accurate, I simply was in love with it. I wanted to participate in the show very much, but the grown-ups did not agree. They said I was still too young. However, I somehow was able to get Seraphim/Ivan the Terrible to agree to permit me to sit at the table on stage in the boyar costume. The day of the show arrived. Everyone was in a excited mood. Someone was getting dressed. Someone was trying out his voice. Someone repeated a monologue. There were many guests: all the many relatives—about twenty people. The room was large enough. There was room for the stage and the audience area. At last, everyone dressed in costumes. I put on the costume of a boyar and sat on stage in my place at the table. It was hot in the house, and the costume was warm. I was to sit in it not less than an hour. It was time to start, but there was no sign of Seraphim—who performed the lead role. This was not like him. He was a disciplined, accurate man. The public was getting upset. Suddenly a shot rang out, and there was loud knocking on the door. Seraphim ran in—pale and with a revolver in his hand. It turned out that bandits had attacked Seraphim, wanting to rob him of the Komsomol's* cash-box. He was forced to run and defend himself by shooting. Seraphim calmed everyone down. The spectators returned to their places. I felt as though I was soaked clear through, but bore it patiently. The curtain opened; we began the show. In spite of the heat, before long, I began to feel myself to be in Seventh Heaven. As usual, the show went on with great success. Everyone was pleased. The performers were called out several times.

We bring away from childhood all that is kind and bright. The First of May—this is when the soul is inspired and rejoices.

Glorious, great First of May—
Holiday of labor and falling of fetters
Glorious, great First of May—
Holiday of labor, and spring, and flowers!
Sisters, put on festive gowns,
Strew the path with garlands of roses.
Brothers, open your arms to each other.
Gone are the years of suffering and tears.

Whole families went out to the parade and walked until evening. They came home tired but jolly and happy. And, customarily, all sat down at the festive table and sang. Wine was not customary. Papa played the balalaika very well, and we sang with his accompaniment.

---

* Komsomol is the Communist Younth Society, an official organization of the Communist Party.

We all loved the Ukrainian songs: *Reveta Stogne, Zakuvala ta Siva Zozulya, Susidko,* and especially *Dyvlyus Ya na Nebo.* Mama and Papa sang very clearly and very melodically. My brother and I also joined in a little, but tried not to interfere. Later on, my brother Vladimir and I learned to sing clearly, and we all sang together. Usually, we sang the melody and our parents split off into harmony. It turned out very pretty. To this day, I remember our musical evenings. I very much wanted to learn to play the balalaika, but Papa categorically forbid me to even touch it. I often dreamed about the balalaika in my dreams and already wanted to hold it. Well, one day, on my birthday, Papa not only allowed me to touch the balalaika, but he gave it to me as a gift. Soon, he began to teach me by giving assignments that were not too difficult. I worked with such pleasure to complete everything Papa required; I so wanted to make him proud. And my efforts did not prove to be fruitless. In a short while Papa taught me to play *Svetit Mesyats, Korobochka,* and *Barynya.* With Mama's help, I picked up a few songs myself. Papa listened to me and was pleased.

A soldier lived in our apartment building. He played the guitar almost like a professional. Papa said that the neighbor knew notes. Once in the evening, from beyond the wall sounded a very lovely melody. Until then I had never heard such a thing. I asked Mama what on Earth melody that was. She answered that it was a very well known waltz, *Over the Waves,* and sang the whole melody through for me. I do not know why, but I wanted very much to play the waltz together with the guitar. That would be great! I on the balalaika, and the neighbor, Nikolai Ivanovich, on the guitar. I felt happy just thinking about it. But, the important military man played the guitar so brilliantly, almost like a professional, that I became even a little terrified. However, my intense desire to play a duet with the guitar overcame all fear. Therefore, I decided all the same to ask Nikolai Ivanovich to play the waltz with me. The neighbor was very surprised by the proposition—such a small child with such stubby little fingers preparing to play a duet with him. Seeing how much I wanted to play with him, he did not begin to insult me and answered, promising, "Well, well, Lyalya child, somehow we will play." That was the result of my request, but all the same hope burned within me. Then one evening, there was a knock on our door. It was the neighbor, Nikolai Ivanovich. I noticed that in his hand he held a guitar—all decorated with mother of pearl. "Well, young man of pleasant appearance, shall we play?" the neighbor asked. With difficulty, I responded, "Yes!" I quickly brought the balalaika. My hands were shaking a little, but the idea that my dream was coming true and I would play a duet all the same gave me both courage and boldness! We tuned the instruments.

"What shall we try?" asked Nikolai Ivanovich.

"A waltz, 'Over the Waves,'" I replied.

"Oho," said Nikolai Ivanovich. "In that case, I will play four bars of introduction for you, and you begin."

Nikolai Ivanovich began the introduction. Lord! How beautiful the guitar sounded! I joined in, and the melody poured out. This was just incomparable bliss! I tried to play very expressively. With its velvety timbre the guitar carefully accompanied me. What I experienced at that time is impossible to describe. I had only one wish—that this bliss would continue as long as possible. However, to my sorrow, the music came to an end.

I began to return to myself. Nikolai Ivanovich regarded me very cordially. He was very pleased with me and advised me to study music. I thanked him. That is how our friendship began. When guests came to the neighbor's, they sang with the guitar. Later, Nikolai Ivanovich invited me, and we played together. I already knew several waltzes and songs.

This was my very first and very earliest participation in an ensemble. I was six years old. After that, began to join family concerts. I Enjoyed playing before the public and before my relatives.

One day, a teacher from my brother's school came to our home. She was working with him on the German language. The teacher noticed we had a balalaika hanging on the wall and asked who played this instrument. Mama replied that her younger son played. The teacher asked me to play something. After thinking a little, I began playing. She listened through almost all of my repertoire. She liked the child musician very much.

The teacher asked,"Sonny, could it be possible for you to play at the school? We are putting on a concert of amateur musicians, and we need artists. What do you think of my proposal?"

I fervently agreed, and Mama gave an affirmative answer. You know, it is so great to play before the public! The day before the concert, we went with my brother to the school. I sat on the stage a little. I played some in the empty hall. This was a dress rehearsal for us. Mama had sewed a bag for the instrument, and I carried my little balalaika there. Now, I would play in public like a real musician!

The day of the concert arrived. I prepared very seriously for the first concert of my life. I asked that they take me to the barber shop, dressed in the best clothes I had with black shoes, white knee-high stockings, dark-blue short pants, white shirt, and a large light-blue bow tie. Mama and Papa went with us to the school. My brother did not leave me for a minute, making sure I did not get lost or break the balalaika. A likable young teacher was conducting the program. When he saw me, he rejoiced greatly, as though Sobinov himself had come. He took me by the hand and led me around the stage for a long time. As a result, he decided to put me on a riser; so everyone could see me.

A pleasant teacher showed me where the performer's room was and gave me some candy. I was nervous and did not start to eat it. I did not know where to stash the candy since I did not have any pockets. I decided to put it in the balalaika bag. I pulled the balalaika out of the bag, tuned it, and strummed a little. After that, I went to look to see what they were doing on the stage and in the hall. It turned out the concert had already started. In the beginning, they showed physics and chemistry experiments. After that, a young girl came out, and sang a well-known Italian song. The young girl was not dressed very well, and was so tall and so plain-looking that

I did not like her at first. However, when she started to sing, it was evident to me that she was a beauty among beauties. The girl sang very soulfully with a ringing voice like a magical little bell. The audience received her warmly. The young teacher I had already met was the master of ceremonies. He read a very funny humorous story. After that they announced the intermission.

They hadsection designated me to open the second part. The teacher carried in a riser, stood a chair on it, carefully sat me on the chair and asked how I felt. I answered that I was alright. "Then," he said, "I will open the curtain." At first, it seemed to me that the hall was empty, and nobody was there. Gradually I began to look more closely, and saw the hall was completely full! I got a little scared, but that same young teacher came over to me and announced me to the audience: "Now appearing before you is the young musician, Lyalya Polekh. He will play for you on the balalaika the Russian folk tune "Shines the Moon." I began to play. Then I played two more short pieces and a waltz. The audience demanded more and more. I was just about ready to play when young little girl approached the stage and held out a pretty doll to me. I was taken aback. In the first place, I was a boy—why a doll? Because the hall resounded with friendly applause, I decided to accept the doll, but I was afraid to get down from the riser because it was high. Then the girl's mother took the doll and put it on the riser. With pleasure, I played my whole program again. The audience still applauded a long time. After this, the master of ceremonies took me down from the riser, kissed me and led me to the wings. I went—holding the balalaika in one hand and the doll I had been given in the other. My parents were very pleased with my performance and my success. I was happy.

TWO

Amateur Activities

M Y RELATIVES, THE PETROVS, began to participate in a drama circle. They performed various plays and musical comedies quite well. I was a spectator at almost all of them. They performed well and with enthusiasm. I enjoyed watching and wanted to perform on stage also, but my age did not permit it. In addition to the drama circle, my cousins began to play in a wind orchestra, and I was lucky more lucky there. They took me with them, and before long, I was playing the alto horn in the orchestra.

The leader of the orchestra was a professional musician, trombonist Yuri Yurevich Gubarev. He knew a lot about orchestras, did arrangements himself, and composed marches. Youngsters and grown-ups who loved music came to the orchestra. For the most part, these were workers from the factory "Red Proletariat" who had never played a musical instrument before. Because of their inexperience, they needed to start with learning very elementary musical theory. Printed charts of scales and intervals were hung in the rehearsal room. Those who successfully passed an examination by the leader received an "elite" card, that con fired the right of several additions to the ration card. At that time, it was hard to receive the elite card; it was given only to the best workers. However, the factory committee wanted very much to have a good wind orchestra and did everything possible to create one.

After the theory of music was mastered and fingering on the instrument was learned, Yuri Yurevich began group assignments with the participants—separately with the clarinets, trumpets, baritones, separately with the altos, tenors and bases. After that, there was combined rehearsals of the whole orchestra.

I remember that long awaited day when the orchestra began performing. It was a real holiday, and it occurred on Aviation Day. The orchestra members arrived early at the factory club house. Yuri Yurevich tuned us up. We began playing a march exalting airmen, *We Were Born to Make the Long Forgotten Tale*. The workers and staff of the factory surrounded the orchestra and listened with great satisfaction. They were proud that now they had their own wind orchestra at the factory. The orchestra opened the solemn part of the ceremony by playing *Internationale*. Everyone stood and listened with bated breath. Later, we played ballroom dances. Everyone was delighted.

The First of May was our most beloved holiday. Early in the morning we assembled at the Red Proletariat factory. Everyone was dressed in holiday best: young ladies in white blouses with red kerchiefs on their heads, men in light sports-jackets and white shirts, each wearing a red bow-tie. The very foremost workers and staff of the factory carried red banners and portraits of leaders.

The command to fall in rang out. The leaders arranged the column. The Secretary of the Party Committee, who led the column, gave the command, "Forward! March!" The orchestra began to play. The column started off. The parade began. The orchestra became the leader, organizer, and soul of the holiday.

In this orchestra, at first I played the alto horn, later, the alto bugle, and after that, the French horn. The orchestra took part in contests and competitions. At first, the results were terrible, but later there were victories—second and first premium. Because Yuri Yurevich Gubarev considered me a capable student with a future, he included me with the five youngsters from the orchestra recommended for training at a music technical school. We organized a competition among ourselves, where each had to play a short piece or a song on his instrument. I played the well-known *Varshavyanka*. After completing the solo, we had to direct a short piece asigned from a list. Fate appointed me to direct a march. My presentation pleased everyone. By decision of the jury, I took first place. From that moment, I began to prepare myself for admission to the music technical school.

THREE

Musical Technical School

A s I WAS GOING to the audition for the musical technical school October Revolution, alarming thoughts were stuck in my head. "Suddenly, I will fail! I will not pass the test! What will I tell the factory, the orchestra collective, and the guys that have such high hopes for me?"

Mama and I arrived at the technical school a little early. For the examination in my specialty, they asked for the C major scale in three octaves, which I played through pretty excellently. In the etude,I rushed the tempo, but did not get distracted and played through to the end. The work by Schumann, *Grozy,* sounded good. After the examination, they asked me to wait a bit. In a little while, the Secretary came out and said I was accepted. I ran like a crazy man to my Mama shouting, "They accepted me!" This was a victory! The first one who should know about this was Yuri Yurevich and the orchestra collective. The very next day I met the factory committee. They clustered around me asking, "How are things? How was the examination?" I replied that they accepted me! I nearly wept from happiness. They lifted me up and began to bounce me like a small child. Everyone was pleased, and I, myself, most of all!

My new life began—the life of a student in the music technical school. The campus of the technical school was an old manor house with a medium-sized garden. For the most part, the students in the wind department had been sent by directors of amateur orchestras. They graduated from this course of study as excellent soloist musicians. Our group of wind players was not very numerous. Most participants were youths with an amateur background, but at the same time, some rather mature individuals were studying with us. I had just celebrated my fifteenth birthday.

The first meeting with my future teacher in my specialty, Vasiliy Nikanorovich Soloduev was memorable. He was a well-known French horn musician, a soloist of the Bolshoi Theater Orchestra, and an experienced artist. At that time, Vasiliy Nikanorovich made an indelible impression on me. He had had a thick head of gray hair, was always well dressed, and wore a bow-tie. For some reason, I was a little afraid of him. He seemed very severe to me. However, as soon as Vasiliy Nikanorovich started talking with me, everything immediately changed. In reality, he turned out to be a kind person.

In the first lesson, Vasiliy Nikanorovich asked me to play something. While I played, he very intently studied the movement of my lips, how I held the instrument, looked at the structure of my teeth, and was touching my cheeks with his fingers. He made me breathe and observed my inhaling and exhaling. After this, Vasiliy Nikanorovich was silent for an extended period, as though he were thinking something over. Then he said, "Valeriy, it will be necessary for you to change the position of the mouth-piece on you lips. You have the position for a trumpeter. Listen, and heed my advice. Do not play the French horn for a week. After this time, come to me for a lesson." I got scared, and said I would forget how to play the horn if I did not practice for a whole week! Vasiliy Nikanorovich said, "Yes, that is the idea. You must, for a time, forget how to play, in order for us to find a new position on the mouth-piece for you lips that will give us the characteristic sound of the French horn and the range. Do you understand me?"

"Yes, I understand, but not to play for a whole week is just terrible!"

"Valeriy, this is all being done for your benefit."

We began everything from the beginning. The new position was not easily obtained. The mouth-piece slid around on my lips, and I was not at all able to keep it in the place Vasiliy Nikanorovich pointed out. In order to establish the necessary position, the instructor asked me to play with dry lips. This was not what I was used to. Earlier, before starting the sound, I would lick my lips. It was slow going, but we made progress. After a time, the mouth-piece was staying in that place for which we had fought so long. Little by little, I began to play scales and the simplest exercises. After half a year, I was already playing etudes and light compositions. The sound became much more pleasant, and my range gradually increased. It became much easier for me to play. How thankful I was to Vasiliy Nikanorovich! However, it must be said that I diligently carried out all directions and his corrections. The teacher was pleased. The wonderful musicians and teachers of the wind department who followed our success were these: M. I. Tabakov, M. A. Shubert, S. P. Grigorev, trumpeter Velchinskiy, and clarinetist Mayorev.

The well-known director, K. S. Saradzhev, led the symphonic orchestra. The string section of the orchestra was quite strong. As I said before, the wind musicians came from amateur orchestras and did not know symphonic music. It was pretty hard. We did not know transposition yet, and were forced to learn everything on the fly. Also, we played serious music: Beethoven's *Fifth Symphony*, Klinnikov's *Symphony*, and overtures. The French horn players especially caught it in Beethoven's *Second Symphony*, where they encountered notes in the high range. We were not very capable yet. Whenever a passage with high notes approached, we broke out in a cold sweat—would we make it or not? K. S. Saradzhev got very upset when we missed the high notes. Still, in concerts we played cleanly. The director praised us.

The ensemble class at the technical school was taught by the wonderful musician P. N. Alekseyev. He taught us a great deal and opened the secrets of ensemble playing. We always attended his lessons with great pleasure because every time we learned a lot that was new and important for our future profession.

Time passed. My course of study was composed of consistent tone, scales, exercises, and compositions. However, I have to say I did not work at it with all my strength—wanting to go to the movies and theater—and this all detracted from working on the French horn. When playing, the muscles of my lips quickly tired, and for the first time, I began to think about how to practice and how very necessary it was. My friend, a horn player named Lesha Serostanov, became an inspirational example for me. He both served in the army and also studied at the technical school. Lesha knew how to organize his time in order to successfully both serve in the military orchestra and study at the technical school while getting good grades. I was arriving at the technical school at eight in the morning, but by then, it was already time for Lesha to take a break. He had been working since seven. Lesha was having very good success. Realizing this and fearing he would leave me behind, I began to apply myself diligently. (We were friends for many years—first at the technical school and later at the conservatory. We also were co-workers in the orchestra at the Bolshoi Theater.)

The head of the wind department at the October Revolution Musical Technical School was the experienced artist, trumpeter Professor Mikhail Innokentevich Tabakov. He followed our progress very attentively, and often attended our tests and examinations. He was strict, often scolded us, bur praised us for doing something special, saying, "Here, you young man, if you will practice hard, you will play well. In such a case, we will already have really good grades ready for you. If you work and get a good grade, take it home. Brag about yourself! Show your parents! Look, do not disregard this precious grade! In the long run, you know, this is your path through life. Just so, young man!"

One day, Mikhail Innokentevich stopped me and took me by the hand. I got scared and began to think of what I had done wrong.

Not letting go of my hand, the professor looked me in the eye and asked, "Do you want to please your teacher Vasiliy Nikanorovich?"

"Yes, I want to very much," I responded. What do I need to do?"

"Well, now," said the professor, "your teacher's birthday is coming soon. You must play something for his celebration."

"But what would I play? I still know so little."

"You will play Handel's *Largretto* for your teacher."

Secretly, I had been dreaming about playing this piece for a long time, but my teacher had been saying, "It is still early."

"I am asking you to play the *Largretto* specifically," continued Mikhail Innokentevich, "because Soloduev has just done an arrangement of this composition for the French horn."

I analyzed the piece with Professor Tabakov, and began to learn it. I learned the *Largretto* by heart, and the moment came to show my work to the professor. Mikhail Innokentevich listened to me very attentively. Then he asked, "What did you play here? Well, look, you played some long tones, but where is the sound? Where are the nuances? Do you know what nuance is?"

"Yes, I know."

"So, Why didn't you execute it? Later, see, this 'adagio' means very slowly, and you are playing fast. You do not understand the style and character of the piece!"

After long explanations and corrections, the professor went through the whole piece once more with me. After a time, I appeared before Tabakov again. My presentation pleased him, and he said I was ready to play now.

The time for the celebration drew near. One day, Professor Tabakov asked me to come to him in a classroom. I noticed that he looked very serious. We were alone in the classroom. Mikkhail Innokentevich picked up his legendary trumpet. At first, I thought the professor was preparing to show me his instrument, but, no! He took the trumpet, warmed it up a little, put in the mouth-piece, and played. Lord! I heard Handel's *Largretto*. I froze. Tears came to my eyes. In the character of the piece, I felt grief, but surprisingly bright and tender. In the middle part of *Largretto* the trumpet played appealingly, triumphantly, but very softly. The sound of the instrument somehow broadened and again went to a sweet tone. I had never heard anything like it in my life! I was entranced. I was ready to kiss the hand of the professor, but understood very well that he would never permit me. I could not contain myself and started weeping. I was overflowing with feelings of joy and thankfulness to the musician, who had drawn back the curtain and shown me that to which I must strive. I blessed the professor. But he smiled roguishly and said, "Valeriy, you are so sentimental! You have simply moved me to tears. Thank you!"

I found myself greatly impressed by what I had heard. I thought, "How will I be playing? You know, MY presentation will not move anyone." And, at the same time, I was insanely happy. You see, I received colossal benefit from association with such musicians. Just think, Tabakov himself had played for me!

Then the day of the celebration came. Teachers and attendees gathered in the hall. The honoree sat in an arm chair on the stage. As always, Vasiliy Nikanorovich was impeccably dressed. Solemnly, in the place of honor sat the whole instructional staff of the wind department. There were many who had come: the professorship of the Moscow Conservatory, the Institute of Military Directors, the academy near the Moscow Conservatory, and others. After all the words of welcome had been spoken, Professor Tabakov declared that now Vasiliy Nikanorovich would be greeted by his student, Valeriy Polekh. How loudly that was said, "Valeriy Polekh," when I had never been called anything but "Lyalya."

I said a few words of greeting, picked up my horn, and tuned it. The nervousness would not go away. I saw the face of Mikhail Innokentevich. He encouraged me, and immediately the fear began to leave, and I began to play. I wanted so very much to play well, and it turned out well. Everyone congratulated me, and my instructor was surprised and praised me. Professor Tabakov thanked me and kissed me. That is how my life went at the October Revolution Musical Technical School.

V. V. Polekh 1937 V. V. Polekh 1938

During time I had free from studies, I went to practices of the wind orchestra of the Red Proletariat Factory. Yuriy Yurevich Gubarev, the leader of the orchestra decided to put on a concert in honor of the anniversary of the factory. Yuriy Yurevich orchestrated R. M. Glier's *Nocturn* for me. The concert went well. Many of the workers and staff of the factory were in the hall. After the performance, the factory committee gave me a gift. They presented me with a dark blue suit. Truly, until then I had never worn suits—if you did not count the one Mama had sewn for my brother and me from a paper raincoat. Here, I wore a felt hat to the concert. The members of the circle surrounded me, touched my hat, and someone even tried it on. At that time, few people wore hats—especially in the working class area where I lived. At various times, the kids had been trying to knock off my hat with pebbles. Now, when they saw me wearing the hat, they said, "Here comes the artist!"

FOUR

Professor Ferdinand Ferdinandovich Ehkkert

*P*ROFESSOR *FERDINAND FERDINANDOVICH EHKKERT was born in 1865
in the town of Prague. He graduated from the Prague Conservatory.
Having received the designation Free Artist, 16 year old Ferdinand
undertook a concert tour as a French horn soloist, playing the natural
horn in the cities of Berlin, Dresden, Zürich, and Prague. Having arrived
in Moscow with an Austrian orchestra, he remained in Moscow forever.
In 1895, he began performing in the Bolshoi Theater and, holding more
than one position, worked as director at the Operetta Theater. In the
opinion of the renowned musicians M. Tabakov and S. Rozanov, who
worked with him in the orchestra at the Bolshoi Theater, he was a horn*

*virtuoso, with brilliant technique, expressive
tone, and solid performing experience. He
played the famous Sigfried like no one else. As
a musician, Ehkkert was known for playing
the "hunting horn" natural French horn. His
playing was notable for full, strong sound and
brilliant technique. He refined the technique
of eliciting closed notes.*

Профессор Ф. Ф. Энкерт

Professor F. F. Ehkkert

He taught his students to beautifully and

22

gently elicit tones. Approximately by the third year, he tried to determine what would be the further creative fate of a student—what position he would occupy in the orchestra. "We need good French horn players," said the professor. "In each part there are specific difficulties that are hard to overcome—even for a master." He gave a lot of attention to sight-reading and transposition. As one of the founders of the Russian school of French horn playing, Professor Ehkkert raised up many first-class musicians, among them Andrushkevich, S. Leonov, V. Polekh, M. Tretyakov, the brothers Yankelevich, K. Tsukkerman, and V. Shvarts. An all-around, gifted musician, Ferdinand Ferdinandovich was a talented composer. He wrote three concerts for the French horn and orchestra, and a fantasia for French horn and piano. He did a whole rank of arrangements and modifications, wrote three operas, two ballets, ten musical comedies, ten military marches for the wind orchestra, over 100 pieces for variety orchestras, songs, romantic songs, and music for dramatic shows.

(The Encyclopedic Biographical Dictionary of Musicians Performing on Wind Instruments)

In my youth, I loved playing in amateur orchestras very much. I especially loved to play in the amateur orchestra near the Moscow Conservatory. The orchestra was led by Professor Boris

V. Kashirin

Emmanuilovich Khaikin. At that time, there was no professional orchestra at the conservatory, and the students in the directing program would go to amateur orchestras for practice. They trusted me to perform the responsible first horn parts. The director was B. Khaikin himself. You can imagine, I very successfully performed the solo from Tchaikovsky's *Fifth Symphony.* B. Khaikin praised my performance a lot. This was so pleasing for me—I had been putting in a lot of effort. Sometimes we were short one or two musicians in the horn section—for one reason or another they could not attend the orchestra practice. At such times, the professor invited French horn students from the conservatory to fill in for the missing horn players. One that I remember was a very kind student, Volodya Kashirin. He helped me, and often let me play his wonderful instrument made by the firm "Kruspe." As for me, I had a rather poor instrument.

Every year during vacation, the student orchestra traveled away for the season. The travel was paid for, and the students were given a little money. For the next summer, the orchestra of students was preparing to go near Kiev to the health resort Sosnovka in the town of Cherkassy.

The orchestra was complete with the exception of one French horn player. Volodya Kashirin suggested me to Professor Khaikin. He agreed. However, I had to pass an audition with Director A. Cherkasskiy who would be directing the orchestra in Sosnovka. I went to his home; he lived on Gorky Street. I pleased the director, and he accepted me. Until then, I had never been to a health resort before, and I was looking forward to staying there.

At last we arrived at Sosnovka. What a wonderful place! All around were the pine trees, the scent of pine pitch, and the Dneper River. N. B. Gogol once said, "Wonderful the Dneper in calm weather." Gentle sunshine and warm water in the estuary—I was enchanted with this area.

I would rise early in the morning and go to the beach. There, I would practice with my horn. The horn would glisten in the sunlight. At ten in the morning, we rehearsed, and evenings, we played concerts.

It was a little hard for me. I did not know the repertoire of the symphonic orchestra. It was necessary to get the parts and master them at home. At times, they were very difficult.

The first horn, Volodya Kashirin,

helped me in every way. He became a wonderful friend. In the free time, I studied to master the horn repertoire. I especially liked the *Concerto* by F. Strauss The *Concerto* is difficult, and I had been wanting to learn it very much. As time passed, I became used to the orchestra. The very hardest parts in the orchestra were on my shoulders. My work on the horn progressed markedly. The technical passages were successful, but as for tone—one could have wished the tone were better. It was the right time for me to pay attention to tone. Volodya Kashmirin remarked to me, "Valeriy, pay attention to resonance. You must sound like a cello. Just like a cello. Play more sustained tones and tonal etudes."

When I felt that the *Concerto* was almost ready, I decided to demonstrate my work to Volodya Kashirin. After listening to me, Volodya said that he simply had not expected I would have progressed so far and advised me to continue to work. He also said, "When we get back to Moscow, I must show you to F. F. Ehkkert."

The following day my Mama would arrive. She would be helping me with my work. She always helped me. Because the orchestra was free that day, I could meet my Mama.

I already had spoken to a friend in the orchestra, and he had agreed to go with me to the train station in the town of Cherkassy. My friend, a bassoonist by the name of Vizyurov, had traveled to Sosnovka from Leningrad. We arrived at the station a little early. I admit I was excited.

I would be seeing my Mama! The train was coming. I saw Mama! She was so sweet and friendly! We embraced and kissed. I introduced Mama to my friend. We found a cab, loaded up Mama's suitcase, got Mama seated, and seated ourselves. It was a dark Ukrainian night. Large stars lighted the path for us. They were enormous and bright. Mama and I held each other by the hand and could not get enough of looking at each other. It was impossible to get enough of talking about how much was happening in Moscow. Tomorrow morning, we would go to the beach. I was happy.

I woke up early and looked at my watch. It was quarter to six. Mama was already preparing eggs, and on the table were hot Moscow pirogies, and tea—English style with milk. "Mama, sit yourself here. Today, I am going to fuss over you! Give me your plate. Here are eggs for you. Here are Zaporozhye for you. Spread butter on them, please. Tea. Tea brewed wonderfully well. Here is the milk."

After breakfast we almost ran to the beach. Mama was enraptured with the hot sand, fresh water, and a baking sun. Mama was sitting under an umbrella. I said, "I'm going to practice a little. I'll play the *Concerto* by F. Strauss for you."

Mama was all attention. Mama liked the *Concerto*. "You know, I liked your performance. You have matured as a performer. In your performance are elements of artistry, and this is wonderful! Do you remember? You always used to look like a girl. Sometimes, on the streetcar they asked you, 'Little girl, are you getting off at the next stop?' You were so angry."

Mama was very musical, and often helped me with advice. When I practiced, she listened, and made sensible observations. "Thank you, my Mama!" The time came to say good-bye to sweet Sosnovka. Such a pity! Nothing lasts forever. "Good-bye, Sosnovka! Good-bye!"

Upon returning to Moscow, I increased my studies. I did not know whether I would be introduced to Professor Ehkkert or not. In any case, the neighbors became significantly tired of my studies. The Strauss *Concerto* began to bore me. I laid it aside for a while.

A month passed after I returned to Moscow. A few days after Volodya Kashirin reported he had spoken to Ehkkert about me, the professor designated a date for an audition. I got nervous, but Mama calmed me, saying, "Think clearly. You have the *Concerto* prepared. When you start to play, remember how we worked with you, how everything has turned out well for you, and you will become calmer in your soul."

Mama and I arrived a little early at the conservatory in order for me to catch my breath and get my mind in order. Then Volodya Kashirin appeared. He took me by the hand and said, "Well, let's go. The professor is waiting."

Mama kissed me, and we went. I entered the classroom. The professor was sitting in an arm chair. Seeing me, he said, "Come in! Come in, young man! What are you called?"

"I am called Valeriy, and my family name is Polekh." I responded.

"Polekh. Are you a Czech?"

"No, Professor, I am Russian."

"Polekh. Polekh. Straight Czech. What are you going to play?"

Besides Volodya Kashirin, there were some other students in the classroom.

"I am going to play the Strauss *Concerto* for you."

"Show me your instrument. I will accompany you." The professor seated himself at the grand piano. I took up my instrument. We tuned up.

He inspected my instrument and made a wry face but did not say anything. He also looked at the mouthpiece. The professor started to play the introduction, and I began to be nervous, but I remembered that Mama stood in the vestibule waiting for me. I began to feel better. I only recollect when I finished playing. How I played I do not recall. Only at odd times during the rests did I glance at the professor. When I finished playing, I got nervous again. What would he say? The professor sat at the piano and did not breathe a word.

Suddenly, he stood and spoke. "You played excellently! Yes, excellently! Young man, sit here, Wait for me. I will return soon."

I seemed to be completely soaked. I took out a handkerchief and tried to wipe my face, but my hand was shaking. "Thank you, Volodya Kashirin!" He came over to me and kissed me. "Valka, what a guy! How you played! How you played!" He had tears in his eyes.

The students came over with congratulations. "Bravo! Bravo!," they said.

The professor appeareed in the doorway. He looked solemn. He came over to me, took my hand in his, and said, "Dear Polekh, you are accepted into the conservatory in the first course."

I ran to Mama and reported the news to her. "I am a student!" I was so happy! Tears gushed from my eyes.

V. Polekh, Professor F. Ehkkert, P. Grigorov at the Conservatory

I began to study at the Conservatory with the renowned Professor Ferdinand Ferdinandovich Ehkkert. How interesting and useful the lessons were! As is the rule, we began with sustained tones. The professor paid attention to our breathing. "The sound flows evenly, without artificial vibration, as they say, unnecessary variation. The beginning of the elicitation of sound has great meaning. The tapping of the tongue—actually there is no tapping—this is the educated expression. When starting the tone, the student must be careful that the starting of the sound should not be a croaking or some kind of creaking or howling." After sustained tones, we played major and minor scales. We often performed etudes with the accompaniment of the piano, with the professor himself doing the improvisation of the piano part. This helped establish the necessary tempo, fill out the intervals, and add exacting intonation. In such fashion, etudes, side by side with their basic assignments of technical order, worked out the problems of the clear, musical, artistic plan.

A. Serostanov, V. Polekh, Professor Shchetnikov

When beginning the study of a composition or concerto, Ferdinand Ferdinandovich first told the students about the composer and played the composition himself on the piano. Great attention was paid to the development of not just beautiful sound, but the individual sound that existed for this student alone. Great attention was given to sight reading and transposition, without which it is unthinkable to be an orchestral musician. At first, when I appeared in the classroom of such an eminent musician, I experienced fear. It was especially hard attending the academic evenings which were attended by the entire staff of supervisory professors: B. N. Tsybin, V. N. Soloduev, M. A Ivanov, A. V. Volodin, A. G. Semyon ov, M. L. Tabakov, S. I. Eremin, G. A. Orvid, V. M. Blazhevich, V. A. Shcherbinin. My legs would shake, and I would be short of breath when I went out on the stage of the Maly Hall or Classroom to perform some composition or other. Ehkkert paid serious attention to this condition. He proposed that I overcome fear by the most simple means. I began to perform a new composition every month at the academic evenings. Toward the end of the year, I stood on the stage more at ease, without any trepidation.

Ferdinand Ferdinandovich was an avid hunter and traveler. When the holidays came, he and his wife, Berta Eduardovna, went traveling. He loved to go hunting lynx. This was dangerous hunting. You hope to God you don't miss, and the shot go wide, and that is the end for you. It is necessary to be quietly lying in wait for the prey a long time.

Hanging on the wall of his bedroom was a pelt of a lynx – his trophy. "I have a story about this lynx," related Ferdinand Ferdinandovich. "I tracked this beast for a long time, and I was terribly tired from the exertion. I felt, 'He is here. Not far off.' At last, there he was! I got ready, aimed, and pulled the trigger. Lord! A misfire! I pulled a second time and the beast fell. But then, to my surprise, a second beast appeared, evidently his mate. She darted to my side, but when she saw the dead beast, the lynx sniffed him, screamed, and went away. I was lucky, or I would not be here with you telling about it."

In the same way, he so interestingly, even theatrically, told stories, and we were ready to listen to adventure stories. Ferdinand Ferdinandovich told us a great deal about the lives of composers and famous musicians.

V. Polekh at Bolshoi Symphony Orchestra

One day, the professor informed me that the following week we would be going to an audition for the orchestra of the All-Union Radio, where the the head director and artistic leader was Nikolai Semyonovich Golovanov. The professor began to work with me intensively. We worked every day and even on Sunday at his home. For the most part we practiced Ehkkert's *First Concerto*, which we would also perform at the audition. Professor Ehkkert turned his attention to the innovations which I had allowed myself. For example, I permitted myself to use *portamento* and *vibrato*.

"From where did you get this?" asked the professor. Ferdinand Ferdinandovich was an adherent of the old German school. In the beginning, my innovations grated on his ears. At long last, the professor got used to my *vibrato* and *portamento* and in his heart, evidently, agreed with me.

The day of the audition arrived. I went with the professor. When we arrived, we saw that the audition was in full swing. We sat in the orchestra pit and began waiting for a call. I caught sight of Golovanov. My hands began to shake. Ehkkert, seeing my agitation, patted my knee with his hand, and I began to feel a little better. Our pianist arrived, Ekaterina Fuks—a wonderful musician.

At last, they called my name. Ehkkert gave me an encouraging nod, as if to say, "Hold on!" and I went on the stage. The pianist gave an introduction, and I began. I played well. Everything came out right: tone, cantilena, and technique. I finished with a final showy chromatic passage. As a result, they accepted me. Golovanov expressed a desire to meet me. He and the professor kissed. Nikolai Semyonovich congratulated Ferdinand Ferdinandovich on the success, and also praised the pianist, Ekaterina Filippovna Fuks. Ferdinand Ferdinandovich was pleased by my performance and just said, "Well done, Polekh!" At the conservatory I often performed at the academic evenings and at concerts.

My professor was ill, and I decided to visit him. While I was at his home, I met the amazing horn musician, soloist of the Bolshoi Theater Orchestra, Sergei Ivanovich Leonov. He asked me to play a little and I agreed. He listened to me and said, "You should be at the Bolshoi Theater." I thought to myself that for me it was still a little too soon for the Bolshoi Theater. Not long after this, they announced an audition at the theater.

The professor advised me to go to the audition. Well, I was working for Golovanov and had played several interesting programs for him. One day at a rehearsal of the Radio orchestra, I approached Golovanov and said an audition for the horn section at the Bolshoi Theater was advertised. Nikolai Semyonovich very understandingly realized that I was wanting to go to the audition at the Bolshoi Theater. Nikolai Semyonovich even advised me to go to the audition. About the Bolshoi Theater he said, "This is the pinnacle of artistry!" In the near future, he would be joining the Bolshoi Theater Orchestra himself. At the audition, I played well, and they accepted me.

One day, I received orders to appear at the military registration and enlistment office. They assigned me to the Military Symphony Orchestra at the Central Building of the Red Army (CBRA). On the designated day, they gathered us draftees at the Central Building of the Red Army, did roll call, formed us up, and marched us from Commune Square to Perekopsky Barracks. This is not far from Sklifosovsky Clinic. As we approached the barracks, we caught sight of the enormous cast-iron gates. The gates were open, and we entered the gates of the barracks—now we were soldiers. They rarely let us out, as they say, "at liberty." At home were my young wife and a baby. We mostly kept in contact by telephone. I rarely was home, and rarely met with Professor Ehkkert. I could not attend my home conservatory.

And then, a national contest of musicians performing on wind instruments was advertised. I, a soldier living behind cast iron gates, decided all the same to take a chance. First of all, I reported to the designated leader of the Central Building of the Red Army, Brigade Commander N. Pasha; "Request permission for me to participate in the contest."

I received permission, but my instrument was very poor—all

covered with "black bread." With such an instrument one could not even think about the contest. What to do? I recalled then my teacher at the school and instructor at the Bolshoi Theater Orchestra, Vasiliy Nikanorovich Soloduev, a wonderful musician and a kind person. Maybe I could turn to him? But what if he did not give me his instrument? I began to feel ashamed that I could even think that way about him. He was such a nice person. So, on a day when they gave me liberty until 2300 hours, I quickly ran to Vasiliy Nikanorovich's home.

After running up to it, I was out of breath. I stood a bit, I composed myself, and rang. His wife opened the door and invited me to enter. Thankfully, Vasiliy Nikanorovich turned out to be at home.

"Valeriy, how is fate treating you? You are a military man. How are things at the barracks? How is my son, Igorick, getting along?" (The son of Vasiliy Nikanorovich, Igor, a violinist, served with me in the military symphonic orchestra.) "What brings you to me? Tell me about it."

"Vasiliy Nikanorovich, I don't know where to start."

"Well, begin right away."

I made my request and showed him my instrument. Vasiliy Nikanorovich was rightly surprised that I could play on such a "clay pot."

"Igor has been telling about how well you are playing. I will give you the horn. Here, look! What an instrument it is! Take care of it, and it will serve you faithfully and truly. I wish happiness and success for you." It really was a wonderful instrument! I kissed my kind teacher.

I began to work, and began to visit professor Ehkkert more often. Ferdinand Ferdinandovich set out a repertoire for me to perform at the contest. The matter progressed. However, practicing in the barracks was bad. For the most part, I practiced in the soldier's latrine. Those who have served in the army know what a soldier's toilet is like. My eyes watered from the chlorine, the air was abominable, and I practiced in such conditions.

My daily schedule went like this: up at six in the morning, light calisthenics, practice, practice, and practice. By eight when the unit woke up, I was already starting to complete my regular required duties. We did strengthening physical exercises, ate a very meager breakfast, and then came marching practice. After this, we marched as a unit to the Red Army Building where, we practiced the concert program with the orchestra for three hours. It must be said, that our orchestra was excellent. All the musicians were excellent; all were conservatory graduates. Many were straight out amazing soloists. The orchestra was led by the Bolshoi Orchestra director Lev Petrovich Shteinberg. The second director was Victor Sergeevich Smirnov, a noble and a descendant of the Russian vodka family. He was the sweetest person — intelligent, with a sense of humor. After rehearsal, we went again on foot to the barracks with instruments and music stands. I led the formation; they had promoted me to sergeant. After a scanty lunch, it was rest time. Each did what he wanted, and I went to the latrine to prepare the contest program. At eleven o'clock it was time for retreat.

The day of the contest was approaching. My work with the the professor was coming to a conclusion. The whole program of three rounds was ready. The instrument was wonderful. I was never separated from it, not even when I slept.

V. Polekh in the CHRA

At last it was the day for me to go to the contest. Today was the first round, and it would be at the CHRA.* I was released from all duties for the day. In the morning I practiced, laid down, and rested, which very rarely happened for me here in the orchestra. I ate lunch and decided to go to the CHRA to get acquainted with the stage, and try the acoustics. I went to the sergeant-major, who was our senior leader in the barracks.

"Please give me a pass for the town."

"Tovarishch Polekh, you, now, will conduct the orchestra in the wash room. Collect the sheets."

"But, permit me," I said. "It is time for me to go to the contest. The leadership freed me from all duties."

"Sergeant Polekh, here I am your leader. If I want, I will release you to the contest. If I want, I will NOT release you. Make ready, fall in your squad, and forward march. Is this clear to you, Sergeant Polekh? After the wash room, go wherever you like. Here is your pass."

There was nothing else for me to do, but just say, "Yes, sir. To go to the wash room."

I took the bag of sheets, the horn, and we left.

Along the way, of course, I ran off, and my buddies helped me out. I ran to the contest, and located the rehearsal room. The pianist was already there. I played a little and began to wait for the call.

My pianist was a wonderful musician. She was a laureate of several contests, Ekaterina Filippovna Fuks. Of course, I was nervous. At last, they called me. We pulled each other by the little finger, something we had always done to calm down. Then we were on the stage. I tuned up, and did not look at the judges. I began with the *Second Concerto* by I. Gaidon. In the beginning I was nervous, but, when I felt everything was going to turn out OK, I calmed down. I played through the concerto, and the audience showed their approval with friendly applause.

---

*   CHRA are the initials for Central Home of the Red Army.

The second work, "Fantasia," music by F. Ehkkert, went surprisingly successfully, and after the end of the piece, besides heated applause, a roar of approval arose in the audience. After the second variation, the roar increased. After the ending of the piece, the hall simply collapsed with applause and a storm arose in the hall. I understood that this was a success, but I was barely standing on my feet, such weakness had overtaken me. To go back out and take a bow at a contest is generally not allowed, but here the public was demanding it, and they permitted me to take a bow, which I did. Again, the hall met me with ecstatic exclamations, "Polekh, bravo! Polekh, bravo!"

The following two rounds went just as successfully. As a result, I received First Premium, 5000 rubles, and the title "Laureate."

The following day, articles appeared in newspapers. My portrait was placed in the newspaper *Red Star**. In gratitude to Vasiliy Nikanorovich, I gave him the a crystal vase, supported by a silver figure of an old man holding a lyre in his hands. I kissed Vasiliy Nikanorovich several times and said that his horn turned out to be lucky. After a short time, I arranged a banquet attended by Ferdinand Ferdinandovich with his wife, Berta Eduardovna; our wonderful pianist, Ekaterina Filippovna Fuks; her husband, a professor of the trombone, Vladimir Arnoldovich Sherbinin; my parents, Vera Alekseevna and Vladimir Vasilevich; and my brother, Vladimir.

After the banquet, I accompanied the Ehkkert couple to the tramway stop. We kissed, and I kissed the hand of Berta Eduardovna. That is how I parted with my kind and wonderful professor.

---

* *Red Star* is the official newspaper of the Red Army.

FIVE

Nikolai Semyonovich Golovanov

M Y MAMA LOVED MUSIC greatly and acquainted us children with music. In the summer, we often went to the Central Park of Culture and Rest. At that time, in the 1930's, in the park were many wooden structures; for example, The Hexagon, a very interesting and beautiful building. In it were restaurants, dining rooms, various buffets, and snack bars. There was a very interesting variety theater. Well-known vaudeville artists performed there: A. Raikin, V. Kezin, K. Shulzhenk, I. Yurevas, and others. There stood, as always, the circus "Shapito." For young children, a large children's town was built. There was both a children's theater and various amusement park attractions. A beautiful library was built there. The entrance to the park began with a structure named "Pavilion of Pavilions," completely made of wood. Located on top of this pavilion was an open-air variety theater named "Rakushka," at which a military band played during summer evenings. Below, under Rakushka, was a brilliant public garden—all in green and flowers. In the garden stood comfortable benches on which listeners sat — lovers of band music. A medium-sized concert hall with the designation "Kurzal" was located in Pavilion of Pavilions.

On Mondays and at various other times, the Symphonic Orchestra of the Bolshoi Theater performed in this concert hall, under the direction of Conductor Nikolai Semyonovich Golovanov. Without fail, we attended these orchestral concerts with Mama. For the most part, the orchestra performed "light" music: the overture to the operetta *Die Fledermaus, Hungarian Dances*, Brahms, overture to the opera *Barber of Seville,* and *Military March* by Schubert. A singer performed *Solveg's Song, Serenade* by Schubert, *The Nightingale* by Alyabev, and in the concert finale Nikolai Semyonovich Golovanov conducted the overture to the opera *Carmen.* For some reason, I always waited for that moment, when the conductor waved his baton and the beat of the cymbals and drums was heard. Then everyone in the audience was enlivened. The elderly folks, who had been dozing, woke up and were not sleepy any more. The bravura, rich music poured out—sometimes thunderous, sometimes gently quiet. The conductor directed the orchestra very energetically, and when prompted by the score, brought forth orchestral sound as though he himself took delight in the sweet bliss being created. Suddenly, unexpectedly, passionately, and imperiously, the hands of the conductor raised, demanding *forte* from the orchestra. *Forte*, and only *forte*, rained down on the listeners like thunder and lightning. The conductor ended the overture, and the concert was over. I recognized that I wanted so much to be a conductor.

A second encounter with Nikolai Semyonovich occurred at a show in the Bolshoi Theater. Mama and I attended the opera *Ruslan and Ludmila.* We did not like the show, which was presented in some new style I cannot put a name to, but the music put us into ecstasy. We sat in box seats on the second tier. I could see the whole orchestra, but most important, to my eyes, was the conductor— Nikolai Semyonovich Golovanov.

I tell you honestly; I was in love with him. It seemed to me that he was a wizard. I was amazed that such a large orchestra was under the control of such a little wand. This wand was doing wonders

Many years later, I was studying at the conservatory with the wonderful instructor, Ferdinand Ferdinandovich Ehkkert, an amazing musician and man. Once, when I came to a lesson with my professor, we worked a little while, and then he suddenly said to me, "Valeriy, get yourself ready. Tomorrow we are going to an audition at the Radio Orchestra. At the Radio Orchestra, the main conductor is Nikolai Semyonovich Golovanov."

When he said this, I even was a little frightened. Oh, Lord! Golovanov himself would be listening to me! Ferdinand Ferdinandovich advised me, "Don't be afraid. Most importantly, you must play well. I will be with you. You will play my concerto. But for now, let's practice."

At the appointed time the following day, the professor and I were at the Radio. The audition began. Twenty horn players were in one place for the audition presided over by Nikolai Semyonovich himself. The professor and I went to the orchestra pit and began to wait. Finally, my turn to play came. There was no time to get nervous. The beginning of the concerto was created to allow the performer to display complete mastery. I succeeded in doing this, and after that it went smooth as butter. In short, the concerto was a success; I played well. I performed last. All the participants in the audition were asked to wait for the results. Everyone was terribly nervous. After a short while, the leader of the orchestra came out and reported, "*Tovarisch* Polekh is accepted. To the rest of you, thank you."

This was my third encounter with Nikolai Semyonovich Golovanov.

I began to work in the Radio Orchestra. As it turned out, working with Nikolai Semyonovich was not easy and not simple. As a conductor, he was very demanding, and I would say, severe. I got used to everything and paid attention. When I was not very busy, I found things to do. I understood that here one did not joke around. Here, precise and very responsible work was being done. I must answer for each note, for each tone, for each measure of music. If something was not just so, they could release one from employment. Nikolai Semyonovich made no allowances. He demanded high quality in everything, and the orchestra was giving that high quality. I began to have doubts. Could I cope with this level of performance that seemed to be beyond me? However, I was committed to cope with this assignment, and come what may, I would cope. At first, Nikolai Semyonovich gave me programs that were not very large and not so hard.

He was a great teacher. I felt he was testing me; he was watching me closely. He even did not shout at me from the podium as he did with others. How thankful I was to that man, and I will pray for him for a hundred years, if one may say it that way! However, something unexpected happened. My chief, who was an amazing horn player and my teacher, got sick, and a very crucial program had to go on. This was Tchaikovsky's Fifth Symphony, where the solo in the second section is very crucial and even the most well-known horn players play it with great trepidation. In any case, I played and played this solo at home. Nikolai Semyonovich wanted to invite an experienced horn player from another orchestra, but when that musician heard that the conductor of the symphony would be Golovanov, he refused to play the Fifth Symphony with him. After this, Nikolai Semyonovich evidently decided to take a chance and give a young man, namely me, the possibility of proving himself.

Rehearsals began. Golovanov was Golovanov. He began to demand large sound from me; "You sat in the place of a soloist. Give!" Unfortunately, I did not have a Golovanovish "Give!" to give. In the first place, I was playing on an ordinary French horn. This horn just did not have large sound in it. At that time there were hardly any double French horns. These instruments were found only in the Bolshoi Theater Orchestra. The director of the theater had ordered French horns of the "Kruspe" system from Germany. And in the second place, I was more of a lyrical horn player, and I still did not have a great deal of experience.

Golovanov demanded and demanded large sound. Truly, I tried to push, but under such a system, the muscles of my lips did not hold up under such an excessive load and began to become tired. I was honestly ready to reveal my doubts to Golovanov, but that talented teacher, Nikolai Semyonovich spoke for me. It was plain to him, that I was a capable musician, even talented, but still young for a professional. At rehearsals, I played a solo well; in my own style, true, but every soloist plays in his own way. Golovanov decided to find me some help, and designated a back-up horn player, "This horn player will help you in the *tutti* places." Praise God! It became easier for me.

The day of the concert arrived. The concert took place in the Great Hall at the Conservatory. I played the symphony rather decently. Nikolai Semyonovich led me out to take a bow, and I stood at the conductor's support neither dead nor alive. I admit, Conductor Nikolai Semyonovich Golovanov had feared greatly for me. After my triumph, Golovanov began to give me harder programs.

It soon became known that the Bolshoi Theater was advertising an audition for wind instruments. French Horn players also would participate in the audition. I wanted very much to play in the audition, but it was impossible for me to abandon Nikolai Semyonovich. Well, you can imagine my surprise when Nikolai Semyonovich *himself* suggested that I go play in the audition.

"Valeriy, go play in the audition. It's opera after all, a really great orchestra, wonderful singers, a great choir, internationally famous ballet, and colorful decorations and costumes. I love the opera myself. Sooner or later they will call me to the Bolshoi Theater again. In a symphonic orchestra, there is only music. The listener must imagine for himself the images the composer has created. Unfortunately, not everyone is able to grasp musical fantasy. In the opera,however, musical images are conveyed to the listener by the singers. the choir, and the orchestra itself. Valeriy, go to the opera. I give you my blessing."

So, I went to the audition for the Bolshoi Theater Orchestra. What joy! They accepted me! I immediately went to Nikolai Semyonovich, threw my arms around his neck, and kissed him.

"Oh, it seems you are emotional," he said. "Compose yourself. I am glad for you. Play one more farewell concert for me."

I went home, thinking all the while, "What a kind, what an

amazing person is Nikolai Semyonovich Golovanov." He was a real father to me.

But you didn't cross him during rehearsal. If something was not just right, you would be smarting, and never mind that you were an experienced artist or a relative, he scolded and brought you back to order. Every concert was a part of his life, a part of his being, and he demanded that everyone involved be just as selflessly dedicated to the sacred matter of music.

However, I did not have long to work in the Bolshoi Theater before I was called to the ranks of the Red Army. At first, I served in the Military Symphonic Orchestra at the Central House of the Red Army. The war began and our Symphonic Orchestra was broken up.

I was assigned to the Detached Parade Orchestra of Brigade Commander A. S. Chernetskiy. In this orchestra, strict military discipline was maintained. After all the activities, we returned to the barracks and barely had time to lay down in bed, or as the say in the army, lay down on a cot.

Orchestra of CHRA* 1939

A rumor went around among the military musicians, that Aleksandr Vasilevich Aleksandrov was inviting singers, dancers, and horn players to join his Red Army Ensemble. In a free time, which happened very rarely for us, I got myself out of the barracks with difficulty and ran to the offices of the Ensemble. I was received by Boris Aleksandrov, the son of Aleksandr Vasilevich, and a second son, Vladimir, who was also in the office. I told them about myself, that I was a Laureate of the All-Union Contest, first premium. The brothers became interested. Boris asked if I didn't have someone who knew me, a solid musician or conductor of course, who could give me a reference. I said, that such a person existed.

"Who? If it is not a secret," asked Vladimir Aleksandrovich.

"It's not a secret, " I replied. "It is Nikolai Semyonovich Golovanov."

Suddenly, I got a little scared. How would Golovanov himself react to all this? However, the die was cast, and as they say, the ships are burning. I would take the risk.

"It would be good if Nikolai Semyonovich, himself, phoned Father, Aleksandr Vasilevich," said Boris Aleksandrovich.

"Alright," I mumbled in terror. On that note we parted.

As I ran back toward my barracks, I was thinking, how was it that I dared to claim that Golovanov was my close acquaintance? Juat the same, I decided to go to Nikolai Semyonovich. He lived on Nezhdanov Street. I rang his doorbell. Nikolai Semyonovich, himself, opened the door. My legs were trembling.

"Oh! What wind has blown you to me? What's up? Come in."

"No," I said. "I'll just stand here. Besides, my boots are rough and muddy. I'll take them off."

"No need to take them off. What is a soldier without boots?"

Nikolai Semyonovich made a request of someone, evidently a servant, and she wiped off my boots with a rag. I entered, and it is too bad I did not have time to look around at the wonderful paintings, busts, and various beautiful statuettes. I thought I had unexpectedly found myself in a museum. I was very nervous, and even forgot where to start to make the request. Nikolai Semyonovich helped me, and began first.

"I see you are nervous. Be bold! What's the matter?"

"Nikolai Semyonovich, I have come to you with a big request. Maybe I am too bold. I decided to appeal to you. I am serving in a military orchestra. Military discipline, daily marching, I could lose my specialty. Besides that, I have a starving wife and small son. Aleksandr Vasilevich Aleksandrov is inviting horn players to his ensemble. He offers very good conditions—receive army rations and to live at home."

"Yes, such conditions in these times would not be bad," observed Nikolai Semyonovich. "How can I help you?"

I felt my hands were shaking.

"Could you recommend me?"

Nikolai Semyonovich was silent for a little.

"Yes, I can recommend you. When would I need to do this?"

"The sooner the better."

"Alright."

"Thank you! Thank you so much! Nikolai Semyonovich, If you could call Aleksandr Vasilevich at the offices of the Ensemble... Here is the telephone number."

"Alright. Leave the telephone number."

I again thanked Nikolai Semyonovich and left.

I did not walk, but more accurately, ran back to the offices of the Ensemble. When I reached Commune Square from Nezhdanov Street, I arrived, so to speak, all sweaty. Boris Aleksandrov met me and said, "Father is asking for you. Go to him in his office. Yes, Golovanov phoned Father and talked with him a rather long time. Go on! Go!"

I entered. Aleksandr Vasilevich spread out some papers. Then he looked at me over his glasses and said, "Rehearsal is tomorrow. Come at two o'clock."

I thanked him and was about to leave.

"Stop! From where do you know Golovanov so well?"

"You see, I was a soloist in his orchestra at Radio"

"Now, go. Do not be late."

So ended my fourth acquaintance with Nikolai Semyonovich Golovanov.

The fifth meeting happened in the Bolshoi Theater. At that time, Nikolai Semyonovich at last had been called to the Bolshoi Theater.

In the Theater, it was decided to present the opera *Khovanshchina*. At the podium stood the head conductor of the theater, Golovanov. He put together the list of performers, artists of the orchestra, and here Nikolai Semyonovich did not forget me. He designated me to be first French horn for the opera *Khovanshchina*. Rehearsals began. Usually, they began at ten o'clock in the morning. At nine thirty Nikolai Semyonovich would arrive with his wooden suitcase and seat himself at the podium, to check off with his red pencil, watching for himself to see which artists of the orchestra came, and when they arrived to study their part. However, the artists of the orchestra were always on the ball and almost always arrived early also. By the beginning of rehearsal, all were sitting in their places.

Nikolai Semyonovich loved precision in execution and did not obtain it with the whole orchestra playing, but began working with individuals. Here one needed to be careful. Every artist of the orchestra needed to know his own part almost by heart. Heaven forbid that some careless musician did not play just the way Golovanov demanded. He would request that the leader of the orchestra not designate such a musician for him in the future. It is true that such incidents almost never happened. Here is what happened to me:

Remember, at the podium, Golovanov is a beast. It seems I mentioned something about that earlier. Suddenly, Golovanov did not like my closed note. I know what sound a French horn produces, I know very well, and am not bad at producing them. But he said to me,"I need a sound like this: listen z-z-z-z-z-z-z-z You are producing some kind of muffled sound."

I told him, "Alright, I will try to find this ringing sound."

No, he wanted the note he needed right away. Fortunately for me, the rehearsal ended and he stopped tormenting me. At the next rehearsal, he again was exasperated with this sound. There was no other recourse for me but to go on sick leave. Later, the leader of the orchestra told me, "Nikolai Semyonovich, having come to the rehearsal and not seeing you in your place, asked, 'Where is Polekh?'

Upon learning that you were ill, he said, 'What a pity! Such a wonderful musician.'"

Here is another incident. The concertmaster of the cellists offended Golovanov in some way. He began to shout at the cellist,"You do not know how to play even a line, and your wife does not know how to sing!" But the cellist's wife was a wonderful singer, working in the Bolshoi Theater. You may ask, what did his wife have to do with this? Such incidents occurred with Golovanov only during work when he was all wound up. Just as soon as Nikolai Semyonovich descended from the conductors podium, he became a completely different person—kind and well-mannered.

Here is yet another incident: for a recording, Golovanov was conducting the orchestra, and a singer was vocalizing Rachmaninoff. Suddenly, Nikolai Semyonovich stopped the orchestra and turned to me, "You are not playing with me. Follow the hand."

I replied, "You gesture in number five was not understandable."

Golovanov answered, "Not understandable? Kindly tell me, what am I supposed to do? Direct with my feet?"

That is how Golovanov was at the podium.

On our own time, we often organized satirical theatrical revues. More than enough people wished to watch our performances. I am glad to report; he loved our satirical revues. He would arrive early and seat himself in the from row. General Semen Aleksandrovich Chernetskiy, who was known to all the wind instrument players, attended. Artists and musicians were coming.

For his sixtieth birthday, we decided to put on a theatrical number. This time, we decided to create a comedic version of an audition committee. A bass who very closely resembled Nikolai Semyonovich served in the choir of the Bolshoi Theater. Nikolai Semyonovich himself touched up his own eyebrows, and it turned out as though he had double eyebrows. They put a little make-up on the artist/bass—Nikolai Semyonovich and made him the chairman of the audition committee. Well, on the day of the performance the auditorium was full. In the auditorium were Antonina Vasilevna

Nezhdanova, and the celebrant himself, Nikolai Semyonovich. The curtain opened. On the stage was a table covered with a green cloth and seated at the table was the audition committee with the artist—Nikolai Semyonovich as chairman. Laughter rang out in the auditorium. The audience could have taken the stage Golovanov for the real one if they had not seen the true Golovanov sitting in the front row. The actor/Nikolai Semyonovich shouted. Out came a violinist—trembling visibly.

"Begin." the committee said.

The violinist shook so hard that he dropped his bow.

"Help him," the chairman told the stage hand. He picked up the bow and handed it to the violinist.

There was laughter in the hall. The violinist started to play the first part of the Tchaikovsky Concerto. After listening a little, Nikolai Semyonovich shouted, "Cadence!"

The violinist was so frightened he fell down. The stage hand grabbed him and carried him off the stage. The audience was very pleased.

"Next!" shouted the actor/Nikolai Semyonovich.

Out came a tuba player—very tall with an enormous tuba-sousaphone. For some reason, the tuba player struggled under the weight of the sousaphone.

"What will you play?" they asked him.

"I...?" asked the tuba player.

"Not I, certainly!" responded the artist/Nikolai Semyonovich.

"I will play Susanina's aria from the opera *Faust*.

"Begin! Begin!"

The tuba player began to blow into the tuba. Nothing happened. He blew some more. Again there was no sound.

"You know," said the tuba player, "There is probably water in the tuba. Wait a moment, I'll empty the water out of the horn."

The tuba player extracted himself from the sousaphone, tipped it, and out of the bell poured a whole bucket of water. With the chairman leading the way, the committee ran off the stage.

THE INCIDENT WITH THE HYMN INTERNATIONALE

This incident happened one day in the theater when *Khovanshchina* was being performed. The show was about to start. Nikolai Semyonovich was sitting alone in the conductor's room. Suddenly, the leader of the orchestra ran in and said, "A foreign delegation has come to our theater. It's obligatory that we play the party hymn, *Internationale*."

Nikolai Semyonovich immediately became upset. "Is there a conductor's score or directions?"

"No, neither one nor the other," the leader replied.

"What to do? I can't do it without a score. How many times through it? Get that clarified, please."

The leader ran to find out. Nikolai Semyonovich was in a quandary—what to do? The leader ran back in and said, "One time through."

"Well, Glory to God! Ask the concert master to come to me."

The concert master ran in.

"Please put the first violin part on the podium. I will conduct from that."

The third bell rang. Nikolai Semyonovich crossed himself and went to play the hymn without a score. The hymn sounded wonderful. How much it cost his nerves only Niklai Semyonovich knows. You know he is a remarkable conductor—without a conductor's score nothing can be done.

ON THE OCCASION OF HIS BIRTHDAY

Nikolai Semyonovich had turned sixty. He arranged a reception at his home for us artists of the orchestra. The leading artists and soloists of the orchestra met at his place on Nezhdanov Street. The honoree himself greeted us. He was dressed for a holiday in a black frock coat, dark trousers with a black stripe up the leg, and a black bow tie. Nikolai Semyonovich seemed tired to us. Actually, he had just recovered from an illness. Our host invited us to the table. The table service interested us. There were unusual decanters, gilded china, silver knives and forks with gold trim, gravy boats and serving dishes shaped like swans, and beautiful gilded candelabras. The first glass was poured and the toastmaster gave a toast to the health of our newly-recovered Nikolai Semyonovich. He sat with us for a while, then excused himself, and went away to rest. We all got up from the table and began to inspect the apartment.

Yes, this was a museum: splendid paintings—for the most part by Russian masters, busts of various well-known and unknown people, a wonderful grand piano, cabinets with vintage books, various china, groups of elegant statuettes, and a bronze. We looked at everything and were amazed at such a collection of rarely-produced art.

Then our host awakened. "Brothers, I see you have not drunk anything, and they say musicians are such mountainous drunkards? Well, I'm joking. Everyone come, sit at the table, fill the vodka glasses to the brim. There, now. I drink to the health of our dear guests. Make yourselves at home. Don't be shy."

So, we did not let our host down after that. The host was forced to refill the decanters again.

"Listen, my kind friends, an incident has come to mind. It was a long time ago—about twenty years or so. In those days, they still did not accept frock coats, dinner jackets, and white bow ties. They considered that this all was a survival of bourgeoisie. Back then, we wore black velvet short jackets to the theater. As I recall now, it was a symphonic concert in the Great Hall at the conservatory. The revolutionary audience in the hall was made up of soldiers, sailors, and anarchists. We had a program of light music. The third bell rang. I came out in a frock coat, of course. In the audience arose noise, an uproar, and whistles. They would not let me begin; shouting, "Bourgeoisie!" at me. I stood, and stood, and then left. I stood backstage, and the noise in the hall became quieter. I came out, and again they did not allow me to begin. I left. In the hall there was almost no noise."

"I came out and immediately started to play the overture to the opera Carmen. I had earlier asked the percussionists to beat the drums and cymbals so that the chandeliers would be bouncing, and they did so. The concert finished with a "Hurrah!" That is how I, Nikolai Semyonovich Golovanov, taught a revolutionary audience to treat the concert uniform, the frock coat, with respect."

All of us guests jumped to our feet with shouts of, "Hurrah! Bravo! We drink to you, Nikolai Semyonovich!" In order to not tire out our host, we quietly dispersed.

THE INCIDENT WITH THE ORGAN.

We were rehearsing *Poem of Ecstasy* by Skriabin in Tchaikovsky Hall under conductor Golovanov. As you know, the organ participates in this performance, but unfortunately, at the finale the organ simply would not stop playing. The orchestra finished the last *fermata,* and cut off the sound, that is to say, finished playing *Poem of Ecstasy,* and you can just imagine—the organ continued sounding. Nikolai Semyonovich did not know what to do. We had in our orchestra a violinist, Lesha Levchenko, who was a jack of all trades, and Golovanov turned to him.

"Lesha, help! Look and see what is the matter."

Lesha crawled into the mechanism of the organ. For a long time he tinkered with it, and crawled out covered with dust.

"Nothing doing! The organ will not listen to me. It's being stubborn!"

"But, we can't change the concert."

"Nikolai Semyonovich, I figured it out. If the organ does not stop, I will use an ax and chop open the main pipe that supplies the air."

They decided to do just that. They sent for an ax. A fireman's ax was brought, but it was very dull. Lesha dug in his famous brief case—he had just about everything in it—and brought out a large file. He began to sharpen the ax, and in a few minutes the ax was sharp as a razor.

"Well, now the pipe will not be temperamental!" said Lesha.

In the evening, during the concert, Lesha stood inside the organ, and held the ax ready in his hands. The finale was approaching. Lesha raised the ax, just one minute, and the pipe was chopped in pieces. Well, Praise God! The organ fell silent in time.

SIX

Semyon Aleksandrovich Chernetskiy

Sub-Warrant Officer Efim Chernetskiy, the bandmaster of a reserve regiment, lived in Odessa. He was poor, as were the majority of the Jews living in Odessa. One day, he found out that the Grand Duke, the brother of Czar Nicholas II, must come to Odessa for an inspection. Efim started thinking. One thought would not give him any peace, but stayed stuck in his mind. Although this thought made him tremble, he in no wise could put it out of his mind. He firmly decided to put this thought into practice—come what may.

S. A. Chernetskiy

It really was going to happen! In a day or two, the brother of Czar Nicholas II would arrive. Good Lord! What was happening in Odessa! All the fences got painted. They ran the legs off the grounds-keepers. Everything was swept. Everything was cleaned. Display windows of stores were washed. Door handles were polished. Odessa was transformed. In place of a dirty provincial town, Odessa was transformed, almost, into a capital city. Everyone was going around in his holiday best, smiling at each other, and tipping felt hats and bowler hats. Ladies rustled in frills, and everyone dressed in his best.

At last, the day of the inspection arrived. The regiment was assembled in the main square. Everything was looking sharp. Everything was shining. Suddenly, the command rang out,"ATTENNNNNSHUN! Dress left!"

The Grand Duke was mounted on a raven black steed. Such an appearance! Such bearing! Good Lord! Like the Czar himself! Handsome! The hymn burst forth, *God, Save the Czar*. The brother of the Czar inspected the whole regiment and, it seems, remained satisfied. The Grand Duke galloped to the center of the formation and loudly called out, "Brother soldiers, whoever has any needs or requests, speak!"

In the square was silence, and suddenly from the distance rang out a hoarse voice, "There is a request." The regiment became agitated. Who dared? Who shouted?

The Grand Duke rode up closer to the speaker and asked rather loudly and severely, "What is the need? Speak!"

They gave the command, "Two steps forward." The soldiers opened the formation, and Efim Chernetskiy stepped forward.

"Who are you, and what is your rank?" asked the duke.

"Sub-Warrant Officer Efim Chernetskiy."

"What is the need? Answer!"

"Forgive me, a sinner. I want to accept the Russian Orthodox Faith."

"What is your creed?"

"I am a Jew. I request, Your Eminence, that you become my godfather."

The regiment again became agitated. What would the Grand Duke answer?

"This is a good thing you have decided. It is agreed to bless you into the Russian Orthodox Church. Tomorrow at three o'clock in the temple. Mister Colonel, arrange everything that is needed."

Then the Grand Duke galloped away. The command was given to dismiss. Soldiers ran up to Efim. "Well, Jew! Well, brave one! We were all gasping. We thought they would lock you up, and look how it turned out! Now, you will be a Russian Orthodox like us. A bucket of vodka for you!"

Efim stood feeling neither alive nor dead. He was thinking, speechless, "Clearly, God has saved me!"

So, the Grand Duke baptized the Jew, and hanged a Russian Orthodox cross on his chest. The Russian Orthodox priest said, "Now you will be called Semyon, son of Aleksandr, and you will carry the family name Chernetskiy." The Grand Duke raised him to the next rank—Warrant Officer. They gave him a silver fifty kopeck piece for passage of his soul.

This true account was told me by a good friend of my relatives, a general. He himself had been an eyewitness to these events.

A short time later, Chernetskiy enrolled in the Petersburg Conservatory. In 1917 he graduated from the Conservatory and, in 1918, took over leadership of the Military Orchestra Section of the Petrograd Soviet. From 1924 to 1929 he was Inspector of Orchestras in the Soviet Army.

I met Semyon Aleksandrovich at the contest for wind instrument musicians. When the contest concluded, it was announced that I had won first prize. At that time, I was in the army serving in the symphonic orchestra attached to the CHRA*. While everyone was congratulating me, Brigade Commander Chernetskiy came over, shook my hand, and congratulated me on my success. He said, "Good man! You did not let the Red Army down!" He also said, "Come to my Model Orchestra."

I thanked Semyon Aleksandrovich. "I will gladly join your orchestra."

"You played brilliantly." Again the Brigade Commander congratulated me.

---

*   CHRA = Central Home of the Red Army

This was in March of 1941. As soon as the war began, our symphonic orchestra was disbanded. Brigade Commander Chernetskiy took me into his orchestra. I served for three years in

the Model Orchestra. This duty was very difficult. We rose at seven in the morning and immediately ran out doors in any weather. Calisthenics. After a meager breakfast, we began drilling—also out of doors. Exercise on the

Zaks, Kaplan, Andreev Aleksandrov, parallel bars and the horizontal bar.
Polekh, Smirnov Kishinev, 1941 Individually, we imitated a bayonet

attack and marching, marching. They trained us to be medical orderlies. We had political training in the barracks. After this was "self-training," that is, we were left by ourselves with our musical instruments.

My strength often failed. I was afraid I would completely lose my specialty because I was continually blowing and blowing on my trumpets and French horns. After a similarly meager lunch, it was quiet time.* I would throw myself on my cot and sleep like a dead man. After an hour, we would rise to practice with the orchestra for three hours.

Sometimes, the brigade commander himself worked with the orchestra until late in the evening. We were playing his amazing marches. When he would shout his well-known, "Shut down! Start up!" we needed to very attentive, and exactly at the time of the division of the march, suddenly stop the sound at the accent of the measure and after a moment re-establish the sound at a strong level. This "Shut down! Start up!" effectively created the impression of movement and saved the march from uniformity by injecting into it a fresh, moving structure. In connection with this action, Chernetskiy was able to direct with his hands in such a way that the effect was

* In Russian literally "dead hour"

invariably enhanced. At the end, Semyon Aleksandrovich would solemnly pronounce his, "Devil take it!" Semyon Aleksandrovich really loved conducting.

There was an incident that occurred at a concert in the Central Building of the Soviet Army. We were playing the *1812 Overture*. The Brigade Commander was conducting. In the finale of the overture, he often was not able to make the change from one time signature to another. He could not catch the "one." He lost it, and that's all there was to it. He was very much aware of this weakness, and for this reason he asked the soloist clarinetist, Victor Petrov—a wonderful musician, to indicate the downbeat of the transitional measure, and everything went smoothly. However, it happened once that the clarinetist, Petrov, was not paying attention or was thinking and did not indicate the transition to the conductor. What a mess! The Brigade Commander lost the "one." What to do? He began waving his finger in a circle, trying to find the downbeat, but did not succeed til the very end of the Overture. Meanwhile, he was repeating all the time, "Devil take it! Devil take it! Petrov, ten days and nights I'll sentence you!"

After the concert, poor Petrov was already prepared to go to the guard-house, but Semyon Aleksandrovich forgave him. He only said his famous, "Devil take it!"

Ensemble of Aleksandrov in concert

Here's another incident. Our orchestra traveled to one of the military units in order to demonstrate excellent marching. The commander of the regiment had suspended training because he was dissatisfied with the military preparation of the regiment. The regimental commander appealed to our brigade commander to show the regiment real preparation. We demonstrated real preparation. Playing a march, our orchestra demonstrated all possible military exercises, and it must be said, performed everything smartly. The commander was very pleased with our exercises and expressed his appreciation to all of us. To his own regiment, he said, "That is the way it's done. Watch and learn!"

You can just imagine the colossal amount of work, and how much effort was expended to be able to do something like this. They drove us terribly hard.

Another time, Chernetskiy drove over to our barracks. He was in a good mood—even jolly. He invited us soldiers over to the grand piano, and said, "Listen, such a new march I have composed!" He began to play. "Well? How about it? How's that for a march? Eh?"

Of course, we were praising the march, shouting, "Wonderful!" Actually, the march was really good. We were asking the brigade commander to play this march again, and we even were beginning to join in singing the melody. The brigade commander was pleased, worked with us a little, and left for home. However, he first took with him the arranger, Zyamu Binkin, with whom he worked on the new march at home.

Once, we were rehearsing a technical piece. Semyon Aleksandrovich himself was conducting. In the music, while the orchestra was repeating the technical passage several times, at that time I had a rest. As a lover of all passages, I very quietly was playing along with the hardest of passages that the orchestra had. However, I made a mistake—I played an extra passage.

Suddenly, the brigade commander said loudly, "Polekh, stand up!"

I was very scared, but quickly stood up. It turned out that I had played the technical passage three times instead of two, and the brigade commander had heard it.

"Devil take it! What are you doing? Testing me? Did you think I was not going to hear your stunt going on? Shame on you! Or did you want to show what technique you have? I heard your technique at the audition! Please be so kind as to play what the author has written and keep your technical stunts to yourself! Devil take it! Do I sit you in a cell? What do you have to say for yourself?"

In a plaintive voice, I said, "Excuse me."

"I forgive you. Sit down."

We were standing in a horse riding arena. ("We" meaning a combined orchestra of a thousand military musicians.) They were drilling us there—marching, marching, marching. The Brigade Commander himself, very importantly, was giving the commands in front of the formation and making remarks about our movement and what was wrong. He guided us to the edge. The brigade commander turned the column around and wanted to give the command "Forward. March!" but did not succeed. A major ran up to him and reported, "Comrade Brigade Commander, Marshall of the Soviet Union Budenniy has arrived."

Goodness, where did the arrogance go? The Brigade Commander became very nervous, began to get his equipment in order, but still did not forget to say his "Devil take it!" Marshal Budenniy came into view. The Brigade Commander hurried to report, but he did not take into account that in the arena there was no asphalt—only some sawdust. The poor fellow tripped and fell. With quick steps, Budenniy hurried over to the fallen man and helped him rise. "Calm down! Calm down, Brigade Commander," said the Marshal. "You have gotten yourself upset."

The brigade commander got up and was preparing to make his report, but Budenniy with laughter said, "No need to report. No need. It will be better to just come with me. I will show you my new mare. It's not a horse, but a fire." They withdrew.

We soldiers were surprised at how, before the eyes of a whole formation, a man could change from an important grandee into a lowly clerk. At the same time, we were sorry for the old man, because he was a good guy.

As soon as the war started, Brigade Commander Chernetskiy brought the famous Knushevitskiy Jazz Band under

G. P. Vinogradov

his command. The jazz musicians became soldiers, and the Jazz Band served as a military unit. The enemy approached Moscow. The Jazz Band was sent to the front, to serve the forward units coming from battle. The Jazz Band performed a great service, encouraging the troops, helping them hold back the enemy. When our units retreated, the Jazz Band gave concerts for the populace. The famous Vinogradov sang his beloved song, *A Mother Bids Farewell to her Young Son*. Listeners cried, hugged and kissed the beloved singer. Near Vyazma the Jazz Band became encircled. For many days and nights, the artists of the Jazz Band walked to escape the encirclement. I remember how, by fives and sixes, they came to us at the orchestra, lice-ridden and starving, but in their hands they held their instruments. That was how they all made it back. The famous singer Georghiy Vinogradov also returned, and he was holding a machine gun in his hand, saying in extreme circumstances it was necessary to use this weapon for defense. For a long time, the jazz musicians were retelling the terrible days and nights they spent in the forests and countryside.

Georghiy Pavlovich and I were great friends. The war brought us together. When he escaped the encirclement, so thin and pale, I wanted so much to do something to help him. Georghiy Vinogradov was a wonderful singer. He had perfect pitch and could read notes from sheet music with complete freedom. When he was enrolled as a student at the Home Hall, concerts were being held in the Great Hall at the Conservatory. Once when Vinogradov was getting ready to go to a concert, he did not have any suitable shoes. He had to ask me to lend him leather boots. Fortunately, mine were well shined. I remember how Vinogradov struggled to pull my boots onto his feet.

Georghiy Vinogradov did a phonograph recording of P. Tchaikovsky's opera *Romeo and Juliet* with Valeria Vladimirovna Barsova. It turned out to be a wonderful recording! When he served in the Red Banner Ensemble of A. V. Aleksandrov, he had special success. He never left the stage without singing four or five songs as encores. There was an incident at a concert for the diplomatic corps.

Vinogradov sang three songs and went backstage. As always, they called a long time for him to come back out. General Aleksandrov asked to send backstage in order that Vinogradov would come out. All the same, Georghiy Vinogradov did not come out. It was a scandal. After this, the publicity organizers of the Ensemble decided to teach Vinogradov a lesson. They organized an open meeting, invited Vinogradov, and he came. It just so happened that Aleksandr Vasilievich Aleksandrov came among those gathered. He asked the chairman, "What is going on here? Why are we gathering?"

"Yes, well. It was decided to wear out Vinogradov singing."

"Stop the execution this instant! You only have to understand," stated Aleksandr Vasilievich, "that Vinogradov belongs to the SOBINOV Ensemble. Immediately, break it off! Do you hear?"

I already wrote about the Red Banner Ensemble needing horn players. I wanted so very much to transfer to the service of the Ensemble, but before me loomed an insuperable barrier—actually two of them. The first was the fact that A. V. Aleksandrov was not in tune with S. A. Chernetskiy. Plainly speaking, they could not stand each other. The second barrier was: would it happen for me? It was absolutely essential that I request a release from Brigade commander Chernetskiy, but he could refuse to let me go. After all, I was requesting a transfer to a man that the brigade commander hated. A few days earlier, Chernetskiy Had been promoted to the rank of general. Aleksandrov was a colonel. General Chernetskiy would make a special point of waiting for the moment when Colonel Aleksandrov emerged from his home. When General Chernetskiy passed by, Colonel Aleksandrov was forced by military law to greet General Chernetskiy. Well, that was the story anyway.

I took counsel with Georghiy Vinogradov about what I should do. Vinogradov advised me to go to Chernetskiy at home and request to be released. To go to General Chernetskiy would be terrifying! Would an ordinary soldier approach a general with a request, and in his quarters? Such a thing just simply was not done! I could be sacked, and rightly so. Subordination in the army is essential. I decided to go. I went! I approached his home. (At that time, the general lived on Big Kaluzhskaya Street.) My legs were shaking. I went up the steps. My legs would not move. I stood on the landing at the top of the steps and took a deep breath. I wanted to approach, but nothing happened. Well, what was I going to do? Go home? No! Once I had decided to go, that meant it was up to fate. I rang the bell. Sofia Pavlovna, the wife of Semyon Aleksandrovich opened the door.

"Oho! Polekh, I can't believe my own eyes. What's with you? " It was evident she wanted to say, "What's the matterwith you? Have you gone out of your mind?" Uncertainly, Sofia Pavlovna said, "Come in."

I went into the entryway. My boots were shiny and clean. I wiped my boots on the door mat anyway.

Концерт во фронтовой полосе

Concert in the frontal zone

"What matter have you come about? What brings you to us? Obviously, it's something you can't put off. You know Semyon Aleksandrov very well—he does not like jokes. How is it you aren't afraid? You are as brave as ten men! Take off your wraps and come in quietly. Himself, evidently, is asleep. What is the matter? Tell me about it."

61

I explained the heart of the matter to her. Sofia Pavlovna listened attentively to me and said, "In such a matter I cannot be of assistance. You know very well the relationship of Semyon Aleksandrovich with Aleksandrov, gently put, it is poor. At just one reminder of the name, Aleksandrov, and he may fly into a rage."

I began to think my case was in a bad way; in other words, this was a failure. I was already preparing to leave, and would have left if at that moment the door would not have opened and Semyon Aleksandrovich appeared.

"Well! I never! Is that you I see, Polekh? And where? As a guest of Chernetskiy himself." But, to himself he was probably saying, "I know I did not call for him." As they say: a miracle in a sieve. "Sit down. Sit down. I see that something is bothering you. Calm down. Devil take it!"

I was silent. I could not speak a single word. Chernetskiy stood up from the chair, paced around the room and said, "Either speak or leave."

Somehow, I immediately came to my senses, and with a shaky voice uttered, "I have come to you as to my own father."

"It is nice to see my sonny boy put in an appearance."

"It is a very serious matter for you."

"Report. I am all attention."

Semyon Aleksandrovich sat. I continued to stand. He did not offer that I should sit down.

"General sir, I feel that I am loosing my specialty, and I am not strong enough or in a position to help myself. I am often starving, I cannot practice, and I barely have the strength to carry out the duties placed upon me by the service. The family is at home, and a small baby, and conditions there are also precarious. So, I came to you for help. You have treated me so well."

"But, excuse me, what can I do for you, eh?

"The Red Banner Ensemble has advertised the audition for a French horn vacancy. The conditions are very good. So, I have come to you to request that you release me to the Ensemble."

"Devil take it! You have given me a problem. Believe me, I sympathize with you whole heartedly, but I cannot help you. I need you myself, besides which, with what kind of status must I release you to some kind of ensemble. What would they give you? What kind of benefits?"

I reported. Semyon Aleksandrovich from time to time scratched the back of his head.

"Yes, such conditions I could not give you. I could install you in the Institute of Military Conductors. You could teach there."

"I thank you greatly, General, Sir, but serving in the Ensemble, I could be working and live at home with the family. In such a case, I could return to my former liveliness and my famous cantilena."

"Devil take it! I cannot release you, and yes, I do not want to."

"General, Sir, I was so hoping in your kindness—you love us so—and in your staunch support of us musicians. Help me and my family."

Concert on the Front

Then I noticed, at the last moment, Sofia Pavlovna made a barely noticeable sort of signal with her gray head, and in her eyes it was as though there were just a hint of tears. Evidently, I had touched a woman's heart. The general stood up from his chair and said, "Devil take it! Alright, it will be as you asked. Go to your Emsemble, but do not say a word about it to anyone. Tell only the Sergeant Major so that he can prepare your transfer. That's all. Go."

I, in some kind of daze, quickly approached the general and kissed his hand. From the unexpectedness, he wanted to say something, but quickly left the room. Tears poured from my eyes. I kissed both Sofia Pavlovna's hands, and said, "You are the kindest woman!" and ran out of the house.

On the street, I caught my breath and silently walked along Kaluzhskaya Street—along the street where I was born. Remembering, I stopped and bowed to the house in which lived an amazing and most kind man. Then I bowed to my own home, where I was headed now with such wonderful news.

Here is another incident I happened to witness. We were rehearsing marches. Captain Zabezhanskiy was conducting the orchestra. Suddenly, General Chernetskiy arrived. He was very jolly and so happy. "Brothers," he addressed the orchestra, I don't know what to do, I'm so happy! I have just been awarded the Red Star Medal. That's why I am so happy."

A baritone player stood up, and addressed the general, "If you don't know what you should do, I know. Throw yourself headfirst out the window, and there you go!"

The General turned white. He was not the sort of man to forgive such an impudent joke. The General shouted, "To the front, scoundrel! To the front!"

The joke cost the baritone player dearly. The following day, the baritone player was sent to the front. The General must have been infuriated to allow himself such a response.

Quite some time passed, and I was serving with the Red Banner Ensemble already. By that time, we had traveled all over many fronts. Well, being on the Western Front, we were serving our fighting units that were beating the enemy. Suddenly, I saw a familiar soldier, who was carrying his mess kit and obviously, getting ready to eat. I approached closer to the soldier. Good Lord! It was our baritone player that had been sent off to the Front! The appearance of the baritone player, I tell you straight out, was not very good. He was thin, pale, and not looking like himself at all. He had a machine gun hanging sort of awkwardly on his shoulder. His appearance was not at all that of a fighting man. Andrei, that was our baritone player's name, recognized me immediately. His hands began to tremble so much that he almost spilled his food, and he began to cry.

"Valeriy," he addressed himself to me, "if you only knew! It is not very sweet for me here. It's really very hard to bear! I am suffering for offending such a good man. It's hard for me. Very hard! He always stands before me insulted. I am so worthless!"

Listening to Andrei, I was thinking, "Really, Andrei is not a bad person."

"You made a mistake, and so you are atoning for your mistake here on the front. Don't turn sour, but find in yourself the strength to be that good fellow that I knew you to be. I promise to speak with the General and tell him that you have repented and ask his forgiveness. I am certain, the General is a wonderful man. He is not evil, and he will forgive you."

Andrei's face lit up. He even smiled—such a good, gentle smile. With that, we parted.

One day, after returning to Moscow, I happened to see the leader of the orchestra in which the baritone player, Andrei, had served. I told him about my encounter on the front.

"Yes," the orchestra leader said, "that's how a man falls because of stupidity. This thing needed to cool down. Who would put much importance on such a man?" I strongly requested of him that, when it was possible, he speak to the General. The leader promised. Later on I learned that the General forgave Andrei and helped him return to Moscow.

That is a man. A MAN, with capital letters. Strict, but with a gentle soul. Semyon Aleksandrovich did so much that was good for us, and for the soldiers. We are all so grateful to him.

SEVEN

Kirill Kondrashin

A CHILD WITH SHAGGY BLOND hair was running along a corridor of the Bolshoi Theater. A stout man with a pleasant face stopped him. "Who are you with?" the man asked the little one.

"I'm with Mama and Papa," the child replied.

"And who are they?"

"Papa is Pyotr Kondrashin. He plays the viola, and Mama is Annechka Kondrashina. Mama plays the violin."

"Oh, that's how it is, eh? And what is your name?"

"I'm Kirill Kondrashin," the boy replied. "My parents are musicians."

"And what are you going to be?"

"I will be a conductor."

"That is laudable. When you grow up, come to my class."

"And who are you?"

"I'm Golovanov, conductor of the Bolshoi Theater Orchestra." He patted the tot on the head. The man with the pleasant face was Nikolai Semyonovich Golovanov.

K. Kondrashin

Many years passed. Kirill was studying at the Moscow Conservatory in the conductor section, and playing in a student orchestra on the percussion instruments. Once when the conductor Nikolai Semyonovich Golovanov was rehearsing the student orchestra, and break time was over, all were in their places, but there was no percussionist. Golovanov shouted, "Where are the drummers?"

Suddenly, the drummers ran in. Leading them all was Kirill Kondrashin, and in his mouth was a slice of buttered bread.

"Stop! Stop! What are you chewing on? Devil take you!" Golovanov addressed the orchestra, "Open up *Dance of the Buffoons*. And you, lover of eating, stand here in my place at the podium. You conduct, and I will listen in the auditorium to see how the orchestra sounds."

With trepidation, Kirill stood at the conductor's podium and conducted. When *Dance of the Buffoons* ended, Golovanov praised Kondrashin, "Good fellow! It seems you are able to conduct not too badly."

My acquaintance with Kirill Kondrashin began with a performance of Rimsky-Korsakov's *Snow Maiden* at the Bolshoi Theater. The performance was directed by Kirill Kondrashin. In this production, the French horn plays quite a large part, and the

presentation is rather complicated. At the beginning of rehearsals, Kirill was sharp in dealing with the horn players. He felt the tone was not right, and he requested we play with a more transparent tone. We began to play with a transparent tone, and again it was not right. During the break, I went to the conductor's room with the horn music and asked him to explain to me all his wishes. Kirill declared, "This is something new! Usually, the conductor explains his desires on the spot, that is, in the orchestra pit." But, he said that he was not against the new method I was proposing. He quite quickly explained his rather interesting proposals. I felt Kirill was respectful in his relationship with me. On my part, there was only a courteous and respectful association with him. Kirill Petrovich invited me to the conductors room another time, and we had a very pleasant conversation. The premiere of *Snow Maiden* went excellently, and Kirill Petrovich remained satisfied with our performance.

Rumors were going around that an orchestra was being put together to travel to the Festival of Youth and Students in Hungary. The rumors were confirmed. Our Youth Symphonic Orchestra was actually going to travel to Hungary. Kirrill Kondrashin was designated to be the conductor. Before long, he phoned me and asked me to head up the horn section. It would be very pleasant to travel to the Festival with Kirrill Kondrashin. He was a young, talented conductor, and the orchestra was full of young people. Kirrill put together a program of Russian music: *Eight Songs* by Liadov, *Stringed Serenade* by Tchaikovsky, and Kamarinskaya by Glinka.

At the Festival, we would participate in a competition of orchestras. We needed to be well-prepared. The musicians selected for the orchestra were excellent: part of them from the Bolshoi theater, from the State Orchestra, and from the Radio Orchestra. We gathered every day, and later twice a day. During the Festival in Hungary, there was going to be an international contest of the participating musicians. I began to practice harder, but there was a problem. The age limit was thirty years, and I was thirty one. They did not list me on the roster of contestants. I was greatly saddened, but did not stop practicing. Summer came. I rented a dacha with my family, and went to practice in the forest. It was wonderful in the forest. In the morning, larks accompanied me, and, in the evening, the nightingales. It was wonderful to be out in nature, and it was easy to breathe.

The day of departure arrived. We were seen off very ceremonially.

A band played. We were all in identical suits. Vocalists, wind instrument players, and string players would participate at the  Festival. The train pulled out. We said farewell to Moscow. On the trip it was merry, in one word, "youth." We arrived in Lvov, and had a one hour layover. Kirrill proposed that whoever wished could wander around the town. They rented a bus. Everyone who wished joyfully got on the bus. The main leader was Kirrill. We began to drive, climbing up the steep mountain and into the town. The bus driver served as our guide. He very graphically explained about Lvov. It was evident he loved his city. The driver showed us the interesting places. Time passed swiftly, and it was time to return to the station. However, there was an emergency. The engine flooded. We all got out of the bus, but the motor was silent. The driver tinkered with it, but nothing worked.

Kondrashin made a proposal. "Brothers, you see, we are on a mountain, and the station is at the bottom of the mountain. Push the bus, and we are at the station."

Everyone quickly boarded the bus, and a few stayed to push the bus. When it was moving, they jumped in the bus, and we coasted down. We were saved! After a few minutes, the train pulled out.

We arrived in Budapest, and a solemn ceremony was organized to greet us. This was nothing to joke about. Representatives of Greater Soviet Union, the victor in a terrible war, were arriving. The welcoming party crowded around our train to see what was happening. Everyone wanted to look at us, shake our hands, and present us with flowers. We went out to the square—it was surprisingly beautiful. An enormous red carpet was spread over the whole square. The meeting began. From our delegation, the Secretary of the Central Committee of the Komsomol brought a word. Shouts of "*Ehlyon* Komsomol! *Ehlyon* Stalin!" rang out. The meeting continued a long time. At the end of the meeting, we got on buses and went to our accommodations.

The next day work began—orchestra rehearsals. Contestants were required to appear before the contest committee in order to draw a lucky number. We sat in the orchestra pit of an opera theater and each waited for his fate. They began to call out the contest tickets. I waited. They gave out all the numbers. There was not one for me, but I did not get upset. I approached the chairman of the contest committee. "Excuse me," I said. "For some reason my name was not called, and I do not have a contest ticket in my hand."

"Your name?" The chairman looked through the lists, and I was not on them. "Will you forgive us? Evidently, there was some sort of misunderstanding. I will add your name to the list, and you draw your ticket."

I had the ticket in my hand—number 26. This was the ticket I had gone to so much trouble to get. They gave us a classroom in a conservatory, and I practiced from morning till night.

One day, there was a knock on the classroom door. A small group of young people entered. They greeted me very politely, and one of them asked, "Are you going to participate in the contest?"

"Yes," I answered, "and I already drew number 26."

"Would you be so kind as to tell us what program you proposed to the contest committee?"

"With pleasure," I said, and told them my program. They were a little surprised.

"You are really going to play F. Chopin's *Waltz in D flat minor*?"

"Yes, I will," I replied.

"Could you play it for us now?"

"I would be pleased to," I assured them.

Among the group of young people they found a pianist, and we started playing. When I finished, the young people expressed praise for my performance of Chopin's *Waltz*. They bowed themselves out. I did not see these people at the contest. Rehearsals of the orchestra also were being conducted every day. Here is a list of the orchestral soloists: Yu. Rentovich, Yu. Silantev, A. Gorokhov, Nelly Shkolnikova, Eh. Grach, T. Dokshitser, N. Sobor, A. Ryabinin, M. Orudzhev, M. Zeynalov, and M. Chepkoy. Kirill Kondrashin grew before your eyes. Now, he was not only in charge of an opera but also a symphony.

My pianist for the contest was Abrasha Makarov—a wonderful master of his work. We rehearsed a lot, but it was not easy because I was staying on the Buda side and Abrasha lived on the Pest side. It was necessary to cross over and back twice each day.

The day of the contest arrived. In the morning, I rehearsed with Abrasha, and we went our separate ways until the presentation at the contest. In the evening, the contest was in full swing, and I was waiting for my turn when, for some reason I was called to the telephone. I heard the voice of Abrasha.

"What's up?' I asked.

He answered, "I can't be at the contest. They've got me busy with foreigners."

"What are you saying? Do you understand what you are saying? You are killing me! I am going on soon, and and you report such terrible news. I don't know anything, but you are simply obligated to appear at the contest."

"Well, alright, Valeriy. If I'm able, I will come."

What was I going to do? My head was splitting in pieces. I had to leave my position, and ask a pianist I was acquainted with to help me. She agreed. We quickly ran through my program, and suddenly I saw Abrasha's bald spot. Well, glory to God! I thanked the kind pianist and prepared myself to go on stage. At the doorway stood the Secretary of the Komsomol's Central Committee. He whispered to me, "Only first place! Only first!" and he showed me his fist. I went on. I played very successfully. The audience rewarded me with friendly applause, and the result was first premium and the title of Laureate. They presented me with a beautiful vase. Also, a famous Hungarian conductor came to hear me for the whole tour, and gave me his photograph with the inscription, "Dear Laureate V. Polekh, I was entranced. Bravo. Bravissimo! I. Shomodi."

After much rehearsal work, at last we appeared at the orchestral competition. Kondrashin was equal to the occasion. We won the first premium. They presented Kondrashin an enormous silver horn. Kirill and the orchestra acquitted themselves wonderfully in the competition program. We received very good press, and photos of Kirill Petrovich and the orchestra were in the papers.

The concluding concert was a resounding success also. The artists of ballet and vocalization presented themselves very well, and we wind instrumentalists did not have mud on our faces either. Our delegation gave several more concerts, and our orchestra traveled around the country.

Here is something interesting that happened at one of my concerts. Suddenly, at the end of one of the evening concerts in which I had played, a young man with a French horn in his hand stood up and commented, "Comrade Polekh, your horn, clearly, has some special construction that helps you play the technical passages so quickly. Please be so kind as to take my instrument and play on it, and we will listen." I took the instrument of this man in my hands and played with the same success. Stormy applause resounded in the hall.

"Thank you very much," the fellow mumbled as he took his instrument from me.

There was another similar incident. As I was walking along the street, some young people approached me, and said, "We heard you at the concert. Please play Chopin's *Waltz* here on the street."

"But won't they take me to the police?"

"Don't be shy. We are listening to you."

I played *a capella*, of course. Hearing the sound, a large crowd gathered. Evidently, they were interested. I played two more waltzes by Chrysler. It was a wonderful time. That is how this beautiful Festival ended.

Upon returning to Moscow, we once more began doing a lot of work with the orchestra, and prepared a new concert program. It included the following compositions: *Capriccio Italian*, and *Scheherezade* by Rimsky-Korsakov, and *Kamarinskaya* by Glinka. The concert took place in the P. Tchaikovsky Concert Hall. The orchestra had great success. The symphonic-concert career of Kirill Kondrashin really began with the Youth Orchestra. Here Kondrashin began to feel that he could live yet another life—one on the symphonic stage. We all felt this at this concert. He directed the program wonderfully.

The All-Union Studio of Gramophone Recording proposed that we record *Capriccio Espagnol* on vinyl. We recorded this composition with great inspiration. Here also, Kirill Kondrashin was equal to the occasion. We began to perform concerts in various concert halls. We performed for the students at the Moscow University with especially great success. Many students who had been at the Festival with us were in the audience. Before long, The Moscow Philharmonic opened a series, and we could perform concerts almost every Monday in the P. Tchaikovsky Concert Hall.

As we were coming to the recording studio one day, we caught sight of Sviatoslav Richter. He had come to record Beethoven's *Fifth Concerto* with us. This was a holiday for us. His playing impressed us. We had never heard anything like it in our lives. It is difficult for me to describe what we felt, and I will only say one thing: this was divine music! From that time on, we began to make recordings with Sviatoslav Richter. We wanted to play and play with Richter. He was an astonishing musician. It needs to be said that Richter loved to record with us. He once said, "When I play with you, I am young. You are such generous people. With you, it is so easy for me."

I am reminded of one of our concerts. P. Serebryakov was playing S. Rachmaninoff's *Second Concerto*. Eh. Gils was playing P. Tchaikovsky's *First Concerto*, and S. Richter was playing Rimsky-Korsakov's *Concerto*. It is thought that Rimsky-Korsakov's *Concerto* is not very interesting, and it is rarely performed. However, Richter wrought a real wonder out of the *Concerto*. The audience was entranced. We musicians were also delighted.

As a person, Kirill Kondrashin was pleasant and always even-tempered. He simply treated us musicians as equals. He was very pleasant to be around. He loved humor. We, somehow, felt like family after we returned from the Festival. Often, some of us artists from the Youth Orchestra would get together. Kirill always was the soul of the society, and the first to take the lead. He was often at my home, at Galya Matrosovaya's, at Nina Sibor's. With him at the table there was no heavy drinking. We played various card games, but generally Kirill would play at *preference*. We always parted happy and only regretted that the evening had passed so quickly. I will always remember the times spent with the wonderful man and musician, Kirill Petrovich Kondrashin.

EIGHT

Timothy Aleksandrovich Dokshitser

T IMOTHY ALEKSANDROVICH DOKSHITSER WAS born December 13, 1921, in the town of Nezhin in the Chernogovskiy Oblast. This small town was known for having one of the finest schools in Russia—the Gymnasia of Higher Science—where N. V. Gogol had studied.

The small town of Nezhin has another other claim to fame—Nezhin cucumbers.

Timothy Dokshitser's father, Aleksandr Timofeovich Dokshitser, was a self-taught musician. He was capable and gifted, played the violin, French horn, and percussion instruments, wrote arrangements for the wind orchestra, and did some music composition. As a child, Timothy began to show an interest in music. His father immediately paid attention to the son's abilities, his excellent ear, and memory. He often took him to rehearsals of the wind orchestra. There, the boy listened with interest and envied at how the grown-ups were able to play the instruments.

T. A. Dokshitser

After a short time he had learned to sing the themes of the orchestra's repertoire.

The Dokshitsers moved to Moscow in the summer of 1932. There, Timothy Dokshitser became an apprentice of the 62nd Cavalry Regimental Orchestra. In this orchestra, Timmy immediately found himself among professional musicians. It was here in the barracks at Khamovnik, for the first time in his life, he heard the music of Tchaikovsky's *Swan Lake* which was played by the cavalry military orchestra. The future musician was overcome by the depth of the music he was hearing. He froze in some sort of stasis and listened and listened. For him, this was the opening of a new world—full of motion, and calling to him. He also would play the trumpet like the trumpeter-musician he knew, but before long there was an encounter that changed his attitude about playing the trumpet.

Little Timmy was taken to the wonderful musician-trumpeter, Ivan Antonovich Vasilevskiy. He became very interested in Timmy's abilities, and accepted him into the school of music affiliated with the college. Having come out of the school of hard knocks, Ivan Antonovich Vasilevskiy treated Dokshitser with great sensitivity. Vasilevskiy was renowned as a wonderful instructor who had developed many musicians. He was exclusively a pedagogic-trainer, a talented rehearser, possessing the rare ability, in a few years of instruction, to instill a good technical basis for the mastery of the instrument. He not only taught how to play the trumpet, but was also a sensitive nurturer and exhorter.

In 1935, Timothy demobilized, and passed the entrance exams for the Central Music School associated with the Conservatory. Professor M. I. Tabakov was in attendance at that exam. From this moment, all of Dokshitser's future artistic life would be connected with the name of this wonderful teacher and person, Mikhail Innokentevich Tabakov. (In a later account, I will tell about my encounter with this generous musician.)

Like Timothy, I was connected with the very kind and sensitive man, Ivan Antonovich Vasilevskiy. Here is my story.

Ivan Antonovich was known to be a wonderful teacher and person. He always helped everyone. For example, R. M Gliere wrote a concerto for French horn and orchestra. My assignment was to quickly learn the concerto and perform it in less than a year's time. I began to work, to study the concerto, and practiced in an artist's room at the Theater. One day, Ivan Antonovich came in. He was interested in what I was playing, and what was this music? When I explained, he immediately advised me to practice with piano accompaniment.

"Well, you see this is the deal, my dear Ivan Antonovich, I do not yet have a pianist, and it is not known when I will get one."

"Valeriy, I will help you. A very good pianist is working in my classroom at the college. I can recommend her to you."

"Ivan Antonovich, I would be so grateful to you! Are you sure this won't be too much trouble?"

"Not at all. Tomorrow, I will negotiate with my pianist. Her name is Nadezhda Ryakina."

On the morrow, I was in Ivan Antonovich's classroom. Nadezhda Ryakina was an exceptional professional pianist. We began to work at her home, at the Theater, and at the college. Ivan Antonovich would come and listen. He enjoyed Gliere's Concerto very much.

Nadezhda Ryakina and I worked hard. The time came to test our performance in public. We played at the College of Ippolitov-Ivanov, in Beethoven Hall at the Bolshoi Theater, and in the college affiliated with the Moscow Conservatory. I appeared with Nadezhda at the Institute for Military Conductors. The whole staff of the Institute came to listen, and many of them were holding the piano score of the concerto. The author of the concerto, Reinhold Moritsevich Gliere, came to the main rehearsal. They listened attentively to our presentation. Our performance was a great success. They praised our music and were very pleased with our execution of the concerto. They called forth the author, Reinhold Moritsevich, and called forth the pianist, Nadezhda Ryakina. I was very thankful to her for playing so beautifully. Also attending the concert was my instructor, Ivan Antonovich Vasilevskiy, whom I kissed.

The wonderful men and musicians, Mikhail Innokentevich Tabakov and Ivan Antonovich Vasilevskiy, helped Timothy and myself to become real professionals. You see, these are our artistic fathers and we, Timothy and I, are their artistic children, and in some measure we are artistic brothers. We did not get acquainted right away, although we both took part in the All-Union Competition of Performing Musicians, and worked near each other during the war.

My first close acquaintance with Timothy occurred at a phonograph recording session. He was recording Rimsky-Korsakov's *Flight of the Bumble Bee* with the Bolshoi Theater Orchestra. He played brilliantly, but the music did not fit because of timing. In those days, recording was done on small vinyl disks.

They took a break. Timothy began training with a stop-watch and found the tempo he needed. You just know how hard that was because the composition is very technically difficult. Timothy called the orchestra back. The recording technician started it up, and the recorder was running. Timothy did the recording just as brilliantly. I witnessed this because I was playing in the Bolshoi Theater Orchestra. We became friends.

One day, Timothy suggested we form a wind quartet. This proposal struck a chord in my soul. We invited a very good musician and individual, trombonist Mamed Zeinalov, and trumpeter, Yashu Gandel. We began to work. We were so on fire that we got together nearly every day. We would come to the Theater at eight in the morning, grab some artistic dressing room, and rehearse until the regular orchestra rehearsal started.

Our repertoire was extremely limited. We possessed a few small pieces, and a quartet by the composer Simon. Timothy appealed to M. I. Tabakov for help. Tabakov told Timothy, that, at the Bolshoi Theater, there had been just such a quartet formed by Professor V. Blazhevich. "Blazhevich quite successfully made several arrangements for a quartet. Find his notebooks," he advised," and you will have a solid repertoire."

We began to search for those precious notebooks. As you may imagine, they were all found in the possession of V. Blazhevich's relatives. In these notebooks were quite a few interesting arrangements. The work heated up again. We began performing with small concerts and programs, and at music schools and colleges, and even a little on the radio. At that time, we still did not have enough experience with ensemble playing, and Timothy proposed that we present ourselves to the well-known expert on ensembles, Aleksandr Fedorovich Gedeke. We continued to work harder. By accident, we found the quintet *Vasiliya Evadda*. Then a tuba player, Lesha Lebeden, joined our ensemble. He was a wonderful musician and composer. We decided to appear before Aleksandr Fedorovich Gedike.

We made arrangements for the meeting by telephone. We dressed in our parade uniforms: black coats, and white bow ties. We practiced a little and got under way. As we were approaching the left wing of the conservatory where Aleksandr Fedorovich Gedike lived, we stopped and froze in our tracks. What did we see? Aleksandr Fedorovich was feeding the birds. Birds were sitting on his shoulders begging. One rather large bird was sitting on his head. We sat on a bench and watched. When the feeding was finished, Aleksandr Fedorovich brought the birds a bowl of water.

Upon seeing us, Aleksandr Fedorovich greeted us, shook hands with each of us, and invited us into his apartment. We were a little taken aback to be entering the chambers of a great musician. Aleksandr Fedorovich politely asked us to be seated and began to ask us all about our work and about life. Timothy told Gedike about our work and what we were playing.

"My kind friends, I would listen to you with pleasure."

We played rather successfully. Our performance pleased Aleksandr Fedorovich, and he said, "I am pleased by you manner of not mistreating the notes. You are not trying to show that you are playing wind instruments. You are controlling your instruments well, and showing the harmony of an ensemble. My advice to you is this: try to attend concerts by such wonderful masters as the Beethoven Quartet, and the Bolshoi Theater Quartet. It goes without saying, this will benefit you. Friends, I thank you for coming to me. I listened to your performance with pleasure. I say this also—you are fully able to perform in concerts."

We thanked Aleksandr Fedorovich for the *Concerto for Trumpet*, *Concerto for French Horn*, and the *Etude for Trumpet*.

"Are you playing my concertos?" asked Aleksandr Fedorovich.

"Yes, we often perform your wonderful compositions." With this we said farewell to Aleksandr Fedorovich Gedike.

An incident occurred, as Timothy and I took part in a concert. While Timothy was playing, I stood backstage and listening. I was thinking, "We have a lot in common—tone and lightness of exposition."

Bogdanov, Dokshitser, and Polekh

Timothy and I went with the Youth Orchestra to Hungary for the Festival of Youth and Students. Kirill Kondrashin was conducting. At the Festival, a contest of orchestras was held. We performed very successfully and won the first premium. They presented us with an enormous horn of plenty. At the Festival, Timothy and I did not just perform as musicians in the orchestra, but also as soloists on the stage. The press wrote that we were not only orchestral musicians, but real soloist artists and equals with the violinists and pianists. We traveled with the orchestra throughout all of Hungary, to and fro. Everywhere the audiences received us with enthusiasm.

In 1955, the Youth Orchestra traveled to Poland for the Festival of Youth and Students. Timothy, as always, sparkled in *Swan Lake*, and played in many towns as a soloist.

In addition to the enormous burden he carried as a soloist of the Bolshoi Theater Orchestra and teacher at the Institute, Dokshitser directed productions at the Bolshoi Theater and studied at the Conservatory in the conductor's department. He also performed in concerts and on the radio. At the Bolshoi Theater, he conducted the operas *La Traviata, Verter, Bank-Ban*, and *Faust.* In the Great Hall at the Conservatory, under the direction of Dokshitser, the Bolshoi Theater Orchestra performed P. I. Tchaikovsky's *Sixth Symphony*, K. Beber's *Overture to Oberon*, and Gliere's *Concerto for Voice and Orchestra.* The critics united in noting the success of the young conductor.

Even after a single visit to the cozy little classroom named for M. I. Tabakov where Timothy Dokshitser worked with students, anyone would long remember the atmosphere of attention, warmth, and high professional requirement. The teaching methods of Dokshitser were mostly a combination of the methods of I. A. Vasilevskiy and M. I. Tabakov, which had as the first order of business that all efforts were directed toward the growth and maturation of the young musician. To this end, he wanted the student to achieve an intelligent mastery of the material. Without fail, Dokshitser would stop a student if he saw that the pupil was doing something mechanically or without thinking. Timothy Aleksandrovich gave especially great emphasis to the development of a culture of tone.

Timothy Dokshitser and his trumpeters at the Bolshoi Theater not only performed well, but were also able to relax well. Annually, on one of those fine fall days, the trumpeters of the Bolshoi Theater would travel to the dacha of their colleague, the trumpeter Sasha Balakhonov. At about that time, Sasha Balakhonov would gather an abundant harvest of fruit and vegetables. He would process fruit drinks, make juices, and pickle little cucumbers. Upon the arrival of the trumpeters, he would bake beans. In addition, the trumpet-playing colleagues would bring something or other. Someone would bring a chicken, someone else shashlik*, and another a bottle of *Russian Mountain***. At last, everyone would be gathered and just waiting for the arrival of the patriarch of the trumpeters, Timothy Dokshitser. Then he would arrive with his dear Fanechka.

The gathering began at Mamed Zeinalov's place, and they were waiting for Mamed's wife, Anechka. They had a large personal plot of land with a volleyball court. Everyone dressed in sports clothes, and the game began. I was not a trumpeter—I played the French horn, but the trumpeters included me as one of their own.

We passed the time happily, and when everyone was tired and sweaty, we directed our steps to the country estate of Sasha Balakhonov. There, the table was already spread, and special gastronomical aromas were wafting into the atmosphere. The first toast was to the friendship of the trumpeters, and, of course, was given by Timothy. The second toast was to the dear ladies, the charming ladies. We raised a glass to the master of the festivities, Sasha Balakhonov. The table was spread with marrow-beans baked in sugar, vinaigrette salad, marinated small cucumbers, a salad of fresh cabbage, carrots, beets, and grated cheese with garlic. We

---

*   shashlik is pieces of mutton roasted on a spit.
**   Russian Mountain Vodka

started on the fruity drinks, the juices, the hot chicken that had been roasted over coals, and the shashlik.

At the table, things went gloriously. There were also anecdotes. Nema Polonskiy, a trumpet soloist told this one:

"At three in the morning, a guy makes a telephone call. A sleepy voice answers the phone, 'Hello.'

"The guy asks, 'Is this telephone number 233-84-56?'"

"The voice says, 'What's this? Are you crazy? I don't HAVE a telephone!'"

Someone told this:

"Mr. Policeman, sir, tell me. Is it dangerous to go on this street?"

"If it were dangerous, I would not be standing here!"

I, Valeriy Polekh, told this one myself:

"In the park next to his Villa, a millionaire architect had three swimming pools built. One had warm water, the next had cold water, and the third swimming pool did not have any water in it at all."

"'Why do you have a swimming pool with no water in it?'"

"'Because some of my friends can't swim.'"

After the rather abundant table, we decided to take a stroll. The trumpeter, Nema Polonskiy grabbed his trumpet for some reason. We decided to make a circle and return to Sasha Balakhonov's. We began with the dacha of tenor Anton Grigorev, but it turned out he was not home. We went on. We came to the dacha of Elizabeta Shuiskaya. Nema Polonskiy took his trumpet and began to play the aria *Martha* from *The Czar's Bride*. Shuiskaya, having heard the familiar and beloved melody, come out of her estate to us.

"Good Lord! Who is this I see? Almost the whole Bolshoi Theater!" Shuiskaya began to sing to Polonskiy with her wonderful voice. "Guys, where did so many trumpeters come from? What are you doing? Are you out caroling? But where is your sack? I could fill it with carrots, beets, and some other things." Elizabeta Shuiskaya was delighted. We talked a little and went farther. "Go over there, where Volodya Ivanovskiy lives. He is known for *German*."

Nema played, "What is Our Life, a Play?" We were already at his gate. After a short while, Ivanovskiy showed himself. With pleasure he struck the pose of German and sang. He sang through the entire first couplet.

"Come on in, guys. Where are you from, the bunch of you?"

"Well, no. We are going farther."

Next was the home of the baritone, Kiselev. It was a pity that he was not home. We went on to the home of Volodya Levashev, the famous Bolshoi Theater dancer. Nema played the theme *Swans*. Out ran Volodya. He did a few dance steps, and flapped his arms like wings. Everyone laughed. He ran off as though he were in a big hurry to get somewhere.

We noticed Uncle Volodya Gavryushov, our three-octave base. Nema played *Loves All Become Submissive*. Uncle Volodya began to join in with great pleasure. He really loved to sing, and sang from morning til night. "Children, let's sing something else, shall we?"

"No, we need to be moving on."

Then I said, "Let's go to my place." And there we were at my cabin, located on my plot of land. Everyone seated themselves around the spacious table. I hurried to the cellar and brought a large bottle of home-brewed kvass*. Also, my mother-in-law, Aleksandra Sergeevna, brought fresh-baked meat pies for the main course. The meat pies were done to everyone's taste, and the kvass quenched the thirst for it was quite hot on the street. My wife, Ludmilla Nikolaevna, went with the ladies to look over our house. Nema and I played a waltz by Chrysler. We sat a little, talked a little, and continued on.

Next was the mansion of Sergei Yakovlevich Lemeshev. It was too bad the master of the house was away on tour. Here, Nema played *Heart of a Beauty*. Everyone laughed.

We turned onto Sobinov Street. We went by the house of A. Krivcheni. He was on vacation somewhere. We approached the

---

* **Kvass** is a traditional Slavic fermented beverage, ... It is classified as a non-**alcoholic** drink by Russian standards

house of A. Geleva—the famous bass. Nema began playing, "Once in the city of Kazan, the Czar himself partied merrily." Right then, Geleva sprang out the gate and sang in his rich bass, surprised to see so many trumpeters. "One minute," Geleva said, and disappeared. He returned with small bouquets of flowers. The ladies were touched, and expressed the general opinion that Geleva was a real gentleman.

The circuit was closed, and we returned to Sasha Balakhonov's where the samovar was already boiling. We drank tea with various preserves. It began to get dark, and everyone began to disperse to to their own Homes. The honorable company of trumpeters warmly and sincerely thanked Sasha for the hospitality. Thus passed a sweet, pleasant, and traditional autumn day of the trumpeters at Sasha Balakhonov's.

The ideological base that served to unite the trumpeters was, first of all, a striving toward a professional social interaction that was truly friendly, mutually enriching, and which came as a change from professional isolation. Life demonstrated that it was necessary to legitimize the unity of musicians and to find a base and form of the work. The Central House of Working Artists of the USSR became such a base. The leadership of the CHWA warmly supported this form of relationship. April 12, 1962, was recognized as the official founding meeting of the Creative Union of Trumpeters. The successful fulfillment of the promise of this union depended on active participation in it of all the leading musicians in Moscow. Interest in the work of the Union spread also to other wind-instrument musicians. The very next year, the Union of Trumpeters was transformed into The Artistic Union of Wind Musicians, and over the course of 21 years, it's constant chairman has been Timothy Dokshitser.

The Collective observed the 60th birthday celebration of Timothy Dokshitser with a small concert at its home, the Bolshoi Theater. On December 13, 1981, the first benefit for orchestral musicians in history was performed. The Golden Age of the soloing trumpet is continuing, and we are glad to recognize that it has given us

a significant phenomenon— Timothy Dokshitser, whose brilliant
talent is so synonymous with our wonderful times.

> To Dear Timothy Aleksandrovich Dokshitser
> In honor of such an anniversary celebration,
> Not stinting extreme effort,
> I wrote this poem for you,
> On the theme of Dokshitser.
> Sixty years is almost a half century.
> But he is a man,
> With such a kind heart and soul.
> Believe it! You have met the best.
> Friends, my toast to Timothy
> He is a storied, epic trumpeter.
> Ta-Ta-Ta-Ra.
> Ta-Ta-Ta-Ta.
> The silver coronet sings.
> I tell you, there is none prettier than it.
> The professor is famous throughout the world.
> His students are growing—
> Both in technique and tone increasing,
> So that they will be just as famous.
> We, wind musicians in the CHWA,*
> May listen to them, a thousand or three.
> Come, listen to the music;
> Find great benefit in it.
> Various debates occur.
> Laureates are playing there.
> For recognition of Timothy Aleksandrovich
> This celebration is necessary.
> Every musician recognizes
> Your organizational talent.

---

*   CHWA=Central House of Working Artists

Warm congratulations flow.
Be forever bold and healthy.
Be jolly, not stern.
Live more than a century, of course,
And love your wife forevermore,
So that all around you is success!
  Respectfully, the Polekhs.

NINE

Kseniya Aleksandrovna Ehrdeli

THERE ARE PEOPLE WHOSE way of life is submitted to an unselfish, purposeful service of one idea, which determines their whole character and the whole style of their lives and energy. In the life of Kseniya Aleksandrovna Ehrdeli, this idea was the love of the harp and the development of a harp culture in our country. Years of ceaseless labor as an artist and teacher, uninterrupted fervor for the art, unquenchable thirst for perfection, and eternal dissatisfaction with achievements—that is the biography of Ehrdeli.

"The years of my childhood," said Kseniya Aleksandrovna, "were spent in the Kherson Province of Ukraine. My father, Aleksandr Aleksandrovich Erdeli, upon completing the the judicial course of study at the Petersburg University, received appointment first to Astrakhan and later to Elizabetgrad. Our whole family moved to his estate, Mirolyubovka. From the Ehrdeli family came people with higher degrees: military officers, engineers, doctors, jurists, and such. I was the first from among them to become a professional musician. When I turned ten, Mother took me to Petersburg to attend the Smolniy Institute. At that time, the Smolniy Institute was the oldest of all the schools for women existing in Russia. It had been established by Catherine II in 1764. The talented harpist, Ekaterina Kyuneh traveled to Smolniy to play a concert. She entranced all the pupils with her playing. At that time, we learned it had been decided to reestablish an old tradition and once more to carry on instruction in playing the harp. A few days after that evening, Kyuneh came to the Institute, and after testing us, chose me and one other pupil. In 1893, a modern harp was ordered from France. "

For Kseniya Aleksandrovna, one may count 1893 as the year she began to work with the harp.

Once, my wife and I went to Olga Ehrdeli's on her birthday. (Olga is Kseniya Ehrdeli's niece.) At that time, we were "home" friends. Her amazing mother, Maria Aleksandrovna had graduated from the Petersburg Conservatory as a pianist, in her own day, and was a broadly educated woman—humorous and smart. Her Papa, Georgiy Yakovlevich had colossal abilities as an artist, engraver, wood carver, and a capable musician. We loved to be in this home because it was always so comfortable there. During the evening of Olga's birthday, Kseniya Aleksandrovna arrived. She had an aura of distinction, and something about her seemed so grand. They introduced us, and we exchanged greetings. Kseniya Aleksandrovna immediately became the life of the party. She knew a great deal, and had lived an interesting life. When she learned I was working in the Bolshoi Theater orchestra, the conversation turned to it. She described her earlier life at the Bolshoi Theater very colorfully, and was interested in knowing how things were going at the Theater. How was the orchestra? Was everything sounding beautiful? "In my time, I've known many wonderful people, played with many, and performed concerts on stage."

One evening, Kseniya Aleksandrovna came to see Olga Ehrdeli, and she was in an excellent mood. She had just come from a concert that was very successful. We spent an enjoyable evening. We had something to drink, and something to eat. Truthfully, at Olga's everything we had to eat was very tasty. Kseniya Aleksandrovna amused us the whole evening. After noisy conversation, Kseniya Aleksandrovna asked for quiet, and she began to talk.

"I remember, when I was at the Smolniy Institute, as soon as I had mastered a small repertoire, I was asked to play the harp for guests and visitors. The Emperor Aleksandr III came to the Institute. He became interested in my successes, and after examining my

hands, asked did my fingers hurt? I was extremely surprised at this attention. Evidently, he had learned from his wife, the Empress Maria Fedorovna, who played the harp, that at first, when one is just beginning to practice, very painful blisters form on the fingers, and afterward the blisters change into callouses."

"This was not my first encounter with the Emperor Aleksandr III. Our first 'acquaintanceship' had a comical character. Soon after starting at the Institute, I became Ill with typhus and erysipelas. They put me away in an isolation room, shaved my head, and spread some sort of white ointment on my face. After I had spent a month in bed, they allowed me to get up. Unexpectedly, one day a bell rang. It was a special bell that announced the arrival of the Emperor and all the Czar's family. It turned out that Aleksandr III had arrived. Making the rounds of the Institute, he directed himself to the infirmary. I had been warned, that when answering a question, it was necessary to add the words, 'Your Imperial Highness.' Striving to accurately fulfill this requirement, I kept repeating to myself all the time, 'Your Imperial Highness.' Suddenly, the door opened, and before me appeared the enormous figure of the Czar. I didn't lose my head. Immediately, I ran forward, made a curtsy, and loudly blurted out, 'Your Imperial Highness!' Everyone laughed, and I was teased about it for a long time afterward."

"Good Lord! You saw the Czar, spoke with him, and even amused him. Kseniya Aleksandrovna, you are a real legend! Tell us more!"

"Oh, I have a lot I could tell you, but at another time."

Kseniya Aleksandrovna attended our concerts with Olga. We performed a series of miniatures. The French horn and the harp sound excellent together. Kseniya Aleksandrovna especially liked *Nocturne* by R. M. Gliere.

The 70th birthday of Kseniya Aleksandrovna was approaching. I decided to participate in the birthday jubilee celebration in her honor. I set some verses to music by Rossini (the aria of Count Almaviva). From the costumer at the Bolshoi Theater, I rented the costume for the Count in the *Barber of Seville*. (This was Lemeshev's costume.) I did not put on the costume at all while I was greeting this artist or that. I was accompanied by the Bolshoi Theater's Stage Orchestra and four harpists—students of Kseniya Aleksandrovna.

The day of the jubilee came. I arrived early, got made up, dressed in the costume— like a real count.* The orchestra was decked out in costumes from *Faust*. We greeted Kseniya Aleksandrovna on behalf of the Bolshoi Theater. Just picture it—the hall was full of spectators and very many important acquaintances. The Great Hall of the Conservatory was filled with excitement—at any moment Kseniya Aleksandrovna must appear. Then she came out, and, to thunderous applause, seated herself in the arm-chair as though on a throne. This day, Kseniya Aleksandrovna was the inimitable, true Czarina of the harp.

At that moment, the welcoming delegation from the Bolshoi Theater appeared, and the stage orchestra struck up the march from

---

*

93

Faust. We marched out. I was in the lead with a bared sword, and after me the orchestra. After playing a little, the orchestra fell silent. The harpists began playing, and I sang:\

Praises the harpists are trilling,
To the Queen of Harpists, Ehrdeli,
Even French hornists are singing.
Oh, how we love our Ehrdeli!
(etc.)

After I sang, I approached Kseniya Aleksandrovna, swept off my plumed hat and knelt on one knee, presented her with the birthday proclamation, and kissed her hand.* Kseniya Aleksandrovna came over to me, and said that she was very touched, surprised, and added, "You sang like a real singer, and looked like a real count."

A short while later, Kseniya Aleksandrovna sent me a photo in

Handwritten note on photo: "To a dear friend, talented singer, Valeriy Vladimirovich Polekh in memory of his performance as a count at my birthday celebration, February 26, 1968. With love to him and thanks. K. Ehrdeli

appreciation. On it was written, "To a dear friend, the talented singer, V. V. Polekh, in memory of his wonderful presentation on the day of my birthday jubilee. With love for him and thanksgiving, K. A. Ehrdeli."

I greeted Kseniya Aleksandrovna when she completed her 70th, 80th, and 90th years. At the last birthday jubilee, I told her that I was already beginning to prepare for her 100th.

---
*

Handwritten note on photo:To the kind talented Valery Vladimirovich Polekh
in memory of my "Holiday of Harps" — (March 21, 1962) and with thanks
for his wonderful performance in it. With heartfelt appreciation, Moscow,
April 1, 1962, K. Ehrkeli

DYNASTY

Olga Grigorevna Ehrdeli was born April 1, 1927. When
she had completed her ninth year, she was taken to the Central
Musical School, and enrolled immediately in the third level.
Upon completion of the school, she entered the Conservatory and
Kseniya Aleksandrovna Ehrdeli's class. In the All-Union Contest of
Performing Musicians she achieved Diploma of First Degree. After
a short time, she joined the Radio Symphonic Orchestra. At the
International Festival in Budapest, she received First Premium. She
began to appear as a soloist around the cities of the Soviet Union. I
got acquainted with Olga at the International Festival in Hungary.
We played together in the Youth Orchestra. Olga and I performed
in the Great Hall of the Philharmonic in Leningrad when I first I
performed the *Concerto for French Horn and Orchestra*, written for

me by R. M. Gliere. At this same concert, Olga played the *Concerto for Harp* by R. M. Gliere, with the composer conducting.

At this writing, Olga Grigorevna has become a professor, a People's Artist, and teaches at the Moscow Conservatory. She invited my wife and me to attend her concert, and promised to send us tickets.

Here is what Professor Kseniya Aleksandrovna Ehrdeli said about Olga Ehrdeli: "Her musical talent, fortunately, combines with a capacity for work, goal orientation, and persistence in attaining intended goals. Her full sound, virtuoso technique, good taste, and artistic charm on stage place her in the first rank of Soviet performers. Olga is very professional, and her musicality is exceptional. The music of her harp captures even the farthest reaches of man's music."

This wonderful, jolly, vivacious woman is a wonderful friend and a very kind person.

Olga has a daughter, Tatiana Shchepalina, who is also a musician. She has graduated from Central Musical School and Conservatory. At present, she is an instructor of the harp at Central Musical School, and Conservatory.

When Tatiana's daughter was born, she was named in honor of her great-grandmother, Kseniya Ehrdeli. She also plays the harp, and has already graduated from the Conservatory, and plays in an orchestra. This continues the tradition established by her great-grandmother, the great artist, Kseniya Aleksandrovna Ehrdeli.

What a wonderful dynasty—a dynasty of artists, a dynasty of exceptional musicians. I have been fortunate to have known these people, who are dear to me.

TEN

Reinhold Moritsevich Gliere

I HAVE ALWAYS BEEN LUCKY with good people. One of the most wonderful is Reinhold Moritsevich Gliere. His way of life is just as beautiful, simple and unpretentious as his outer appearance. Look at the portrait of Gliere.* The first thing it brings to your attention is his handsome appearance, which you combine with modest dress, the way he holds himself, an emphasis on accuracy, and hints of a sort of elegance. No carelessness, and nothing superfluous jumps out at you. Lively, hazel, expressive eyes are framed by thick eyebrows. The gaze is cordial and benevolent. The lips are ready to form a kind smile, and just on the verge of expressing gentle words. That is a incomplete portrait of the Great Maestro. I will give you a clear example of this intelligent man.

One evening, my telephone rang. I picked up the receiver and said, "Hello."

Note on photo: "To dear Valeriy Vladimirovich Polekh, in token of sincere affection and devotion. 21—1959 R. M. Gliere"

*

"This is Reinhold Moritsevich Gliere speaking. Greetings, Valeriy Vladimirovich. How are you getting along? How is your health?" inquired Giere.

"You know, Reinhold Moritsevich, I live for your kindness, and your wonderful concertos."

"Yes, Valeriy Vladimirovich, the concerto really turned out pretty well. Listen, Valeriy Vladimirovich, I have the honor of inviting you to my birthday celebration tomorrow. Please, I will wait for you at the restaurant on Miusskaya Street, and expect to see you about seven in the evening. Good-bye."

I had just hung up the receiver, when the phone rang again.

"Please be so kind as to call Ludmilla Nikolaevna to the phone. Is this Ludmilla Nikolaevna? Greetings! Good Day! How is your precious health? How are you getting along? This is Reinhold Moritsevich Gliere speaking."

"Hello, Reinhold Moritsevich.! This is Ludmilla Nikolaevna speaking. How are you getting a long? How is your health?"

"Glory to God, I am well! You are very kind, Ludmilla Nikolaevna. Be so kind as to attend my birthday celebration. I would be very glad to see you at my party. Valeriy Vladimirovich knows where I live and where the restaurant is located. Please, I ask you. All the best to you. Good-bye."

We attended the birthday celebrations of Reinhold Moritsevich Gliere several times. Artists connected with the creations of this remarkable composer were always there. Such evenings were merry and very relaxed, and often turned into merry satirical revues. Gliere really enjoyed it when I came up with a parody of famous singers. Usually, M. Rostropovich accompanied me, but when he was not there, K. Kondrashin took his place. Once, when Reinhold Moritsevich was inviting me to his birthday party, with a laugh he said, "Valeriy Vladimirovich, do not forget to bring all your famous singers with you."

I became acquainted with Reinhold Moritsevich Gliere at the Bolshoi Theater during the rehearsal for his ballet *Bronze Horseman.*

As we were finishing the correction of the ballet's music, I had not even once noticed the presence of the author at the rehearsal. It must be noted, that at the Bolshoi Theater, we were rather accustomed to composers at the rehearsals not being able to sit in one place, but they would be running first to the conductor and then to the concertmaster. Often, this interfered with the work. I wondered why the author of the music was not there. It was explained that Reinhold Moritsevich had attended all the rehearsals, but he'd quietly and modestly sat in the spectator hall. He only discussed his impressions with the director of the show, Yu. F. Faier, during breaks between sessions. I was also invited to one of these conferences. My impression of Reinhold Moritsevich was that he seemed to be an unassuming man of extreme spirituality. His knowledge of music seemed limitless. He conducted the conference graciously and simply, asked questions, He asked our opinions about the horn parts in the ballet, and listened attentively to my explanations. He said, "Who knows the instrument better than the performer? It behooves us to pay attention to the performers, and we must learn from them."

I expressed the wish that our leading composers would write more for wind instruments. "Yes, we are lagging in this *genre*," Gliere admitted, "and I agree that we must write more for wind instruments." Taking advantage of this, I proposed to Gliere that he take the initiative and write a concerto for French horn and orchestra. Such a promise was given me.

One day, M. Person, the biographer and administrator of Reinhold Moritsevich Gliere, phoned me. "Hello, Valeriy Vladimirovich. I am calling for Gliere. He has very strongly requested that you come to his home. He is preparing to decide some details about a future concerto. If it would not be too difficult`, fetch your instrument along with you."

I gladly agreed. "Tomorrow, at four o'clock."

The following day at four o'clock, I was there at Gliere's. He received me well, even affectionately, and asked me to wait a bit. "I very much ask forgiveness, but I have students."

After a short time, Gliere brought in a small silver decanter, a silver liqueur glass, and some kind of sweets on a silver tray. With a sort of gentle smile, he strongly urged me to strengthen myself and left the office. I was left alone in the office. To tell the truth, I did not touch what had been offered. I was sure that I would need to play, and that is what happened. Coming into the office, Gliere immediately began quiz me about my instrument, and about my possibilities in regard to range. He asked about tonality, and the character of the instrument's sound. Gliere attentively wrote my answers in a fat notebook. At the end of the conversation, Reinhold Moritsevich asked me to play a little.

"You, obviously, brought music with you."

"Yes, I brought it," I answered. "I want to acquaint you with the possibilities of performance on our beautiful and difficult instrument. What would you like me to begin with?"

"First of all," said Reinhold Moritsevich, "I am interested in cantilena, the quintessential sound of the horn. Do you agree that I am right?"

"Yes, you are completely correct. For each instrument, cantilena is essential, especially for such an instrument as the horn."

Reinhold Moritsevich sat at the piano, and I put music on the stand. "Good Lord! This is my *Nocturne*. I wrote this in my youth."

We began playing. It was great to play together with a composer, and especially with Gliere. I can't remember when I had been so inspired playing this composition. When he finished playing the *Nocturne,* Gliere said, "Bravo! You are a cello, a vocalist! Valeriy Vladimirovich, how would it be if we played something classical? Well, for instance, my beloved V. A. Mozart? Obviously, you know he wrote four concerti for the horn, and a concerto rondo. Here, I am looking at the music, and I am wondering, how would it be if we played the first part of Mozart's Fourth Concerto? How does that seem to you?"

"Good."

We played the Mozart concerto. Gliere remained pleased. "Such lightness, and the cantilena is completely different—somehow airy and completely without any pressure. Incomprehensible."

"You know, Reinhold Moritsevich, I will play the first part of the R. Strauss Concerto."

"Play. This is interesting. Yes, you have mastered timbre and mood, you know. I like Strauss. The horn sounds very good with him. Valeriy Vladimirovich, couldn't you play something typical of a stage play?

"Now, I will play you the waltz by Kreisler, *Beautiful Rosemarin.*"

"Yes, this is really the stage—performing freedom. The performer does whatever he feels like, and has nothing to be shy about. Valeriy Vladimirovich, all my textbooks, obviously, are out of date. Times are changing a great deal. Several accepted rules have ceased to exist. I will have to completely change my attitude toward the French horn. In the beginning, I thought there would not be sufficient technical possibilities—yes, and possibly range also. Now, as they say, 'the shackles have fallen.' I can compose freely, and nothing will hinder me. Valeriy Vladimirovich, I am starting to work! Valeriy Vladimirovich, play something else for me."

I played the D-flat minor Waltz by F. Chopin. Gliere was thunderstruck. "You are a real virtuoso on the stage."

"Reinhold Moritsevich, let me tell you about an incident that happened to me. As a student at the conservatory, I supplemented my stipend by demonstrating the possibilities of the French horn to students in various departments. Once, I was invited to a class in instrumentation, and I went to the class of a well-known professor. I was asked to play something that had cantilena. The professor explained that the French horn was an instrument of pure cantilena and had very extremely limited technical possibilities. I played the French horn solo from Tchaikovsky's Fifth Symphony. All the students listened attentively. This was a well-known solo. The professor asked me to play something technical, and told the students that now they would hear the indistinct sounds of the technical piece. I played the waltz by Kreisler, *Beautiful Rosemarin.*

At the conclusion of my playing, noise and uproar arose in the classroom. The students were shouting, 'What's that you said? That the French horn is not a technical instrument? And what are we hearing? Brilliant technique! What's the deal?' The students asked that I play something more. I played the first part of V. A. Mozart's First Concerto, which caused the students to stamp their feet in delight. The professor was confused. He only said he had never heard anything like it. 'Bravo to you, French horn musician. You have put me down.'"

"Thank you, Valeriy Vladimirovich, for the story. You know, that is similar to what happened with me also. Thank you for the demonstration of your remarkable instrument."

With that, we parted. I left with the hope of playing a wonderful, new concerto in the near future.

One winter night in 1951, a small car stopped near my home at midnight. I looked out the window. Who could be coming so late? I recognized M. Person. Good Lord! Yes, it was for me! Right away, I ran to open the door, and in truth, at the door stood M. Person. We greeted each other. My heart skipped a beat. Could it really be the concerto? The concerto I had been waiting for so long? "Valeriy Vladimirovich, Reinhold Moritsevich requests that you come to his place right now."

So, in the winter of 1951, in Reinhold Moritsevich's apartment, I played the just-completed concerto from a hand-written score. This wonderful composition conveyed a strong impression to me. I was in ecstasy from the music of the concerto. I had just a few observations and suggestions, which Gliere accepted without argument. He commissioned me to do a finished edition of the concerto. After this, I went to Reinhold Moritsevich's home many times. We labored over the concerto quite a bit before we felt it was ready for a performance. In preparing for the premiere, I played the concerto with piano accompaniment. I played the concerto at the Ippolitov-Ivanov Music College, on the stage at the Moscow Conservatory, and in the Beethoven Hall at the Bolshoi Theater.

My performance at the Institute of Military Conductors was a serious test. The hall was full. They introduced me, and I began to play. After my performance, there was a judging of the music of the concerto and the presentation. The author of the music, Gliere, was in attendance in the hall. The music of the concerto and its presentation received high marks. The listeners aplauded the author of the music and the performer for a long time. I was already preparing to leave the stage when a young major rose in the audience and asked me, after performing such a difficult concerto, could I play the D-flat minor Waltz by F. Chopin?

L. N. Polekh

"Alright, I will play Chopin's waltz for you."

The pianist went over to the piano, and we played the waltz by F. Chopin. The audience was delighted. So ended the painstaking work on the concerto of Reinhold Moritsevich Gliere.

The time to perform the concerto drew near. With my wife, Ludmilla Nikolaevna, I traveled to Leningrad on March 10, 1951. We were met at the train station by musicians from the conservatory and Professor P. Orekhov. After warm greetings, they took us to the European Hotel. The rehearsal was scheduled for eleven o'clock in the morning. In the hotel, I did a small warm-up on the horn, and we went to the rehearsal. Gliere was already rehearsing with the orchestra in the Great Hall of the Leningrad Philharmonic. The hall seemed majestic to me with beautiful columns, and lovely chandeliers. The whole hall struck me with its grandure. I thought to myself,"What a place to get to play in!" The rehearsal went well. The orchestra was excellent. Gliere was a wonderful conductor. I calmed down. Then Olga Ehrdeli came also. She was going to play Gliere's Harp Concerto.

The first performance of Gliere's Concerto for Horn and Orchestra was performed May 10, 1951 in the Great Hall of the Leningrad Philharmonic. I was accompanied by the Symphonic

Orchestra of the Leningrad Committee of Radio-Information, directed by the author. Backstage, they told me that the administration of the Philharmonic was very concerned about the attire I would wear on stage. They calmed down when they saw me in a frock coat. I looked at the hall—full house. Even the upper loges were packed. When I go on stage, I like to meet my wife's gaze. Her gaze always calms me down. The third bell. I checked myself in the mirror— everything seemed in order. Then Reinhold Moritsevich was there. He looked at me, took my hand, and said, "With God, let's go out." I played with emotion, and what I had planned all turned out right. For an encore, we played the finale. We were called out several times to take bows.

Gliere was pleased with my performance. He hugged and kissed me. My wife and I went out walking about the streets of Leningrad. The city was lit up for the holiday* and everything was lovely. It was springtime—May. People were out walking, and feeling jolly. It is a wonderful city, and we love it so.

Reinhold Moritsevich's composition has had great success in the world. In the composition, *Concerto for French Horn no. 91 in C-flat Major,* Gliere strove to create an extended symphonic composition filled with a rich emotional content.

V. V. Polekh with spouse 1939

The main part of the concerto was noted for its willful character, its rhythm created the impression of a masculine marching step. The second theme, expressed by the solo horn, was notable for a bright lyrical-vocal character, responding in the best way possible to the specific tonal character of the instrument. In the concluding division of the section, heroic coloration became the predominant significance. The middle section of the concerto was written in a slow tempo. The poetic music of this section was closely reminiscent of a romance

---

*   May Day

105

between the horn and the orchestra. The opening was peaceful and placid, but the second division was written with an excited, restless manner. The finale of the concerto is the embodiment of a picture of a people's gaiety. Here, the theme of a daring dance has something in common with the themes of lyrical deep emotion and extreme soulfulness. The performance of this composition, written with such love and mastery by the author, demanded excellent command of the instrument and tonal and technical gifts in completion of the development of this wind apparatus.

Gliere's concerto has entered the repertoire of many Russian and foreign horn musicians, and has become a favorite composition. It was, and is, included in the required audition programs of performing musicians across Russia and internationally, and it has won a deserved popularity, both among us and beyond the borders. Phono-recordings of this concerto have sold in all music stores of America and Europe. One famous American horn musician expressed this idea: "Your concerto is an emissary of the Russian school of performance, and everyone who performs this  concerto will remember with thanks the creator and performer of this wonderful concerto by Reinhold Gliere and Valeriy Polekh." In his *Concerto for the French Horn*, Gliere showed the enormous increasing possibilities contained in this instrument performing in the capacity of a solo and a concerto, and how great was its emotional range, extending from the powerful commanding sounds to lyrical soulful vocal melodies.

Soon after the premiere, Gliere informed me, that we would repeat the concerto, but in Moscow, in the Columned Hall of the House of Unions. We met a few times before the performance to correct and adjust something or other. It was going to be wonderful to play in Moscow, in our home city, and in the Columned Hall.

The acoustics there were wonderful, and the hall was so smartly decorated and festive. The day of the concert arrived, and the hall was overflowing. From the wings looking out at the audience, I saw familiar artists of the Moscow Orchestra. The conductors had come. I saw Yu. F. Faier, K. P. Kondrashin, and Boris Aleksandrov. I don't think I caught sight of them all. They were all interested in hearing a colleague. You see, that did not happen often. The concerto went successfully. I performed quite well and played freely and emotionally. We came out for bows several times. Gliere was satisfied. We were greeted by friends and attendees from the audience. The House of Unions is a wonderful hall!

The jubilee birthday celebration of Reinhold Moritsevich Gliere was in the Great Hall of the Moscow Conservatory. Everything was conducted very ceremonially. The jubilee committee was on the stage. Present were notable people of art, many musicians, and artists from various cities and republics who had come to congratulate this wonderful composer and marvelous person. One delegation followed another. Reinhold Moritsevich sat on the stage in the golden arm-chair. I brought a greeting from the artists of the Bolshoi Theater. The stage orchestra played the march from the ballet, *Bronze Horseman*. I was made up to look like A. S. Pushkin. I had my hair done like Pushkin, sideburns like Pushkin, and a corresponding costume. A make-up artist had been specially invited. He tried very had to create a real likeness, and they say he succeeded. The musicians of the stage orchestra were dressed in costumes from the times of Peter the Great. A ballad I had composed was read. The ballet directors G. Ulyanov, O. Lepeshinskaya, I. Petrov, S. Koren, Yu. Faier, M. Reizen, and I. Kozlovskiy went with me. We kissed Gliere, and he was touched.

The All-Union Studio of Audio-Recording proposed to Reinhold Moritsevich Gliere and me that we do a recording the concerto on a disc. I was experienced with recordings. I had recorded the concerti of V. A. Mozart, C. Weber, and many miniatures. When my wife and I arrived at the studio, Gliere was already rehearsing with the Bolshoi

Theater Orchestra. I also played a little, and the recording started. We played the entire concerto twice, and the audio-producer shouted from the recording booth, "The recording is done! Everything is great! I congratulate you! A tremendous thank you!"

In our day, the concert was performed and recorded by the best horn musicians in the world: Professor of the Leningrad Conservatory, V Buyanovskiy; Professor of the Dresden Conservatory, P. Damm; Professor from Essen, G. Bauman; Professor from Munich, G. G. Pitska; and others.

Alexander Shamilevich Melik-Pashayev

I T WAS JUNE 13, 1931. In the Bolshoi Theater, *Aida* was about to be performed. The conductor was a young debutant— Alexander Shamilevich Melik-Pashayev. With excitement, the audience awaited the beginning of the show. Slowly, the lights went down. All eyes were straining toward the orchestra, and suddenly, the first notes of the overture flowed out. This first performance

A. Sh. Melik-Pashayev

of Alexander Shamilevich met with great success. The musicians of the orchestra playing with him in this show put a high value on the gifts of this young maestro. His performance became a noteworthy musical event. The renowned conductor of the Bolshoi Theater, V. Suk, attended the performance and was ecstatic about what he heard that evening. This brilliant beginning of his career did not go to the head of the young musician, nor cause him to "rest on his laurels." On the contrary, he very passionately plunged into serious and difficult work. What are characteristic features that distinguished the creativity of Melik-Pashayev, and what is the reason for his creative success? First of all, Alexander Shamilevich was in love with the theater. He knew the theater really well; and, surprisingly, clearly understood the performance possibilities of an orchestra, a choir, and soloists. He was able to utilize these possibilities for the creation of an highly artistic performance. He was notable for colorful artistry and fine artistic taste, great creative desire, and colossal ability to work. Uncompromising demands on himself and on others, and high professionalism created an atmosphere of genuine creativity. I am laden with recollections that call to mind isolated episodes in the artistic life of Alexander Shamilevich Melik-Pashayev.

The lights went down, and Alexander Shamilevich walked to the conductors podium. I saw his welcoming and inspired expression. He stood at the podium, greeted the orchestra with slow nods, captured the gaze of all those with whom he was appearing that day to work, and, as though hypnotizing the musicians of the orchestra, and gathered their attention to himself. Alexander Shamilevich took up the baton. His whole appearance was transformed. His face was serious and pleasant, and everything about him was sharp. One more moment, and his hands were raised. At this moment, the orchestra was completely under the control of his hands. Alexander Shamilevich "created" the production. Everything has come from him. He has controlled everything. There was not a presentation of an orchestral soloist, instrumental group, singer, or choir that Alexander Shamilevich has not prepared beforehand. It is not that he did not have faith in the performers. No. The many performers themselves knew their parts satisfactorily well, but the director led everyone from the beginning to the very end as though he were tugging and slacking-off invisible threads, guiding these many instruments, and delving deeper into the music, to read the most concealed secrets hidden in the conductor's music score.

The artistry of Melik-Pashayev was crowned with glory by an exceptional nobility and an enchanting romanticism. Alexander Shamilevich wrote, "Opera is not a concert in theatrical costumes, but an active spectacle in which the singing and music are closely connected with its dramatic existence." Standing at the the podium,

Alexander Shamilevich made high demands of us performers—superlatively high demands. A culture of high level performance was necessary in order to make real all the intentions of this amazing artist. In justice, it is necessary to say that it cost us a great deal of work and colossal effort to fulfill the desires of the conductor. However, he inspired us with his own enthusiasm and his surprising belief in what was happening on the stage.

In bringing to fruition his creative desires, Alexander Shamilevich understood very well that he did not do this alone, but together with a large artistic collective. Like a true artist, he valued the creative individuality of the artists and did not denigrate their initiatives. On the contrary, he encouraged the efforts of those who were striving for artistic freedom and their free and thoughtful creative activity. When playing productions with Alexander Shamilevich, I always spontaneously felt such freedom. As an example, this was one incident. At Radio, the aria of Micaela from the opera *Carmen* was being recorded. The orchestra was being directed by Alexander Shamilevich. At the beginning of the aria, the horns played a short but rather expressive piece. Usually, this solo was played at an even volume, but I wanted to give this musical phrase more expressive color. I began this theme with a gentle *pianissimo*, then gradually increased the sound—took it in culmination to *forte*, and did a reversing diminution in sound, ending the phrase at *pianissimo* once more. Alexander Shamilevich was very pleased, and requested that in the future this solo be played with just the same nuance at the Bolshoi Theater also.

Artists who just passively participated in the creative process disturbed Alexander Shamilevich's effort, "displacing" him from the creative state. On several occasions, the inspector of the orchestra assigned one performer or another to an Alexander Shamilevich production, and praised the performer, alleging that he he had mastered his instrument well. "Yes, he has mastered the instrument well." responded Alexander Shamilevich. "Only, I very strongly ask that you do not designate him for the production. We have not found a common language." A musician may have mastered his vocal apparatus or instrument yet not have a sufficient feeling for the essence of the production, not understand the style of the composer, remain indifferent to the musical forms, and not know how to catch the listener with his performance. Such a musician could not please a director like Alexander Shamilevich.

Alexander Shamilevich had extremely flexible and expressive arms and hands. Persuasive logic, natural gestures, and the expression of the eye—all this helped him to communicate his intentions and express to us, the performers, feelings analogous to his own with startling exactness.

In the opera *Aida*, at the very beginning of the Overture, there are two "empty" quarter notes, and the conductor has two silent motions. (At this time, the orchestra does not play.) The attack does not come until a sixteenth note on the third beat when the first violin comes in. Usually, during this musical pause, the conductor makes inexpressive motions, just a schematic counting of these beats, completely unconcerned as to what effect these motions of his hands have on the further character of the orchestra's performance.

Alexander Shamilevich has taken a completely different approach to this presentation. Having stood at the conductors podium, greeted the artists of the orchestra, and waited for complete quiet in the hall, he would pick up the baton and turn to the side toward the first violinist. The gaze of the musicians was directed toward his hands, toward the face of the conductor, and toward his eyes—in which, like a mirror were reflected his thoughts, feelings, and his internal state. Just as a sorcerer could determine the future fate of a man with two gestures of his fingers, so Alexander Shamilevich, with two movements, could foreordain not only the tempo, but also the character and internal content of the musical performance. To do this is in the power of only a wonderful conductor.

Alexander Shamilevich Melik-Pashayev wrote, "...My soul is in the operas with starkly expressive dramatic collisions, with stormy fireworks of passion, and waves of gentle lyricism— operas with

Pompei-like form and dynamic saturation of the orchestral sound such as more closely correspond with the fulfillment of my individuality." The true masterpieces created by Alexander Shamilevich set in the beauty of the Bolshoi Theater were *Othello, Aida, Carmen, Absalom and Eteri, The Queen of Spades, Boris Godunov, Cherevichki, William Tell, Francesca da Rimini, Falstaff,* and *Fidelio.* I had the good fortune to play *Fidelio* with Alexander Shamilevich. In this production the horn players met extreme difficulty. Our assignment, in general, would turn out to be mainly overcoming these difficulties, in order to play everything "cleanly" and in unity with the conductor. But this was not to be. Alexander Shamilevich set before us such high artistic demands that we were forced to drop all other affairs and concerns and devote all our mastery, all our many years of experience, and all our free time to assimilation of the exceedingly complicated orchestral parts. The results of this enormous pedagogical and artistic-creative work of Alexander Shamilevich were not slow to be talked about. The production received general recognition. After *Fidelio,* everyone usually felt a little lift and a holiday spirit. They did not disperse to their homes immediately, but discussed the production for a long time. It was as though they had lived through what had just been presented, and had been-surprised and endlessly enraptured by the fresh inspiration and captivating, romantic talent of this great maestro.

The great service of Alexander Shamilevich also includes being a great teacher, and raising up a whole constellation of wonderful singers and musicians, who comprise the golden stock of performing artists of the Bolshoi Theater. Here is an example of the arduous effort of Alexander Shamilevich in establishing a repertoire of new performing soloists in the orchestra. I was chosen for *The Queen of Spades* which I had never performed before— though it was true that I had done a few rehearsals under the direction of Alexander Shamilevich. After playing the production, according to established tradition, I went to the conductor to learn what his opinion was of my playing in the just-finished production. Alexander Shamilevich expressed his satisfaction with respect to my performance. In connection with that he gave a few suggestions of how to play one or another phrase. There were three proposals. I thanked Alexander Shamilevich for the direction. After working at home on these phrases that he had shown me, I achieved definite success. At the first production, I noticed that Alexander Shamilevich listened to me very attentively. After each of the indicated phrases, he turned in my direction and, with a slight tilt of his head, gave me to understand that he was satisfied with my execution. In such moments, surprisingly tight connection between a conductor and a performer are established. We do not avoid such contact in our art.

On one of the hum-drum days in the Annex of the Bolshoi Theater, a no less hum-drum production went on. It was significantly shabby at times, and betrayed an indifferent relationship of the lead director who was gray-haired and bored with the production. Ordinarily, such productions do not give pleasure to either the performers or the audience. Unexpectedly, upon arriving at one of these productions, we found that, due to the illness of the conductor directing this production, on this particular day the conductor would be Alexander Shamilevich. In the orchestra, everything was in motion now. A great deal of preparatory work was going on. Artists of the orchestra were going to the orchestra's area where they were beginning to study diligently the difficult passages. Wind musicians were gathering in groups and "tuning up" the choral passages. The lights went down. To the conductor's podium strode Alexander Shamilevich.

It was not possible to recognize this production. The soloists were not only singing cleanly, but demonstrating true mastery. The choir and orchestra were at an inaccessible height. The execution was striking and emotional with contrasts ranging from poetic *pianissimo* to heroic *fortissimo*. The soloists of the orchestra were brilliant. A cascade of technical passages were played with extreme expression. All in all, the production was a premiere, a holiday of operatic art. After the performance, everyone was excitedly congratulating

Alexander Shamilevich on the success. A little tired but happy, he accepted the congratulations, and we were happy too.

In the 1950's in Moscow, there was a youth orchestra composed of musicians from the best orchestras in the capital: Bolshoi Theater, All-Union Radio, and Municipal orchestras.

We all were wanting very much that Alexander Shamilevich would direct one of the symphonic programs although he had not appeared on the concert stage for a protracted time, but directed only operatic productions. Just the same, I proposed to Alexander Shamilevich that he direct our orchestra. He heard me out with great attention. When I stopped talking, he thought a while. Then with a heavy smile, he looked at me and said, "Valechka, " (He always called me that.) "you know, lately, I have been thinking more and more that I should return to symphonic conducting. However, it seems to me that the time still has not come. I do not feel myself sufficiently prepared for such responsible performances." After this conversation, I decided that Alexander Shamilevich did not want to overload himself with extra work. At that time, he was carrying a heavy burden—being the head conductor at the Bolshoi Theater. However, later I understood the reason for the refusal— Alexander Shamilevich could not simply conduct; he would have needed to start living still another creative life.

Happily, after fairly long interval, Alexander Shamilevich returned to the concert stage. He presented Tchaikovsky's *Sixth Symphony* with the Bolshoi Theater Orchestra in the Columned Hall of the House of Unions. This was his favorite work, and he conducted the symphony beautifully. The performance of Beethoven's *Ninth Symphony* under the direction of Alexander Shamilevich in the Bolshoi Theater re-established a beautiful tradition of the orchestra presenting symphonic concerts in its home theater.

This tradition had its beginning long ago. Even in the first days of the Soviet power, the Bolshoi Theater Orchestra, under the direction of Oscar Fried, performed symphonic programs. This tradition was birthed on the base of the prominent performance culture of the

Bolshoi Theater Orchestra and the first-class conductors working in the theater at that time. I was a participant in the performance of Beethoven's *Ninth Symphony* under the direction of Alexander Shamilevich and recall this concert with great excitement. The symphonic orchestra was situated on an improvised stage, and behind it was the praiseworthy choir of the Bolshoi Theater. The spectator's auditorium was freshened up to look its best, and the soloists of the opera were in front. Alexander Shamilevich Melik-Pashayev was at the conductor's podium. It was unforgettable.

TWELVE

Sergey Yakovlevich Lemeshev

M Y ACQUAINTANCE WITH THE wonderful artist Sergey
Yakovlevich Lemeshev happened at the Annex of the Bolshoi
Theater. Truly, I became acquainted with his voice first. You see, I
had the good fortune to play in productions that Sergey Yakovlevich
took part in. These were *Rigoletto, La Traviata, Lakme, Werther,
Eugene Onegin, Dubrovskiy, Fra Diavolo,* and others. To play with
Sergey Yakovlevich was a singular delight. He had a rare musicality,
artistry, a handsome appearance, unusual vocal timbre, and, in a
word, unending charm with a Russian soul.

We became more closely acquainted during
the production *May Night,* an opera directed by
V. V. Nebolsin. The premier took place in the
morning on the first of January in the Annex
of the Bolshoi Theater. The cadre of soloists
was amazing: S. Ya. Lemeshev, V. Borisenko,
and M. D. Mikhailov. In the overture to
this opera, Rimsky-Korsakov wrote a quite
interesting part for the horn. He displayed an

S. Ya. Lemeshev

amazing knowledge of the instrument. In the final act of the opera,
the horn responds very beautifully with the tenor. A magical duet
develops. Here, the soloist French horn musician must demonstrate

outstanding mastery. I worked hard to find the necessary sound quality. As a result, I adopted a few subtleties in the ensuing duet with Sergey Yakovlevich. It must be said that in the performance I played successfully. After the production, the musicians congratulated me, and the conductor, V. V. Nebolsin, said some pleasant words to me. It was especially pleasant for me, when my former teacher and instructor of the Bolshoi Theater, Honored Artist of the Republic, V. N. Soloduyev came over to congratulate me. I was already preparing to go home when Vanosha, who worked for our orchestra, came over to me and said that S. Ya. Lemeshev asked me to come to him in the dressing room. You must know I was gripped by agitation. With a frozen heart, I went to Sergey Yakovlevich.

"Ah! There's the guy that played so sweetly on the horn today! Bravo! I will tell you, you are a real melodist! Rightly, a vocalist in playing on the French horn! Reveal to me, if you please, your secret. How is it that you were able to draw such cantilena out of the horn? Let's get acquainted," said Sergey Yakovlevich.

I introduced myself, "Polekh, Valeriy, a student in the Second Course at the Moscow Conservatory. You know, Sergey Yakovlevich, I'm Laureate of the All-Union Competition, and received First Premium."

Sergey Yakovlevich laughed, "How about that! You have a whole list of honors. Bravo, Valeriy! Evidently, you are working with Professor Ehkkert. Yes, there's a wonderful musician. You know, he once was a soloist himself with the Bolshoi Imperial Theater. I have to tell you an interesting story, Valeriy. For the First of May and the Seventh of November celebrations, Professor Ehkkert arranged holiday concerts early in the morning before the parades. Wind musicians gathered—for the most part students, but mature, veteran musicians also. They all loved these traditional holiday concerts. A wonderful wind orchestra gathered. The conductor-inspirer, of course, always was Ferdinand Ferdinandovich Ehkkert. You know, I had the good fortune to get acquainted with the professor by accident. Once, I was going along a corridor in the conservatory, and coming toward me was Ferdinand Ferdinandovich.

'Young man, hello, how is your success? You are not letting your work slide?'

'You know, professor, I'm not letting my work slide. I'm studying excellently.'

'Well, wonderful! Wonderful! Say, I have a request to make of you. Would you be able to sing in our concert?'

'I'd be happy to sing in your holiday concert.'

'Tell me, please, do you know the revolutionary song, *Tormented by Heavy Slavery*? I have it orchestrated for a tenor.'

'Yes, I have heard this song.'

'In that case, come with me into the classroom.'

We went in, and the professor sat at the piano. After we sang it the first time, the professor said, 'Dear Serozhenka, in your singing, there is a lot of lyricism, but this is a revolutionary song. Give it more pathos.' We sang it again. 'There, now it's wonderful. I will await you at the concert.'

The concert was a success! Professor Ehkkert himself directed wonderfully. After the concert, everyone went to the parade..."

At that moment, it was reported that the car for Sergey Yakovlevich was there. He gave me his hand, and we parted. After going out on the street, I was still under the influence of this charming and dear man for a long time. Standing in the service entrance, I observed how his aficionados surrounded Sergey Yakovlevich asking for his autograph.

Sergey Yakovlevich and I did not see each other for an extended period of time. We did hear each other. In the theater, he sang and I played. Truly, fate brought us together all the same. I was elected to the Party Bureau of the theater. Because Sergey Yakovlevich was was a member of the Party Bureau, we began to encounter each other at meetings. One day something unpleasant occurred. A reporter wrote a satirical article, a lampoon, in a central newspaper about I.O. Kozlovskiy and S. Ya. Lemeshev, giving them pseudonyms.

One was Lohengrin Lohengrinovich and the other was Mantuan Mantuanovich. The satirical article was titled "On High D," and in it, the reporter simply insulted the famous singers. He wrote, that they were thieves, taking a lot of money for a performance. Because Sergey Yakovlevich was a Communist Party member, the Secretary of the Party Committee needed to investigate the goings-on. A commission was appointed to bring clarity to what had happened. They named me chairman of the commission. We asked the reporter for evidence, which he was not able to give us. Then the commission demanded an apology from the miscreant. The author of the article twisted every which way and defended himself, but gave an apology all the same. Sergey Yakovlevich was not very upset by the events. He said, "The reporter made a very good advertisement for me!"

The Local Committee of the theater gave dacha plots to. employees of the Bolshoi Theater, and it happened that our lots were side by side. The construction of houses and, where-ever it was possible, planting of fruit trees and bushes drew us together. We began to drop in on each other as guests fairly often. Our birthdays also turned out to be side by side. Mine is on July 5th, my wife's is on July 9th, and Sergey Yakovlevich's is on July 10th. On occasion when Sergey Yakovlevich and his wife, Vera Nikolaevna, came to our place for a bonfire, we celebrated our birthdays in warm company.

Every July 10th was a special day. In the morning, aficionados of Sergey Yakovlevich began to arrive—one delegation after another. On this day, Sergey Yakovlevich locked himself away on his property. The gate in the fence was locked. Enormous bouquets of flowers flew over the fence. The aficionados brought whole baskets and boxes of candy. These greetings continued until the evening itself.

Sergey Yakovlevich rarely went out—only when relatives sometimes came. When all the fans had departed, Sergey Yakovlevich went out to rest. About nine in the evening, he received local guests. They gathered on the veranda—six or seven people.

On hot days, Sergey Yakovlevich went swimming and stopped by for me. We would walk quietly, almost not speaking, and enjoying nature. Our stream, the Desna, was clean and not very cold. Having taken a dip and settled down on the bank, Sergey Yakovlevich loved to watch the clouds. "Valeriy, should we slip over to the station and drink a cold beer?"

"No, Sergey Yakovlevich, you shouldn't have beer. Let's go over to my place; that would be better. I'll treat you to some home-made kvass.

When we were done building, and our houses had begun to look pretty good, it seemed it was necessary to register them. We got together (S. Ya. Lemeshev, N. S. Khanaev, V. A. Gavryushev, and I) to travel to the town of Narofominsk to officially register our structures. I must say it was pleasant to be going for a drive in such company. We rode gaily along, and there was no end to the anecdotes and stories. We drove up to the Area Council building and began to go up the stairs. Some likable young girls ran out toward us, but, when they caught sight of us, they stopped, and for some reason ran back in the building.

While we were looking for the reception room, these same young girls approached us, and after looking at Sergey Yakovlevich, they burst out, "Hello, Sergey Yakovlevich!"

"Hello, dear ones. How can we find the reception room?"

"You probably came to register your construction?"

"Imagine that! You guessed it."

"Aha, give us your documents."

"Well, I'm not alone. Some other People's Artists are with me."

We went to the reception room. We did not have to wait long. Acquaintances of our two young girls came out from the Secretary and, holding out the documents, said our houses were now registered.

"How ever can we thank you?" Asked Lemeshev. Smiling, the

121

little girls held out clean sheets of paper and asked for an autograph. Sergey Yakovlevich wrote them some very beautiful words. The girls were happy.

We went out on the street. Khanaev smiled and said, "Well, Seryozha, now we see that you are truly famous. Bravo!"

"All this is wonderful," observed Sergey Yakovlevich, "but the matter deserves to be sprinkled. Valeriy, lead us to a tavern."

To a tavern? Yes! To a tavern! I was in agreement. We drove over to a tavern, parked the car, and went in. The establishment turned out to be not so very high class. The table cloths were not fresh, and in vases, there were flowers that had long since withered. Near the bar, two waitresses quarreled. For a time, they did not pay us any attention. All the same, one soon approached. Catching sight of Sergey Yakovlevich, she was astonished, then delighted, and confused us by running out to the adjoining establishment. Later, she was staring and signaling her friend. At first, we could not understand anything, but later, everything became clear. One of the  waitresses approached our table. With quick, obviously habitual motions, she took the vase from the table and left immediately. The other, with the same quick movements began to spread a clean, starched table cloth. The first brought a rather nice vase with fresh flowers. She also appeared before us lightly rouged, in the cleanest little apron, and with a pretty head-dress on a rather dear little head. Having looked at Sergey Yakovlevich, with a mezzo-soprano voice declared, "Order."

We were a little dumbfounded, but Sergey Yakovlevich, not at all confused, asked in his tenor voice, "Dear fairy, what do they call you?"

"I'm called Liza."

"You know, there is a song that goes, 'My Lizochek, so very small, so very small.' May I honor you with the name of 'Lizochek'?"

Liza laughed happily and said, "You know, it's so pleasant to talk with you." Not taking her eyes off Sergey Yakovlevich, she handed him the menu card and disappeared.

"Friends, today is a day of miraculous transformations. Everything is like a fairy tale, and there is even a magic table cloth."

The girls brought us two trays of snacks. During the little party, Sergey Yakovlevich kept us occupied with a variety of interesting stories. He told us of an incident that happened at the resort named "Silver Pines."

"You know," began Sergey Yakovlevich, " this was my favorite vacation spot. One day I was sitting on the veranda with my dear wife and a friend. It was hot, and my wife was sitting there with us crocheting something. My better half always is very strict with regard to spirits. She keeps track of me very strictly. But you know, it really was necessary to mark my wife's birthday somehow. I tried to think up a way, and then she, herself, said to me, 'Seryozhenka dear, set up some good strong tea for us. You are allowed that.' I was pleased and ran to the refreshment room. After a little while, I brought the tea—two glasses for us men, and a cup for the wife. In a small bowl were lemon and sugar cubes. We sat and drank the tea. We drank decorously and genteelly, not hurrying. But then the wife began to feel dissatisfied. 'Seryozhenka, is it from the tea that your tongue is so loose?' I said, 'Evidently, it is from the heat..' 'And you are flushed beyond all measure. Give me your glass. Well, how about this tea! Something about this tea smells like cognac. Seryozhenka, I know you are a big schemer, but today you have out-done yourself. You drank cognac and not once did you grimace. You are a real artist—playing your role excellently. For such mastery I will forgive you. Thank you for congratulating me at least.'"

My wife, Ludmilla Nikolaevna, and I attended Sergey Yakovlevich's concerts many times. The auditorium was always overflowing.

In Sergey Yakovlevich's repertoire were Russian folk songs and romantic songs. The audience awaited with excitement the vocal and spiritual wonder. Sergey Yakovlevich would go out on the stage, and a thunder of applause would greet the beloved singer. He would bow in greeting. The wonderful pianist Olga Tomina accompanied Sergey Yakovlevich. When Sergey Yakovlevich sang, he completely captured the auditorium. No one was disinterested or bored. The audience flowed with the singer in one spirit and one frame of mind. Everyone listened to him, charmed by the marvelous voice. It is impossible to describe this. One simply had to be there at the time in the auditorium and enjoy his singing. The strength of his artistry was the great strength of soul of a great singer. The stage always was converted into a glorious garden of lilacs, cyclamen, roses, and chrysanthemums.

After a concert, my wife and I went to congratulate the singer-magician on his success, but it was almost impossible to reach Sergey Yakovlevich because so many were wanting to express their delight to the singer. However, with great difficulty, we reached Sergey Yakovlevich and expressed our feelings to him. Sergey Yakovlevich asked us not to leave and invited us to his home. People kept bringing more and more flowers backstage. Llittle by little, the public at last began to depart, and we drove over to Sergey Yakovlevich's. My wife and I were with Olga Tomina in one car, and Sergey Yakovlevich and his wife, Vera Nikolaevna, were in the other. Approaching Sergey Yakovlevich's place, we saw a crowd of fans—again with flowers. He got out of the car, and young girls threw themselves at him. Sergey Yakovlevich, with restraint, thanked them and politely said good-bye. We were already expected. The table was set, and from the table rose very tasty gastronomical aromas. It must be said, that we loved the comfortable apartment of Sergey Yakovlevich and Vera Nikolaevna. At the table, the first toast, of course, was raised to the amazing talent of the singer. In no wise had the. concert tired Sergey Yakovlevich. All the while at the table, he was telling us stories about his rich life-experiences.

"You know, once I had a concert in which I did not make a single sound. Here is how it happened. I was invited to a concert at a location out in the country. I agreed, but suddenly became ill, and had a bad head cold. What was I to do? I telephoned the Secretary of the Regional Committee. I told him what was what; that Sergey Yakovlevich had gotten sick. The Secretary was in a panic; the public had been informed and everyone was waiting with excitement for the beloved singer. The solution was unexpected; I was asked to simply sit on the stage. 'Just let them look at you. Our people love you so much.' I got myself all wrapped up and drove out there. They placed an arm chair on the stage for me. They announced to the audience that I had gotten sick and would not sing. In the auditorium arose a terrible noise, but when they found out I had arrived after all, it soon quieted. Then they opened the curtain, and greeted me for a long time. I spent the whole concert on the stage while my colleagues performed. This was the single instance where I went out on the stage and did not sing. What doesn't happen in this world?"

The front door bell rang, and more flowers were brought in. We immediately found ourselves in a marvelous garden. The enchanting odor, the aroma of flowers intoxicated us. Everyone got up from the table and spent a long time enjoying the wonderful flowers—especially the roses of every shade. Sergey Yakovlevich invited us to the drawing room where a tape recorder stood on a grand piano. It turned out, the whole concert had been recorded on tape. Immagine, we listened to the whole concert again.

Strolling among the rooms, we located Sergey Yakovlevich in his office. Here we found a gold maple leaf that stood near him on a table. This had been a gift of the most devoted aficionados of Lemeshev. Sergey Yakovlevich was very excited about this gift. You see, it was made from a multitude of gold knick-knacks each fan brought to a jeweler. They ordered a golden maple leaf made with the inscription, "*To the singer of love, To the singer of our sorrow.*"

THIRTEEN

Ivan Semyonovich Kozlovskiy

I N MY CHILDHOOD HOME, the phonograph was often playing. We had a variety of phonograph records. Of the vocal records I listened to, I liked the singing of the artist Ivan Semyonovich Kozlovskiy best of all. He performed the aria of the off-stage singer of the opera *Rafael* and the song of the Duke of Mantua from the opera *Rigoletto*. The record was already very badly worn, and had a lot of hissing and noise on it, but with great pleasure I wound it up and wound it up. I had a liking for music and singing already.

I. S. Kozlovskiy

Near us on Kaluzhskiy Street, was a textile technical college. Concerts were performed on important holidays in the concert hall of this technical college. Among those who appeared were the distinguished artists A. S. Pirogov, V. V. Barsova, S. Yudin, B. Zlatogorova, and S. Ya. Lemeshev. Sometimes, we kids were allowed to go into the spectator hall of the technical college. It was a holiday for us. Once when we were there, as I recall it was May day —

my favorite holiday, we had gotten seats close to the stage, and we heard the master of ceremonies announce, "Now, the artist of the Bolshoi Theater, Ivan Semyonovich Kozlovskiy, will appear." I was dumbfounded. "Guys," I said, "now Kozlovskiy is going to sing!" Ivan Semyonovich did not just come out, but somehow ran out onto the stage with a smile on his lips. He was tall, well-built, and beautifully dressed in a frock-coat.

Ivan Semyonovich sang the aria of Vladimir Dubrovskiy from the opera *Dubrovskiy*. He sang wonderfully, and the audience applauded him in a friendly fashion. Suddenly, he sang the song of the Duke from the opera *Rigoletto*. I was in ecstasy—I was hearing and seeing Kozlovskiy himself! For me this was a double holiday. I remembered this concert my whole life. This was my first encounter with Ivan Semyonovich Kozlovskiy.

The second encounter with Ivan Semyonovich happened at the Front. At that time, I was serving in the Red Army Ensemble of Song and Dance with Aleksander Vasilevich. At that time, we were performing for military units on the Ukrainian front. Our troops were freeing settlement after settlement, and town after town. On the Ukrainian front, an enormous advance of our units was being readied. The Ensemble received orders to serve the units on the Ukrainian front, to give several concerts on the Front Line. We needed to raise the fighting spirit of the soldiers. An improvised stage was prepared in the forest. Soldiers built it from young fir and birch trees.

We were already sitting on the stage, and the soldiers were arranged around us when a staff-car arrived. Ivan Semyonovich Kozlovskiy emerged, and the general that escorted the famous singer everywhere on the front was with him. While Ivan Semyonovich was greeting everyone, we stood and shouted, "We serve the Soviet Union!" He was touched.

We began the concert. Ivan Semyonovich took his famous guitar and sang several songs in Ukrainian. After that, he approached our director and whispered something. The director told us, "We will sing 'In the Forest on the Frontal Area.' " I was all eyes looking at him and thinking, "Well, a meeting, and in this song I have a beautiful supporting part for the horn that is played along with the singer." We played, and Ivan Semyonovich sang. You know, it was not for nothing he chose this song—we were actually located in the forest and on the Front Line. We came to the very place where I was to play together with the singer, and I began to play. Ivan Semyonovich immediately began to listen attentively—who was this joining in with him? It turned out to be a quite melodic duet. Thus, we played the whole three verses.

Afterward, Ivan Semyonovich approached me, shook my hand, and said, "Well! We would like to have you playing like that with us in the Bolshoi Theater. Thank you."

"You know, Ivan Semyonovich, I am an artist of the Bolshoi Theater. Now I am serving my time in the army, and will come to you again."

"What is your name?"

"I'm Polekh, Valeriy."

"I must remember that name. By the way, what a beautiful instrument you have. I love the horn very much; especially the solo in the second part of P. I. Tchaikovsky's *Fifth Symphony*.

With that, I parted with the great singer. All the same, my dream of personally meeting Ivan Semyonovich had been fulfilled.

The war ended, and I returned to my beloved Bolshoi Theater. Also, I met Kozlovskiy again. Rehearsals for the opera by C. Gounod, *Faust*, were going on, and Ivan Semyonovich was performing the title role. In one place, Faust's well-known aria has a *fermata*, and everyone knew that Ivan Semyonovich was a great master of holding the long *fermata*. In this aria's *fermata*, we needed to hold as a duet. Kozlovskiy held, and I held. Kozlovskiy held, and I held. At some moment, Ivan Semyonovich was silent—out of breath, but I still held.

Kozlovskiy came out on the proscenium and asked, " Who, here, held the fermata?

I stood and said, "It was I, who held it."

"Good man! If you are able to hold longer than Kozlovskiy, honor to you and glory! Yes, this is, I know, my acquaintance from the Front! I remember your name—Valeriy Polekh. Bravo! Bravissimo!"

One day, something unpleasant happened. A satirical article under the title On High D appeared in a central newspaper, and the author's name was Narinyani. In this satire, he poured mud on our praiseworthy singers. However, he did not indicate the real names, but gave them the names "Lohengrin Lohengrinovich," and "Mantuan Mantuanovich." It was not hard to guess that it was about Kozlovskiy and Lemeshev. Ivan Semyonovich was terribly angry and insulted. This Narinyani called them thieves, who were taking a lot of money. Ivan Semyonovich called the Bolshoi Theater Party Committee on the telephone. At that time, I was the Deputy Secretary of the Party Committee. I heard Ivan Semyonovich out, and promised to investigate. That very day, I went to Kozlovskiy's home. I was very nearly not allowed in to see him—he did not want to talk with anyone. Just the same, he did receive me.

Here is what he told me: "On my own time, the Chairman of Artistic Affairs called me to his office, and said that the Minsk operatic theater was in a melt down, and concert life was freezing up.

Would it be possible for me to travel to Minsk and give a few operatic and concert presentations that would correct the problem. I agreed and named a price. The chairman agreed.

Ivan Semyonovich went to Minsk. There was a real emergency there. The public was not attending the opera. The artists were leading a depressed life – they had not gotten wages for several months. He sang several operatic spectaculars to a full house in spite of greatly higher ticket prices. The concertss had great success. The artists and the public embraced him. The artists received wages and the city came alive culturally,

Following such a momentous effort, he did not sing for nearly a month. He needed ti rebuild he previous form. After all this, an article such as this appeared.

Culturally, the city came to life. After such a gigantic effort, he did not sing for almost a month, necessarily, to reestablish his previous form. After all that, an article like this appeared.

I promised Ivan Semyonovich to get to the bottom of everything and set everything right. I reported to the Secretary of the Party Committee, and he, in his turn, decided to summon Narinyani to the Party Bureau of the Theater. Narinyani appeared at the Party Bureau. We showed the accuser all the errors of his accusation. Narinyani stuck to his story, defending it. We threatened him with legal proceedings. In the end, he agreed to give his apology. By the way, Ivan Semyonovich showed me a document, signed by a high-ranking leader, that said, "Certificate given to the People's Artist of the USSR, Kozlovskiy, Ivan Semyonovich, in that he sang a great quantity of very well done concerts, from which the proceeds went to the support of the growth of culture and for which thanks are given to him."

Our next encounter happened under the following circumstances. I was on tour in England with the Bolshoi Theater as Second Director of the trip. There I became acquainted with the horn musicians of the Covent-Garden Opera Theater. I played my horn for them. My playing made a good impression. The horn players of the theater were very pleased by our Russian style of performance. As a mark of our friendship, the British horn musicians gave me a work by the composer B. Britten, Serenade, for tenor, French horn, and orchestra.

When I returned to Moscow, I showed Serenade to conductor Gennadiy Rozhdestvenskiy and Ivan Semyonovich Kozlovskiy. We decided to perform the work in the Great Hall of the Conservatory. I was a little concerned because the great singer had invited me and I would be working with him. The day of our appointment arrived. I went to the house on Nezhdanovaya Street. I rang the bell. The door was opened for me. I took off my wraps. At that moment, a small window in the wall opened, you know, such a window as a cashier has. Through the window, with the voice of Ivan Semyonovich, someone said, "Ah, it's you. Go on in. Someone will guide you." I entered a large room. Silence. No one was to be seen. Suddenly, I heard a voice, and not simply a voice, but a pleasant tenor, and from somewhere up above was heard, "One minute, and I will be with you." Only then did I notice the stairway leading upward.

Ivan Semyonovich very lightly descended the stairs. He looked me over from foot to head. It seemed to me that Ivan Semyonovich was pleased with my appearance. Ivan Semyonovich himself looked great. He was tall with a fresh handsome face, and beautiful hands. He was dressed in a lightweight, black velvet, short jacket, slacks in the style of Max-Linder with a gray stripe, and was not wearing house-slippers but shiney black boots. He invited me to sit. Ivan Semyonovich asked me if I
remembered life on the Front.

"Yes, Ivan Semyonovich, I remember, and not rarely. We were in such tight spots that at night we were not sure of waking up again. The Front is in my dreams. War is war."

Ivan Semyonovich looked at me with a gaze that was at the same time welcoming and questioning. We went to the other half of the room, where a grand piano stood. On the piano stood a porcelain vase with the image of Ivan Semyonovich on it.

The large room was divided in two halves by a movable wall. Later, I learned the half of the room where the grand piano stood was for artistic work. For example, if we were working on a composition or song or arguing with regard to this or another production, then nothing should interfere or distract from the flow of the creative work. However, suppose one wanted to bring up some other subject, or make inquiries, or tell some sort of anecdote or story; in that case, Ivan Semyonovich would rise from the chair and ask the conversationalist to cross over to the other half of the room. There, we could raise any subject. Perhaps you would say this is an eccentricity or something of that spirit. No! And again, no! With this I cannot agree and do not want to! I only understood how good this system was after I had "cooked in this juice."

Ivan Semyonovich terribly disliked any sort of gossip or vulgarity. The stories of Ivan Semyonovich were notable for wit and elegance. As an intelligent man, he loved to speak himself, but he was able to listen also.

The door-bell rang, and the pianist, Petya, arrived. He was an old friend of Ivan Semyonovich and a wonderful accompanist. What a misfortune had happened to Petya! In 1941, he had gone to the Front,

and returned with a wounded hand. The palm of his right hand was shattered. He could not play the piano any more. Ivan Semyonovich did not leave Petya in a lurch. He helped him for several years, located doctors, encouraged in every way, and instilled hope in his spirit for recovery of health. And Petya began playing—
tentatively at first, carefully, and later at full strength.

Ivan Semyonovich very scrupulously analyzed Britten's *Serenade* with us. He asked me to pay attention to the fact that the composition was very hard. "We will have to put in a lot of work in order to perform this work at a high level." I agreed with him. In reality, the composition turned out to be very complicated. It begins with an off-stage solo by the horn. This is the prologue, which must convey the mood of *Serenade*, and to do this demands a whole palate of colors and the tightest of nuances. The sound must be magical. Here, the author made use of the wonderful closed note of the French horn that is performed with the help of special mutes—metallic, cardboard, or plastic. The effect of a distant echo was achieved. In the composition, the interval jumps between notes were very uncomfortable, and open notes suddenly changed to closed notes.

Other complications came up also. We each sang and played well individually, but our goal of unity was not achieved when playing together. Then Ivan Semyonovich took the artistic leadership into his own hands, "I am the singer, and you must imitate me in timbre, in character, and nuance. You must support me and do everything that I do. If you do everything better than I, then it will be an honor and a glory for you."

So, here appeared my best quality, to sing on the horn. The combination of the extraordinary voice of the singer and the sound of the horn must produce an indistinguishable impression. Ivan Semyonovich came to rehearsals exactingly prepared for work. Ivan Semyonovich was a wonderful musician, and he had almost no problems. However, we had one mutual problem—learning to understand one another. It was "Together!" and "Together!", and again "Together!" We worked, and once more, not stinting the effort, we stayed up late—till midnight. Once, when we had stayed late, as Petya and I were preparing to leave, Ivan Semyonovich proposed, "What do you say, Petya, maybe we could have a little drink?"

"With exceeding great pleasure."

Petya was a great one for sitting in glad company. I phoned home and asked my wife not to become alarmed. We had decided to take a little rest.

"But won't you disturb Ivan Semyonovich's rest?"

"No, this is on his initiative."

The next day, we rested after the tiring work. Our work was nearing completion. The concert was arranged for the Great Hall of the Moscow Conservatory. Our program attracted interest. The concert was attended by musical Moscow. Onto the stage strode Ivan Semyonovich and the conductor Izrail Borisovich Gusman. The lights gradually began to dim. I was standing in the wings, and feeling nervous. Taking myself in hand, I started playing. The notes of the horn carried into the darkened hall. I felt I was playing a prayer that I performed before the audience. After performance of the prologue, the lights came up in the hall, and I went on stage. A competition began between vocal effort, emotion, virtuosity, and musicality. The contest ended with victory for both. This was a victory of indefatigable, fanatic labor. The hall resounded with deafening applause. We went out many times for bows.

Backstage, a great many artists and important musicians came to greet us. The great Marshall and Four-Times Hero of the Soviet Union Gyeorgy Konstantinovich Zhukov came with his spouse. Also, my happy wife came. Afterward, *Serenade* was performed in the city of Gorky at the Festival of Modern Music with the Gorky Philharmonic Orchestra. At that time, Ivan Semyonovich Kozlovskiy introduced a few innovations. He asked that a French horn be hung behind the orchestra on the rear wall. As soon as I began to play my prologue off stage, in total darkness the beam of a spot-light illuminated the French horn. It created the illusion that the horn was playing itself. You may imagine that this made an impression!

Time flies so swiftly. It seemed just a short while ago that I joined the Bolshoi Theater, and it was already my jubilee—25 years. We celebrated in the VTO building. The hall was full. Five of the leading artists of the Orchestra were celebrating their jubilee. Many of our friends and artists from other collectives were in the hall, and also the directors Yu. Faier, V. Nebolsin, K. Kondrashin, S. Sakharov, and orchestral soloists A. Buravskiy, T. Dokshitser, M. Chepkoy, and others. K. Kondrashin began the evening. He congratulated the guests of honor for the jubilee, and also said he always felt great pleasure working with such venerable artists. We were greeted by Yu. Faier, V. Nebolsin, and S. Sakharov. Ivan Semyonovich Kozlovskiy and Maxim Dormidontovich Mikhailov came on the stage. As always, Ivan Semyonovich came out with a small basket, like they always have in hotels. Maxim Dormidontovich Mikhailov proclaimed a toast in his low bass voice, "You have done well, men. You are serving the country and Fatherland well." Then he closed by singing in a deep bass voice, "Many Years." From off-stage, Ivan Semyonovich brought out a small trombone and played Valentine's aria from the opera *Faust.* Thunderous applause and delighted cries of "Bravo! Get Ivan Semyonovich into the Bolshoi Theater Orchestra!" rang out in the audience.

After this, Ivan Semyonovich spoke a few words of greeting. "You know, I remember an interesting incident. A violinist brought an alarm clock to the theater. He had just gotten it from the repair shop, and fearing it would disappear, he brought it with him into the orchestra pit. He wound it up and set it and prepared for the start of the production. *Eugene Onegin* was being put on in the Annex of the Bolshoi Theater. I was playing Lenskiy that time. At the most tragic moment, when Onegin must kill Lenskiy, the alarm clock began to ring very loudly, resounding through the whole theater. The violinist was very startled. He tried to grab the alarm clock, and stop the ringing; but in his haste, he dropped it. Because the clock was round, it rolled under a chair—ringing all the while. We were laughing ourselves to death. Onegin was so weak from laughing that he dropped the pistol. So it happened, because of the alarm clock, Lenskiy remained alive, and the curtain closed. They wanted to fire the violinist, but, because he had saved a man's life after all, they gave him a reprimand as punishment and let him stay in the theater."The audience really enjoyed the story, and Homeric "Ho-Ho's" resounded in the hall.

We watched Maxim Dormidontovich Mikhailov carry Ivan Semyonovich's overshoes onto the stage. He placed them on the floor and put his knees in them and thereby became short and fat. He then did a comical skit the audience found funny. As a finale to the skit he was doing, Maxim Dormidontovich put the overshoes on the feet of their owner. The fact is, at that time, the only one wearing overshoes in Moscow was Ivan Semyonovich.

Ivan Semyonovich looked around the auditorium, and, seeing my wife, Ludmilla Nikolaevna, there said loudly, "You see sitting before you in the second row a likable blond lady. This is the wife of today's jubilee celebrant, Valeriy Polekh. It takes a lot of patience and feminine tact to be the wife of such a busy man. Valeriy, I congratulate you for your jubilee, but even more so for your kind and charming wife."

Ivan Semyonovich descended the steps from the platform, approached Ludmilla Nikolaevna, and kissed her hand. That is how the jubilee evening ended

A small group came with us to my place to continue the festivity. I invited Ivan Semyonovich to share the evening with us. He thanked me and agreed. It was not far to walk. My wife and I took Ivan Semyonovich by the arm and escorted him to our home. With us also came the wife of Marshall N. N. Voronov, Nina Sergievna, M.D. Mikhailov, and a singer from the Bolshoi Theater, S. G Panov. Ivan Semyonovich continued to entertain us along the way. We arrived and went straight to the table, because we were all starving. Ivan Semyonovich took off his overshoes, left them in the entryway, and went to wash his hands. I gave him a fresh towel, and he carefully dried his beautiful hands, combed his hair before a cheval-mirror, checked himself from foot to head, and only then entered the sitting room. He sat down at the table and immediately got down to business. He asked that drinks be poured.

"You know," he turned to me, "I see you and everyone sitting in the orchestra pit when I am on stage. I look at you and study you. One time, one of the violinists, seated at the last position, was playing while sleeping, and snoring softly— maybe to himself. Wind instrumentalists, on the other hand, are always tending to business."

"Faier or Golovanov don't let anyone sleep. They wake them up right away with their gestures."

"During a break you don't have time to sleep either. You love to visit with each other. However, I love the wind players in general."

It's true, the toast was a little long, and mouths were watering. We drank and snacked. There were a lot of snacks, but everyone liked the marinated sevruga sturgeon that had been sent to us from the south. Ivan Semyonovich especially liked it. He was devouring it with a great appetite, and kept repeating, "Valeriy, save the fish. I'll come over to eat sevruga in the morning."

Ivan Semyonovich told us a comical story that had happened to him on the stage at the Annex of the Bolshoi Theater during the production of *La Traviata*. "In the third act, when Alfred insults Violetta, I was so exhausted that, in order to rest a little, I leaned against a column. The column was a fake made out of cloth, and of course it did not hold me. I went flying from the set into the wings—continuing to sing. I was told about it afterward; it was very comical that a singer fell heels over head. The audience liked the trick very much and rewarded me with applause like you never heard before. Valeriy, save the fish. Don't forget that I'm coming tomorrow."

Ivan Semyonovich danced a little with my wife. The evening passed very, very pleasantly. I escorted Ivan Semyonovich to his home, and we parted.

—ɯ—

One evening, Ivan Semyonovich phoned me. He made a request, "Valeriy, go right away to a store and buy a bottle of vodka. You see, it is very necessary to visit Maxim Mikhailov. He is ill, and cannot leave his house. The doctors have prescribed home confinement. It is necessary to encourage him because he is completely despondent. He lives across from you on Gorky Street."

We agreed where to meet. Ivan Semyonovich quickly found the apartment. We rang the bell, and the wife opened the door. How she rejoiced! "Take off your things. Go on into the room. How glad our Maxim will be!"

We went in, and saw the sick one himself in a beige robe seated in a high-backed, green arm-chair. The master of the house attempted to get up, but Ivan Semyonovich sat him back down in the chair. We greeted each other in the Christian manner, and kissed on three sides. Maxim even cried a little, wiped the tears with the sleeve of his jacket, and repeated, "Here now, you did me a good turn. You did me such a good turn."

I stood the bottle on the table. Maxim Dormidontovich immediately became more animated. His wife went out to deal with household affairs, and we discussed politics. She began to set the table. There appeared dill pickles, a favorite snack of the master of the house. She set out *kulebiaka* pie with meat and eggs, a little herring with onion, and brought a hot potato. We opened a bottle, a native forty-proof, poured it into sizable glasses, drank and snacked. Ivan Semyonovich made a toast in honor of the master of the house and his precious health. Conversation continued. Maxim Dormidontovich asked how our concert at the Great Hall of the Conservatory went. "It seems you performed the work of the English author? I strongly request that as soon as your record comes out, you send it to me. I will listen to this music with great pleasure."

The conversation went more cheerfully. The Russko-Gorkaya vodka was taking effect.

"Listen, Vanya," Maxim Dormidontovich addressed Kozlovskiy. "Let's sing my beloved duet by Vilboa, *Unpeopled is Our Sea.*

Ivan Semyonovich sat at the grand piano, and they began. Good Lord! What inspiration! What marvelous voices! In my opinion, they had never sung like that, and when they stopped singing, they both had shed a few tears. In order to lighten the atmosphere, I told them an anecdote. "A young artist was preparing to go from the theater to a snack bar. Friends told him, 'You should buy yourself a suit-case for traveling.' 'What for?' 'To put your slacks, jacket, and underwear into it.' 'But what would I wear to go out to eat in then?' " I told of an incident that happened with our famous singer, E. Shumskaya. She was singing *Snow Maiden* in the Bolshoi Theater. "I was standing and singing," recounted Shumskaya. "My aria was so gentle and so quiet. Suddenly, laughter burst out in the audience, louder and still louder. What was going on? Maybe I had done something wrong that was eliciting this laughter? I looked around and Good Lord! What did I see? In the middle of the stage stood a fireman with a teapot, and he was listening to me sing. He stood there a while and walked off. They nearly fired the fireman."

The singing went on. Ivan Semyonovich sang *Reveta Stogne* and *Divlyus Ya na Nebo*. Maxim Dormidontovich sang *Dubinushka*. On that note we parted. It was a marvelous evening.

Nature has given Ivan Semyonovich a magnificent voice. To describe it with words is very difficult. Many have tried, and I will try. Nature has gifted Ivan Semyonovich with a glorious voice, and a timbre that is delicate and, I would say, divine. He has an irreproachable — and the cleanest — intonation, and absolute pitch. Ivan Semyonovich has a golden sense of proportion. Rare diction. Like the great Kachalov, he conveys each vocal word to the listener. Boundless diapason. Difficulties with diapason do not exist for him. Like a bird, he sings completely unconstrainedly, freely, and easily. After hearing the singing of Kozlovskiy, the great Shalyapin said, "This Russian singer sings like a bird!" Ivan Semyonovich absorbs everything that is needful to become still better. He is very inquisitive. He is ready to see everything and to hear everything. He attends nearly all the concerts in the Great Hall of the Conservatory, and his permanent seat is in the Conductors Loge on the first level in the corner. He is at almost all premieres. He loves our own and the visiting instrumentalists. He loves to listen to excellent singers. Ivan Semyonovich is like an encyclopedic-dictionary of music. He has heard a lot and knows very much. He knows mythology, poetry, the history of Rome, and he is acquainted with the music of very many composers.

That's the kind of person our great Ivan Semyonovich Kozlovskiy is.

FOURTEEN

Vitaliy Mikhailovich Buyanovskiy

MIKHAIL NIKOLAEVICH BUYANOVSKIY (VITALIY's father) was a French horn musician, teacher, Honored Artist, and the son of a flutist of the Court Orchestra. He graduated from the Petersburg Conservatory (the Class of Ya. Tamma), and was awarded the Gold Medal and Diploma of a Free Artist. As a result, his name was engraved on the marble plaque listing the graduates of the Leningrad Conservatory.

His son, Vitaliy Mikhailovich Buyanovskiy, was born August 28, 1928. The creative path of V. M. Buyanovskiy as a orchestra member, began quite early. In 1946, after successfully completing musical high school in the class of Professor M. N. Buyanovskiy (his father), the eighteen-year old Vitaliy passed the audition for the S. M. Kirov Opera and Ballet Theater. The orchestra was headed up by B. Eh. Khaikin, D. I. Pakhitonov, V. A. Dranishnikov, and S. V. Eltsin.

He continually served as a soloist—working on the most difficult French horn repertoire and presenting concerts at the Conservatory, on television, and on the radio. Vitaliy Mikhailovich has given great effort to

M. V. Buyanovskiy

concert work. At his instigation, the young Leningrad composer, A. Zatin, wrote a concerto for piano, French horn, and trumpet with orchestra. Listeners recall the amazing concerts of V. Buyanovskiy with singers, "Sonata Evenings with Virsaladze. " The genre of chamber music occupies a special place in the concert activities of Vitaliy Mikhailovich.

V. M. Buyanovskiy is no less talented as an instructor. Having inherited a great deal from his father, the oldest professor at the Petersburg Conservatory, Vitaliy Mikhailovich follows performance traditions of the Russian school in his instructional activities. Great attention is given to the various types of ensemble.

I first met Vitaliy Mikhailovich in the Great Hall of the Leningrad Philharmonic when I traveled to Leningrad to perform R. M. Gliere's concerto. The entire class of Professor M. N. Buyanovskiy [the father] attended a rehearsal in the hall of the Philharmonic. By good fortune, at the same time, I became acquainted with the wonderful person and French horn musician, Pavel Orekhov. He came to meet me at the train station, accompanied me to the Philharmonic, and showed me where it would be best to stand on the stage during the performance. That evening, Pavel Orekhov played in the orchestra that accompanied me. R. M. Gliere had already been rehearsing with the orchestra, and now they began to rehearse with me. After the rehearsal, I again met with Pavel Orekhov, and he introduced me to Vitaliy Mikhailovich Buyanovskiy, who was still a young horn player.

In the evening, the concerto went very well, and I was out several times for an encore. Professor M. N. Buyanovskiy came back-stage, and congratulated me on the success. He said he was hearing me for the second time. "The first time," said Mikhail Nikolaevich, "I congratulated you in Moscow when you, Valeriy Vladimirovich, were victorious with First Premium in the All-Union Competition." After the concert, we went out on the street. The city was beautifully illuminated, and the young people were happy and smartly dressed. We loved Leningrad, this incomparable city.

My next encounter with Vitaliy Buyanovskiy occurred in Moscow at the Academic Building. A group of Leningrad musicians had come, and Vitaliy Mikhailovich was among them. I was at their concert with my wife and daughter. Vitaliy Mikhailovich played V. A. Mozart's *Fourth Concerto*. During the intermission, we greeted him—this man who was already tall and handsome.

After a short time, Vitaliy Mikhailovich sent us a letter inviting us to the First Seminar of French Horn Musicians. We accepted the invitation, and on November 20, 1978, arrived in Leningrad. We were very pleased with the way the seminar was organized, and most of all applauded the organizer and inspirer—Vitaliy Mikhailovich. With a short introduction, he opened the seminar. There were several very interesting performances by young horn students, and Vitaliy Mikhailovich, himself, performed and demonstrated an amazing *belcanto* on the horn. The ensemble came forward. This was a large horn choir conducted by Vitaliy Mikhailovich. With this the seminar ended. Then I composed a dedication to the first seminar.

To the First Seminar of French Horn Musicians in Leningrad

French Horn players in Leningrad
Gathered together as on a parade.
Both young and old came here,
All came to the First Seminar.

This First of Convocations
Exceeded all expectations.

Methodological themes shared
French horn problems hard
Were raised by presenters
At the First Leningrad Seminar.

These are soloist presenters,

Gifted French horn players

The Old School you've left behind
All-powerful Tamm.
And these, Tamm's successors,
Are truly wonder workers.

If still alive were Tchaikovsky,
And he heard how Buyanovskiy
In his *Cantabile Andante*
Performed with such *belcanto*
I tell you without irony
He would write another symphony.

Virtuosi, please be me believing.
You, at the concert in the evening,
Yourselves were evidently made certain,
And were not a little surprised.
I am envious a little of colleagues.
The vocal cycle and sonati
Were all written so professionally
And performed with real genius.

I traveled here from Moscow,
To receive, as your Orekhov
With the French horn made
Such first-class artistry.

You, inspired the convocation,
Now receive our recognition.
All musicians have remarked on
Your great talent for organization.

It is your right to be *avant garde*.

143

At this First Leningrad Seminar.
BRAVO!
BRAVO!

Valeriy Polekh, Honored Artist of Russia, November 20, 1978. Composed while standing, leaning one elbow on the grand piano at the end of the evening which had proceeded with such great success.

Vitaliy Mikhailovich introduced us to his wife—delicate, sweet, and statuesque as a ballerina. Vitaliy Mikhailovich invited us to his home. When we came to Buyanovskiy's, we were met by an enormous, pedigreed tom cat. After meeting the guests, he jumped into a rocking chair. We sat at the table and Tanechka informed us that this gentle cat would not leave the rocking chair until he had shown us his acrobatic act. We all prepared ourselves to watch. The cat began to move the rocking chair—gently at first, and then harder and harder and rocked so strongly that we really thought he would roll right out of the rocking chair. However, at that moment, he slowed the movement and stopped the rocker. We began to applaud the cat. He looked at everyone as though to say to himself, "Hey, I am something else!" and ran off.

For the occasion of the end of the seminar, Tanechka baked a wonderful pie. A small company assembled—about ten people. A horn player from the Republic of Georgia brought an excellent wine, a couple from the Asian republics obtained a basket of fruit. There also appeared strong wines, an olive salad, and various snacks.

I brought the first toast—to the instigator of our celebration, such an indefatigable organizer; "You, Vitaliy Mikhailovich, strove with all your might to produce the seminar, even set up chairs yourself, and played excellently. Enormous thanks to you. I bow before you. You are a magician! Hurrah!" Then Pavel Orekhov arrived with his wife. The second toast was raised to Pavlik, as he was called. Following that was a toast to the sweet, charming ladies.

Thus ended this wonderful, miraculous day—the day of the First Leningrad Seminar.

When Vitaliy Mikhailovich came to Moscow, he always stayed with me. I would meet him early with my car, and we would come to my place. Here, we shared so many conversations and opinions over a cup of coffee. We could never run out of things to talk about.

There was an interesting happenstance. One time when I went to meet Buyanovskiy at the train station, what did I see? There, stood a long line of generals—evidently to greet someone important—and walking to meet me came Vitaliy Mikhailovich. We greeted each other, exchanged a Christian kiss of greeting.

I remarked to Buyanovskiy: "Look how many generals are here to greet you!"

He looked and said, "So many generals! What a great honor for me! So, Valeriy Vladimirovich, give them the command to stand at ease."

We had a good laugh.

It happened that Pavel Orekhov sent me a letter inviting us to his birthday jubilee. After thinking a little, I got together twelve horn musicians. We practiced a jubilee program and traveled to Leningrad for the jubilee of our friend Pavel Orekhov.

Horn musicians from many Republics came to celebrate the jubilee. Professor Pavel Serebryanikov, the director of the Conservatory, conducted the whole program. We liked him very much. He was so pleasant and intelligent. Our presentation was very successful. I addressed a few words of greeting to the honoree of the jubilee. I directed all our musical program. Vitaliy Mikhailovich prepared an extensive program and also played a solo himself. Pavel Orekhov was very touched by our presentation — in as much as such a group of Moscow horn musicians had never before been in Leningrad. The evening concluded in a tavern.

One summer, Jimmy Decker, the well known French horn musician, came to visit me from America. We had met before in Los Angeles when I was on tour in that area. The American horn musician spent several days in Moscow. I went with him to museums, showed him Moscow, and we attended the Bolshoi Theater. He enjoyed being with me at the dacha. In general, he was pleased with my reception. When it came time to part, I drove him to the airport.

After a short time, he sent me a letter of invitation to a seminar of French horn musicians that the University of Los Angeles was putting on. He asked me to send the documents necessary for me to participate in the seminar. In the letter, he wrote that horn musicians from the whole world would be coming to the seminar. I prepared the documents and sent them to the address in Los Angeles. After a short time Vitaliy Mikhailovich Buyanovskiy also received the same invitation. The two of us agreed to travel to the seminar together.

Valeriy Vladimirovich Polekh and James Decker

So there we were, Buyanovskiy and I, in America! Jimmy Decker met us and drove us to the hotel. I participated in the activity of the program. I needed to give three lectures on the theme "French horn artistry in the Soviet Union," and during the concluding concert direct a-horn choir consisting of sixty French-horns. I want to tell about the work Buyanovskiy did at the seminar. He had to conduct three demonstration lessons with the horn musicians who had come and play a solo program.

I attended his demonstration lesson. I had never heard how he was going to conduct it. I liked his system. In the large room in which Buyanovskiy conducted his lesson, horn musicians sat in rows. Buyanovskiy asked those in the auditorium, "Who would like to participate?" A horn musician, who was not very young, went up. Buyanovskiy greeted him and asked a few questions: How many years had he been playing the French horn? Where did he study? In which musical institution? Where is he working now? And where is he living?

Having received the answers, Buyanovskiy took in his hands the instrument of his student, examined it, and said, "Yes, this is of the firm 'Conn' in rather battered condition, the mouthpiece also is of the firm 'Conn.' Would you play a scale?" The answer was in the affirmative. "Please play F sharp Major," requested Buyanovskiy. Unevenly and incompetently, but all the same he played.

"Do you play the etudes of Kling?"

"Yes."

Vitaliy Mikhailovich took his own instrument and showed how we play a scale.

"Now, play the scale yourself. Well now, you see, you have already begun to play much better and more competently."

Aditionally, he demonstrated a principle which must always be followed by performers. This is rhythm. This is a counting technique, but if this etude is cantonal, it is necessary to perform such an etude like a concert.

"Please play the piece," Buyanovskiy requested. The student played *Romance*, by Saint-Saens.

"Thank you! You played without mistakes, but where are the nuances? Here, listen." Buyanovskiy took an instrument and began to play. "Well, what do you say?" asked Vitaliy Mikhailovich.

"You play beautifully," responded the apprentice.

Vitaliy Mikhailovich was explaining and demonstrating how one needs to carry the note, and how to breathe, how it is necessary to hold the support and the diaphragm. Buyanovskiy succinctly showed how this is done.

"Please, play and try to put into practice all that I talked about here."

The apprentice began to play with more assurance, the sound poured out more freely and beautifully. The apprentice left very pleased with the lesson.

In the J. Decker home, Long Beach, CA

It was like that for about ten people. To all, Vitaliy Mikhailovich gave instructions and answered questions of interest. In the concluding concert, Vitaliy Mikhailovich played his solo program beautifully, and they did not let him leave the stage for a long time. My turn came at last. All sixty horn players were on the stage. I had earlier arranged with the concertmaster of the horn choir so that at the moment of my entrance, all the horn players, in unison and lightning fast, raised their horns high. The American public appreciated this effect. (Americans love a variety of effect pieces.) I played "Hymn of the City of Leningrad," by Reingold Moritsevich. The audience was pleased, and long expressed their acceptance with extended applause.

Vitaliy Mikhailovich signed my picture in the program. I signed Vitaliy Mikhailovich's picture in the program. Buyanovskiy and I both got acquainted with many famous horn musicians.

I thanked Jimmy Decker for the wonderful organization of the symposium. In the evening, we were guests at Jimmy's. He has a very cozy home. Near the house, a nice little cabin-cruiser stood on the water, and we went for a little ride on the water. Jimmy had a bar in his house, and we sat down in his bar with pleasure.

The next day, about ten horn players gathered with us in the hotel. We were staying in a four-room suite. Our new horn-player friends did not come empty handed. They brought many tasty things. Late at night, all our guests drove off. The two of us remained, Vitaliy Mikhailovich and I, and what to talk about?

In the James Decker home.

I said, "How great this is! Now we have so many new friends."
"Yes, this is very good!" Buyanovskiy confirmed.

Los Angeles, 1982

149

It is impossible not to agree with the what D. D. Shostokovich said about V. M. Buyanovskiy: "His artistry is exalted and strong. Characteristically, he has irreproachable artistic taste, a nobility of sound, emotional restraint, and the subtle ability to express the ideational-formative content of a composition in agreement with its character and style."

FIFTEEN

Larisa Leonidovna Artynova

T HE MUSIC COLLEGE ON Merzlyakovskiy Lane was in a small three-story building. Inside the building, working conditions were crowded, and even the basement area was used. The sheet-music library and classrooms were down there. These basement classrooms were mainly used by the winds—that is, by students who were playing wind instruments. They located us there for a reason—so we wind instrument players would not disturb the other departments with our piercing sounds. The office of Director Blyuman was located in a small room on the first floor. Adjacent to this crowded office was the general office where two dear women sat. One was in charge of the scholastic area, and the other business affairs. They conducted all the business of the college.

I was recommended as a teacher to the Director of the college by Professor S. N. Eremin. Blyuman invited me into her office and said, "You are a famous musician. You appear on stage as a soloist. Couldn't you put together a little concert for us? That

This reminds me of so much..

way, we could get a little more closely acquainted with you, and it would be pleasant to hear your presentation. The fact is, we have never heard a French horn on the stage." I assented. One beautiful day, the instructors and students gathered in the small auditorium of the college to listen to a French horn Musician. My presentation was met with enthusiasm. On her own authority, the Director signed me up as a teacher in the college.

At that time, the sectional instructor over the horn class at the college was Anton Aleksandrovich Shchetnikov, who had been my teacher at the October Revolution Technical College. Here, we met again. Anton Aleksandrovich was very glad and helped me in every way to establish the new specialty. I set to work. The work turned out to be not so easy. It was necessary to teach the young person who had just come from amateur status to play the horn. Some rather good students began to appear for me.

At that time, our oh so thoughtful and intelligent Director became ill and, to our great regret, left the college. A new Director, Larisa Leonidovna Artynova took her place. The word went around that she was a business-like and capable leader. Also, as Secretary of the Party Organization of the college, she showed herself to be a sympathetic and principled friend. Of course, she had realized long ago that such a famous college could not be located in such crowded conditions. She began to make arrangements. The fact of the matter was, that a general-education school adjoined our college. The new Director, Larisa Leonidovna, put forth a lot of work and effort to join this school facility to our college. This was the Director's first great success. After colossal rebuilding and re-equipping, the new facility began to fully correspond to the parameters of a musical college.

The Director changed the old facility into a music school. By this means, Larisa Leonidovna had both a music school and a wonderful college. The Director changed the entire first floor over to a support area—accounting, housekeeping section, a rather spacious teachers' room, a rehearsal hall, the Director's office, and the Deputy Director's office. Auditoriums were put on the second, third and fourth floors. On the second floor was a very comfortable concert hall with an organ. Aditionally, there was an elevator. Larisa Leonidovna fought for all this. The leader of the housekeeping department, Galina Vasilevna Krasnoperova, was an efficient woman, and her housekeeping was always exemplary. The accounting department was ruled by three Ninas: the head accountant, the book-keeper, and the office worker. The accountants and I were very good friends. Whenever I came into accounting, the three Ninas would try to keep me with them as long as possible by making a variety of light conversation. One Nina admitted to me, "You always give off a delicious aroma, and we always try to keep you with us in order to breathe that Parisian scent a little longer." I loved what was a secret sin—to sprinkle myself a little with perfume.

In the scholastic area presided Eugenia Petrovna. Some of the old-timers simply called her "Zhenya." The First Deputy of the Director kept to himself in his office. This was Aleksandr Ivanovich Lagutin.

Lastly, there was the Director's office. The indomitable, businesslike Larisa Leonidovna, who was simultaneously gentle, angry, and strict was located in these premises. She was always on the run and did not sit in her office. Just think how many teachers and how many students there were, and she had business with all of them. If it were necessary, she would take notice of all, listen to all, give advice to all, or make a request. I almost forgot; she also taught music literature. The youngsters respected her, but they also feared her.

There was a great flood of students who wanted to attend our children's music school. Larisa Leonidovna decided to construct another floor. The Deputy Director of the the College and the Director of the Music School was Zoya Konstantinovna Leonova, the choirmaster. She had at one time graduated from our college herself. In the music school, she led the children's choir. She was a wonderful person—kind and sincere. The keeper-of-the-keys in the school was the well-known, exceptionally "young" Vera Semenova

Petrova. (Just between us, she was close to ninety.) She walked without a cane, and quickly, quickly. Her discipline was strict. The kids feared her, but respected her. When I had a break, I went to Vera Semenova, sat across from her, and she would begin to reminisce. "Do you remember, Valeriy Vladimirovich, when I still was working at the Conservatory? I always noticed you. You always had some unusual collars and neckties. You were a dandy."

Larisa Leonidovna loved her symphonic orchestra very much—passionately loved it. She invited the very capable, young conductor, Leonid Nikolayev and entrusted the orchestra to him. It must be said, she did not miscalculate. Nikolayev worked enthusiastically and hard, so that the orchestra would sound professional. He succeeded in this endeavor.

The Director watched over the orchestra a great deal. She traveled with the orchestra to concerts at various institutions. The orchestra even performed in the Great Hall at the Conservatory. The famous conductor from West Berlin, Herbert von Karajan, advertised an International Competition of Youth Orchestras. Larisa Leonidovna decided to try for good fortune, prepare for the competition, and take part in it. She expended a lot of strength and health in the preparation for this competition. At last, the orchestra left for Berlin led by Larisa Leonidovna and conductor Leonid Nikolaev. In West Berlin, our orchestra achieved great success, and as a result, Herbert von Karajan awarded the orchestra First Premium.

Larisa Leonidovna paid a lot of attention to the dormitory. She Understood that the dormitory needed to be like a family home. With all her might, she tried to create coziness there and a little bit of comfort. It was necessary to have a good buffet, dining room, and good showers. The rooms needed to be clean and neat. In the beginning, The dormitories were crowded. Larisa Leonidovna constructed another story. It became easier to breathe. In the dormitory, were kind adults who had been recommended by Larisa Leonidovna, and they kept track of everything. There was even a man in the dormitory whose specialty was rearing children. When the music school was being remodeled and I had to temporarily work in a small auditorium in the dormitory, I saw with my own eyes how orderly it was. Of course, it goes without saying, that the Director, Larisa Leonidovna, kept track of everything.

On the grounds of the College stands a solid building with the designation of swimming pool. This was also the brain-child of Larisa Leonidovna. She tormented herself so very much going around to various departments requesting and pleading to be given the possibility of building a swimming pool so that the children would not need to travel to the ends of the Earth to go swimming. That "energetic lady," Larisa Leonidovna, succeeded. Now we have our own swimming pool. We go swimming.

The librarian was Mila. From morning till late at night, she was passing along knowledge to the students. "Come to us in the library. Take knowledge without charge—just learn." She trained so many people, and from her golden hand, we received so much knowledge. I remember as I was putting together a text book I needed rare musical material. When I went to Mila in the library, my request was always filled with a smile on her pleasant lips. She climbed among the shelves, set up a ladder, and somewhere, high up near the ceiling itself, found what I needed, and was happy to have helped me and my project. I was always going to the library and to Mila, kind Mila, wonder-working Mila. She would invite me to have some strong-brewed tea, and always asked how she could help me today. Her expression sometimes seemed a little angry, a little tired, and sometimes a little humorous, but there was a pleasant kindness that shone in Mila.

I recall our Party meetings. All the instructors always assembled, and the members of the Party attended the meeting as though it were a holiday. As was always the rule, a chairman of the meeting and a secretary were elected. Larisa Leonidovna, as a rule, sat in the first row of the auditorium and always participated in the process. If she felt she needed to speak her piece, she spoke it. She kept track of everything, and kept it quiet in the hall. She followed the proceedings of the meetings very closely. If a little noise would arise in the hall as we were starting to talk among ourselves, Larisa Leonidovna would rise and turn her face toward the assembly. Immediately, quiet would prevail. The instructor from the Regional Committee of the Party Would come to the meetings. Business matters were dealt with, but there was also laughter and humor—there was everything. I remember almost no instances, in the course of forty years, when we uncovered some sort of dirty dealing or anything of that sort. For many years we had a friendly Party family, and for a fact, Larisa Leonidovna led this family. I would like to add that students Larisa Leonidovna raised and graduated from the college would return after they finished the Conservatory and work again under the wing of Larisa Leonidovna.

In the college, we had a tradition. The first Monday of June was "Health Day." At eight o'clock in the morning the three groups gathered: first year, second year and third year students. They traveled by electric train to three separate stations. Each group boarded the train together at their designated stations. The leader of each group would designate at which station they would leave the train. All three groups would exit the electric train and go on foot and gather together at the designated point—Peredelkino. Experienced instructors would guide the groups. Under the leadership of experienced teachers, usually the physical education and civil defense instructors, from three different locations the groups would direct themselves to the designated point—Peredelkino.

I will permit myself to describe how the first group went. My daughter, Lyudochka, and I already were at the Kiev station at eight o'clock in the morning. (I loved the Health Day very much and always went with my kids.) We bought tickets. The people began to arrive, someone called roll, and we got seated on the train. The girls and boys in the pleasant compartment sang songs—drowning out the beat of the wheels. It was evident that all the surrounding passengers liked our singing because everyone tried to sit a little closer to the singers to hear real singing. They even started to sing along.

That's how we traveled to Solnechnaya Station. The command was given to exit. We got off, crossed the railroad tracks, and entered the forest. It was such a beautiful, radiant morning. The sun was shining. The air was clean and smelled of the forest. The girls gathered lilies of the valley and violets. Soon, everyone had small bouquets. When we had boarded the electric train, it had been cool, but now everyone was beginning to unwrap themselves. The sun had done its job and warmed the children up. After an hour of travel on foot, the military instructor, Boris Ivanovich Zharov, gave the command for a halt.

When the halt was over, we went farther. We were walking in the forest, and it gradually began to thin out. Suddenly, before us opened a wonderful oasis. We were standing on a height, and below us opened a beautiful panorama: wonderful, ancient pines; the aroma of pitch in the air; and a picturesque stream with clean, transparent water. Along the stream stood benches painted various colors. This was Peredelkino. We saw Larisa Leonidovna. She was already bustling about with regard to the buffet. In the heat, how pleasant it was to drink cool kvass or a fruit drink and eat buttered bread. The sports equipment booth was opened for us, and we could rent bicycles, volleyballs, and soccer balls. Our famous military instructor, Boris Ivanovich, had already prepared various competitions in running and jumping. He was a great master at thinking up ingenious games to play. The heat was doing its work, and everyone was taking off heavy clothing. Larisa Leonidovna was keeping track of everything and everyone. I sat with Lydlochka on a bench by the stream. Suddenly, two pleasant heads burst forth from the water—yes, two of my students! Surprised, I said, "The water is cold, how can you stand to swim?"

"It's nothing!" responded my sportsmen. "We are hardened people."

That is how the first Monday in June went.

TRADITIONS

On a beautiful day, Larisa Leonidovna would gather all the returning students in the college. The students got on buses and went to the museum-home of P. I. Tchaikovsky in Klin. Larisa Leonidovna had established this tradition. Upon arriving in Klin, the participants entered the museum-home—a holy place for musicians. It was the rule for all the participants to assemble in the hall. Larisa Leonidovna delivered an introductory speech, and the student tickets were handed out.

One of the best students who had completed the college was permitted to play the grand piano on which P. I. Tchaikovsky himself had once played. After viewing the museum, the youngsters left—full of all manner of joyful hopes.

I think Larisa Leonidovna loved Soviet Army Day very much. All the instructors of the college would wear their medals, and war veterans would attend on this holiday. Larisa Leonidovna also wore her medals. Everything was very serious. The orchestra played, and the veterans were looking sharp and festive. The students looked at us with completely different eyes, and evidently thought, "Wow! So that's what you are, and we didn't know!"

Larisa Leonidovna always invited military men to bring heroic battle banners. The military lector related the heroic histories of these banners. In addition, Larisa Leonidovna always invited a well-known Hero of the Soviet Union who would tell in gripping fashion of his legendary actions.

After the official ceremony, the amateur artists of the college performed, or masters of the circus were invited, or young artists of the dramatic theater performed. The evening was always serious and interesting.

It was also a tradition at the college to put on an amateur theatrical production every ten years. The youngsters began preparation many months in advance. They memorized whole scenes, wrote scripts, and prepared operatic excerpts—with a comic theme, of course.

Graduating students and alumni of the college would come from other cities. Our jokers, and we had more than a few, prepared various very funny excerpts from the life of the college. I have kept an interesting photograph showing the hall, full of instructors, and all, as one, are laughing. That's how our amateur theatrical production went.

SIXTEEN

Nikolai Nikolaevich Voronov & Semyon Ilich Makeiev

O NE DAY, I WAS painting my dacha house. I had made a special scaffold, climbed up on it, and began to paint. Suddenly, I saw a small auto approaching. I saw it was a BMV make, and a general got out. He went into his personal plot, which was directly across from our dacha. After a little while, the general came out of his plot, glanced around and caught sight of me.

"God preserve you." shouted the general when he saw me.

"Thank you," I replied. At that time, I was finishing the painting work on my property.

"Whom are you renting to?" asked Semyon Ilich Makeiev. "And who lives here?"

"I live in this house, but I rent to my mother-in-law."

"How are you paid?" asked the general. "Payment for painting, of course, is a bottle."

"Ha, Ha! Such payment is very much in fashion now."

"Yes, you're right,' responded Semyon Ilich. "They rarely take money. More and more it's spirits."

S. I. Makeiev

"Comrade General, I am climbing down now. I ask the favor that you enter my cabin. We'll have some tea, and maybe, as we are becoming acquainted, also a glass."

"With pleasure. I'm not in a hurry."

We went into our house. The general inspected my abode. He seemed to like my place. While we were looking around the house, my wife was setting the table.

"Let me introduce you, Comrade General, this is my wife, Ludmilla Nikolaevna, and I am Valeriy Vladimirovich."

"I am very pleased, and I am Semyon Ilich. Valeriy Vladimirovich—this is a name I am acquainted with. No doubt, you know there is a famous lady singer, Valeriya Vladimirovna Barsova?"

"Let me tell you of an interesting incident, " I replied. When Valeriya Vladimirovna turned sixty, they had a jubilee celebration in her honor, and I brought greetings from the Bolshoi Theater. The leader announced, 'Valeriya Vladimirovna will be greeted by Valeriy Vladimirovich Polekh.'"

"Just think!. What a coincidence!" said the general. "My wife, Sofia Grigorievna Panova, you know, also sings in the Bolshoi Theater. She is a soloist and an Honored Artist."

"Here is what happens. Sofia Grigorievna sings on the stage and I accompany her in the orchestra."

"So, you play in the orchestra? Wonderful! Ludmilla Nikolaevna, do you work at the Bolshoi Theater also?"

"No, Semyon Ilich. I just am helping my husband."

"A wonderful answer! So, let's drink to our wonderful wives."

That was the start of a very pleasant acquaintance with the family of Semyon Ilich and Sofia Grigorievna. Time passed. Semyon Ilich built his house, and we became true friends.

We developed a strong friendship, and really lived like a large family. We got acquainted with Semyon Ilich's daughter, Natasha, and in turn, we introduced them to Ludmilla Nikolaevna's mother, Aleksandra Sergeievna. We introduced them to our daughter, Lyudechka, and our son, Valeriy. In the summer, we passed the time happily, and in the winter, we would meet on Gorky Street because we lived on the same street. We got along well. Semyon Ilich and Sofia Grigorievna turned out to be wonderful people. As our kids grew up, Natasha got to know Valeriy, and they became friends. Natasha and Valeriy fell in love with each other, and we all began to expect a wedding soon.

Semyon Ilich had an old and very close friend, Marshall Nikolai Nikolaevich Voronov. They were both army men, and they both even had served in the Czar's army—two tall, stately grenadiers. Nikolai Nikolaevich achieved the rank of marshal and Semyon Ilich achieved the rank of general. The Voronov and the Makeiev families had been friends for many years. The Voronov family often came to the Makeiev dacha. Semyon Ilich introduced my wife and me to Nikolai Nikolaevich and his wife Olga Sergeievna. These were very pleasant and courteous people.

We began to get together often. Nikolai Nikolaevich always had a story to tell, and we listened with pleasure to his stories from the time of the Civil War and from the time of the Second Great Patriotic War.* He talked about music and about theater. However, Nikolai Nikolaevich did not just talk—he loved to listen to the person he was talking with.

Once, somehow, the conversation got around to mushrooms. It turned out that Nikolai Nikolaevich was a confirmed mushroom hunter. Right away, he proposed that we go for mushrooms on Saturday. Everyone gladly agreed. The long-awaited Saturday arrived. My wife and I rose when it was barely light out, had a little breakfast, got ready, and went across to Semyon Ilich's, but Nikolai Nikolaevich's car was already standing at the gate. Because Nikolai Nikolaevich knew where mushrooms were to be found, he drove us to an excellent location.

It was a thick forest of ancient trees: firs, pines, and the occasional birch tree. The forest was a little dark and damp and mossy. The soil

---

* The Second World War

was just right for mushrooms and the aroma of mushrooms went through the forest. In the beginning, we came across russula and chanterelle mushrooms. Later came brown cap, white, and orange cap. Nikolai Nikolaevich took only the heads. He carefully cut them off with a small knife and placed them in a basket. The bottom of the basket was lined with ferns so the mushrooms would not be crumpled. We spread out in different directions.

Nikolai Nikolaevich
Voronov

Interestingly, as I was stooping to pick a mushroom, it seemed to me that I heard a noise, and not just a noise, but music. I stopped and listened. The sounds faded. Again, the sounds were audible. Again, I was hearing chords and harmony, and then, I was hearing a symphonic orchestra. It couldn't be, but I was hearing Tchaikovsky's Sixth Symphony! At first, I was even a little scared. The sounds of the symphony got closer and then moved farther away. I looked around. Nikolai Nikolaevich was picking mushrooms almost next to me. I began to move away from him, and the sound began to get softer. I drew nearer to Nikolai Nikolaevich again, and the symphony was playing again.

"Nikolai Nikolaevich, what is going on? I hear music. Put my mind at ease. Is this true?"

"Yes, Valeriy Vladimirovich. it's completely true. You are hearing music, and the music is located in my pocket. This is a small radio receiver." The music poured out and poured out.

"Well, this is Tchaikovsky's Sixth Symphony."

"No, this is not magic. It's the latest word in technical equipment. When I was in Paris as a guest of Charles de Gaul, he presented me with this little wonder. Valeriy Vladimirovich, this is my very favorite symphony. Here's a big stump. Let's sit down and listen."

We heard the voices of our ladies. "What's happening? What's that music?"

"Yes, this is our receiver playing. We are listening to the Sixth

Symphony of Tchaikovsky. Please, sit down. Look, such a charming stump. Be seated and I will spread my raincoat for you."

We listened through the final part of the symphony. Ludmilla Nikolaevna remarked that the symphony sounded magnificent in such magical surroundings.

"You know," said Nikolai Nikolaevich, " we have coniferous nature and magnificent music. Well, alright, and what about our harvest? Show our trophies," said Nikolai Nikolaevich. "Here are my trophies: forty whites, also brown caps, and orange caps. What do you have there, Valeriy Vladimirovich. Show us"

"I have thirty whites, twenty orange caps, and also brown caps."

The ladies also showed their trophies. With this harvest we turned toward home. Tired and happy, we returned home with full baskets and wonderful memories of the Tchaikovsky music.

It was winter, and there was a light frost. My wife and I were at the dacha sitting in the little house we had built ourselves earlieer. We'd had a stove installed, and we lived in this little house until our big, comfortable house was built. We called this little house "The Temporary." This day, we had come to clean it up and put it in order. We tidied up, chopped firewood, and fired up the stove. General Semyon Ilich Makeiev and Marshal Nikolai Nikolaevich Voronov had decided to come visit us at the dacha in our little house that Semyon Ilich had nicknamed "The Winter Palace."

On the appointed day, we drove to our estate. We got out of the car. The weather was wonderful. The sun was shining, and the snow glittered. The general called Nikolai Nikolaevich over to his place. I hurried to my property and took along a shovel and scoop to clean the road. There was a lot of snow, and I really wanted the guests to be able to walk on a clean road. I opened the door to The Temporary and went in. I began to quickly heat up the stove, and the fire sort of flared up. I went out on the street and began to clean the road. I returned to The Temporary. Oh, Good Lord! Smoke and soot! What was the matter? It turned out, I had forgotten to open the stovepipe damper. Again, I began to tend the fire and the fire got hotter. I took a big piece of plywood and began to wave it from side to side in order to drive the smoke and soot out of the house. This turned out to be no simple task. I was driving the smoke and soot out of the house, and all that filthy stuff was flying right back in and tormenting me. Sweat was pouring off me like hail. I saw that my guests were already coming toward me. I continued waving the plywood and driving out the smoke. I quickly shut the door to the street in order to warm up the place at least a little.

The door opened, and the guests came in. Nikolai Nikolaevich apologized for being detained at Semyon Ilich's place. In his hands, Nikolai Nikolaevich was holding a case. It was a rather impressive looking suitcase. The table was already covered with a fresh white table cloth, and Nikolai Nikolaevich placed his case on the tablecloth. It was too early to take off coats because it was still cold in the house.

Nikolai Nikolaevich opened the case, and it turned out to be a magic tablecloth. Revealed there were jellied meats, ham, cheese, and baked chicken cut in thin slices. Also, white and dark Borodinsky bread, hot tea and coffee in thermoses, sweets, candy, sugar in small lumps with special tongs for it, and khalva.* There was also dishes: cups with saucers, plates, and even salt and pepper. All these viands came out of special plastic boxes. Nikolai Nikolaevich took all this out and arranged it very attractively on the table. Two bottles of cognac—Armenian and Moldavian. I was busy with the stove, and the temperature rose noticeably. We were able to take off the overcoats. Soot was flying everywhere, and when it was possible, I caught it. We sat down, and Nikolai Nikolaevich raised the first toast. We drank to the host of "The Winter Palace." The first glasses flew like eagles, and the snacks were regal, especially the sliced fish.

---

*   khalva — a paste of nuts, sugar, and oil

I always listened with pleasure to the pure Russian speech of Nikolai Nikolaevich. We were sitting, drinking, and eating, but I noticed how Nikolai Nikolaevich would catch some floating soot and make it look like nothing was going on and there was no soot. He, himself, completely freely caught it and made it seem as though nothing were happening. At meal time, guests exchange interesting memories. Nikolai Nikolaevich reminisced.

"Stalin was about to arrive to accept a new canon. (I must explain that both Nikolai Nikolaevich Voronov and Semyon Ilich Makeiev were artillery officers.) So, there we were, waiting for the canon, and the canon had not arrived. No canon. No canon. What was the matter? Everyone was waiting and expecting Stalin. At last, the canon rolled up. I was in charge, Head Marshal of Artillery Voronov. Stalin's cortège was in sight. We were all sweating. The canon had gotten stuck in the mud along the road. Somehow or other we cleaned it up and presented it for judgment, and not just for judgment, but for judgment by God. Don't forget, at that time Stalin was God for us. He inspected the canon, and gave the order to fire a few salvos. Stalin seemed to be pleased with the test. However, Stalin was a riddle of a man. Before driving away, he looked at me with his penetrating gaze and said, 'Headman!' I snapped to attention. 'I saw how you wiped the canon with the edge of your overcoat. I am reproving you. Be thankful that I am in a good mood today, or else!' And he rode away. At last, we could breathe more freely. Stalin could have thrown us to the wolves."

We each drank another glass, and decided to go for a walk. After the walk, we switched to tea. So ended an amazing day spent in "The Winter Palace" with Marshal Nikolai Nikolaevich Voronov and General Semyon Ilich Makeiev, wonderful men and excellent neighbors. I still have the two empty cognac bottles. On them, I have inscribed, "Here in the Winter Palace, this bottle was drunk with Head Marshal of the Artillery Nikolai Nikolaevich Voronov and General Semyon Ilich Makeiev" and the date.

A warm autumn arrived. Nikolai Nikolaevich invited Semyon

Ilich, Sofia Grigorievna, me, and my wife, Ludmilla Nikolaevna, to his dacha in Barvikha. Because he was a thoughtful and attentive person, Nikolai Nikolaevich sent his governmental staff car for us. The ride was comfortable and soft; in a word, we rode wonderfully. The landscape at Barvikha is enchanting, and we liked it very much. The summer-like days of early fall were in full swing. The leaves had not turned yellow, but it smelled like autumn. Nikolai Nikolaevich and Nina Sergeievna met us joyfully. It was so wonderful in the garden we did not want to sit in the house. The bright drops of the purple rowan* outlined the autumn scenery. Nina Sergeievna showed us her estate. Not far off, stood the white columns of a Moorish summer-house. We could not pass by such a charming object. We entered the summer-house and arranged ourselves on some very comfortable arm-chairs. The figure of Nikolai Nikolaevich was imposing, and his powerful height was outstanding. In contrast to these, his actions and voice were soft and somehow gentle. All the appearance of Nikolai Nikolaevich reminded me of the great composer, S. Rachmaninoff. Nikolai Nikolaevich recounted to us the history of this Moorish summer-house. I will give his account.

"Once in Germany, I drove with my adjutant from Berlin to Dresden. The city was completely smashed. That is what the Americans endeavored to do—to destroy the Second Florence. The city reminded me of the picture, *The Death of Pompei*. Among the continuous ruins, I noticed a summer-house that by some miracle was still intact. We stopped, got out, and walked in the direction of the summer-house. Yes, the Americans had been there. The summer-house was ransacked and covered with scars. In spite of that, we sat in it for a moment. I liked it so much that I felt sorry for it. I left feeling sick at heart. In Dresden, during a conversation with the city's commandant, I wanted to talk about my encounter with the summer-house and about how it had made an indelible impression on me. The commandant looked at me, and seeing my sorrow, said,

---

*   purple rowan — mountain ash

'Take it. It's all going to be torn down for scrap anyway.' 'How can I take it?' 'Well, that's our affair. If you like it, take it!' As a result, the commandant ordered the soldiers of his engineering unit to carefully dismantle the summer-house, and provide for setting it up. A short while later, the dear summer-house arrived in Moscow for us. Now, you know what path the summer-house has traveled, and now, the summer-house adorns our garden."

They invited us into the house. We were ecstatic about the dacha. Everything was comfortable and warm. There was a large room for entertaining, a spacious dining room, a billiard room, and the office for Nikolai Nikolaevich was very pleasant. There was a very darling boudoir for Nina Sergeievna, and an airy veranda. Flowers were all around. A large oval table was supplied with various tasty hors d'oeuvre and wines. They invited us to the table. Truly, everyone was noticeably hungry. After the goblets were filled, Nikolai Nikolaevich gave a toast for the health of the dear guests, and added that for him and Nina Sergeievna it was so extremely pleasant to eat and drink in such warm company. There were other toasts. As always, Nikolai Nikolaevich was attentive and pleasant. They served pineapples in champagne. Conversation at the table flowed pleasantly and abounded in light jokes and witticisms.

As always, Nikolai Nikolaevich was on a high level. He told elegant and quite humorous anecdotes. "In the park next to his villa, a millionaire architect built three swimming pools. One had warm water, one had cold water, and the third had no water at all. 'Why a swimming pool with no water?' they asked the architect. 'The fact of the matter is, many of my friends do not know how to swim.'"

My turn came to amuse the guests. "One farmer telephoned his neighbor, who was also a farmer. 'Jackson, do horses smoke?' 'What's the matter with you? Have you lost your mind? Of course not!' 'Then, that means your stable is on fire!'"

Nina Sergeievna told an interesting anecdote. "Doctor, is it true that those who eat a lot of carrots have good eyesight?' 'Of course! Really, have you ever seen a rabbit wearing glasses?'"

After lunch, we went to the living room. Nikolai Nikolaevich asked me to sing something. "Sing. You are a quite a master at imitating great singers."

I sang several parodies. Nikolai Nikolaevich liked my singing, but regretted that there was no instrument, a piano, at the dacha. He promised, that there definitely would be a instrument the next time I came.

One day, Nikolai Nikolaevich phoned my son, Valeriy, and asked him to ride with him to a music store and help him pick out a good instrument. My son, Valeriy, was studying at the Conservatory, and he had perfect pitch. That's why Nikolai Nikolaevich turned to him.

We learned with pleasure that Nikolai Nikolaevich and Nina Sergeievna were putting on a New Years Eve party at their dacha. Also, we learned that the Polekh family and the Makeiev family were invited to the party. The day of December 31st arrived, and Nikolai Nikolaevich sent a car for us. We went out on the street where snow was falling by the shovelful, got in the car, and went for the Makeievs. They were already prepared.

When we got to the point on the main road where we should turn off to Nikolai Nikolaevich's dacha, we could not find it. The road was completely congested with snow. What to do? Suddenly, in the distance appeared a man with a lantern in his hand. The man made signals with the lantern. Glory to God! We learned the man with the lantern was Nikolai Nikolaevich. In valenkiy boots* he was clearing the road for us. In patent leather dress shoes and light boots, we tramped through the snow with difficulty, but we got there. After the snow and blizzard, how pleasant it was to find ourselves in warm accommodations and to shake the snow off ourselves. Nikolai Nikolaevich fussed over Sofia Grigorievna, and got down on his knees and massaged her feet. I also brought back to order the

---

*   valenkiy boots —warm calf-high felt boots with rubber lower parts and soles

frozen feet of my wife. At last all the feet were warmed up and we proceeded to the living room. We were met by a tall richly decorated fir tree, a fire in the fireplace, and soft comfortable easy-chairs. After sitting in the living room and chatting, we directed ourselves to the billiard room.

Nikolai Nikolaevich invited Semyon Ilich to play a game. He accepted the invitation. I became an enthusiastic spectator. Nikolai Nikolaevich began adroitly to chase the balls into the pockets. Semyon Ilich was defeated. Victory was awarded to Nikolai Nikolaevich.

The clock struck eleven, and the host and hostess invited us to come be seated at the table. The doors to the dining room were opened. The table was decorated with great taste. On both sides of the table stood lighted candelabras. There was silver, crystal, and porcelain bowls filled with fruit. Fifteen minutes remained until the New Year. Nikolai Nikolaevich requested that wine be poured into the goblets. He pronounced a toast: "Friends, we will drink to the old year. This is in some measure somber, because we are parting with one more year of our lives. However, we are optimists. How have we spent this past year? In my opinion, not badly. We have gotten together often, attended the theater, and, you will remember, we even were at the circus. So, we drink to the old year. Hurrah!"

The chimes struck twelve. The champagne swirled in the goblets. Everyone stood and greeted the New Year. They shouted "Hurrah!" several times. Everyone ate with a good appetite.

Semyon Ilich brought a word: "Friends, I am hoping, that the New Year will be still more interesting and more meaningful. I think everyone agrees with me. I wish for everyone strong health and to get together frequently. Hurrah!"

I drank to the health of the ladies—the dear ladies. My wife, Ludmilla Nikolaevna, thanked the host and hostess for a marvelous evening. Addressing Nina Sergeievna, she also said, "You are always able to give joy and pleasure." After supper, everyone adjourned to the living room. A rather new piano stood in a prominent place.

Nikolai Nikolaevich said, "Valeriy Vladimirovich, we ask that you be the first to try out the new instrument."

I sat at the piano, and played a few chords. "I will sing a few parodies of singers you all know."

Nina Sergeievna clapped her hands and remarked that Nikolai Nikolaevich loved my parodies very much.

I began with Ivan Semyonovich Kozlovskiy, and then came Sergei Yakovlevich Lemeshev, L. Utesov, Byul-Byul Orly, and A. Vertinskiy. They told me later, that when I sang Vertinskiy, Nikolai Nikolaevich had tears in his eyes inasmuch as Nikolai Nikolaevich was sentimental. When I began to sing the operatic Kachalov, Nikolai Nikolaevich asked me, "Do you know who you did a parody of?"

I said, "Yes, I sang Kachalov."

"You sang my son-in-law. Kachalov is the husband of my daughter."

I had to sing a second time:

"Gardens flower greenly, and in them lovers stroll.
They stroll and gaze upon the world.
For strolling lovers, world's concerns
Matter not at all."

Nikolai Nikolaevich was very pleased. Later Sofia Grigorievna and I sang the duet of Violetta and Alfredo from the opera *La Traviata*. Sofia Grigorievna sang a solo very well. She is a wonderful singer, a rare singer. We enjoyed ourselves for a long time, sang together, and danced.

We began the New Year beautifully. The snow stilled, and the moon appeared. We all went out into the garden. What a beautiful winter. The trees were all dusted with snow, and every little branch glistened like a storybook picture. Nina Sergeievna asked everyone to go in the house; the frost was getting stronger. Noses were turning red, and patent-leather boots and shoes were beginning to freeze stiff. Quickly, we went in for tea—for hot tea. So ended our New Years party. It was as though everyone were a little younger, and new life was starting in the New Year.

Once, when I was strolling with Semyon Ilich in his garden, he asked me, "How about you inviting Nikolai Nikolaevich and Nina Sergeievna to your dacha?"

I replied, "With great pleasure. Only I ask you to come to an agreement with Nikolai Nikolaevich as to when would be a good time for him to be my guest. I need to prepare seriously for this visit."

"Good, Valeriy Vladimirovich. I will let you know."

At last, the designated day and hour of the visit came. It was the end of summer. The morning turned out to be sunny, but not hot. We rose a little early and got everything ready. When we saw Nikolai Nikolaevich's car coming, we all went out to greet him. There were pleasant hugs, kisses, and greetings. We went into our dacha.

Nikolai Nikolaevich said, "Semyon Ilich has been telling us what a master craftsman you are, and how many interesting things you have made. Is this the sitting room?"

"This is the dining room. I made all the furniture myself. For example, this is a side-board made from redwood and also around the mirror."

"This is good work," observed Nikolai Nikolaevich.

"Here is the dining table. As you can see, it is made to look like a chess board, only with a larger aspect, and it has of two tones— brown and cream. Look at the the doors of the cupboard, the sides repeat the same pattern as in the table. They are finished in the same tones. This decorative bench is made according to an American magazine; but it also really incorporates my ideas."

Nikolai Nikolaevich was surprised. "Such mastery! Where did you get the material? The sideboard is made of redwood and again, has such a wonderful polished finish.

"I bought all the material at the "Children's World" store. They have a department there called 'Do It Yourself.' There, they sell various leftovers that come to the store from mills and factories.

Earlier, they simply burned these leftovers, but this is valuable material."

"Your success is simply astonishing," marveled Nikolai Nikolaevich. "And a piano?"

"This is a very old instrument from the French firm, Pleiele. Our grandparents even played on it. Lets go into the bedroom. This dressing table was made from the same material, only I added a different tone—light-blue with white. It seemed to me that such a tone would be gentler and lighter."

"Where did you get such a large and splendid mirror?" Nikolai Nikolaevich asked with interested.

"This is from an old dresser. The dresser itself got old and was falling apart, but a mirror is forever young. Look, what a headboard! This is an ultra-modern headboard. Yes. When I was abroad staying in various hotels, I looked closely and got familiar with it. Notice, the headboard is solidly, firmly fastened to the wall, but the bed itself moves independently wherever you wish. The chairs are also light-blue with white. The wall serves as the back of the dresser, and as a result the dresser is strongly knit to the wall. Once a craftsman, who had come to paint the room for us, asked permission to move the dresser. I told the craftsman to try. He actually tried, but laughed loudly and said, 'That's a good one! You fooled me.' Over here is Granny's room. This also is my work, a night-table and chairs. Notice the apple-green color. We once bought an apple-green dresser, and I had to make the whole room apple green. The side-board is also my work."

Nina Sergeievna and Nikolai Nikolaevich were astonished. They liked my work very much. We went out on the veranda. There also was my work, a buffet and a dining table. "Everything we have seen is my hobby and my passion. Enormous thanks to you, Nina Sergeievna and Nikolai Nikolaevich, for the positive valuation of my labor."

From the veranda, we descended the colonnaded stairs to the garden. Nikolai Nikolaevich and Nina Sergeievna were delighted with the stairway. Nina Sergeievna observed that it was as though we were guests of the Lariniy's or the Dubrovskiy's.

"Look! What roses! Good Lord, what a marvel! What colors and aroma!

However, Nikolai Nikolaevich continued to admire the stairway. "You know, if you look at this from below, this is very good. And whose work is this? Is it also yours, Valeriy Vladimirovich?"

"No, this is the work of a master craftsman. Yes, he pleased us."

"I must get a photograph of these marvelous roses. But what is this above the roses—some kind of transparent roof?"

"You know, roses do not like rain. They immediately loose their beauty. However, in good weather I open the roof, and the roses are warmed by the sun. Here, in our small vegetable garden cucumbers and onions grow. This is dill. These are turnips and carrots. Over here tomatoes are growing. This is a water pipe that we use for putting water on the garden."

"And what is all this that has grown? Some kind of vine?"

"Well, this vine is called green peas. Try it, Nikolai Nikolaevich."

"It's very tasty. I'll try it with pleasure," and he cut a few pods. "How amazing. May I cut some more?"

"Of course. Of course. Help yourself. We have ten apple trees, and as you can see, the apples are ripening. In front of the veranda itself is an English lawn. We cut the grass here often, and then it looks good. We are also growing black currants, gooseberries, and raspberries."

"Yes, I can see that. This is our 'Winter Garden.' It is obvious, that you have built from the ground up, and it is good."

From nearby, Nina Sergeievna noticed our conversation. "I am sure this is your work."

"You have guessed it, dear Nina Sergeievna. This is the work of my hands."

"You know, this conversation is similar to a conversation in theNeskuchniy Garden* —an exact copy," remarked Nina Sergeievna.

Then our Grandmother, Alexandra Sergeievna, came out.

"This is my mother. Allow me to introduce you, please."

"This is my cherished one," said Semyon Ilich, kissing Aleksandra Sergeievna.

"You know," said Ludmilla Nikolaevna, "on our property was not even a tiny tree nor a bush. Our head gardener is my mother. Just think of all the gardens you see here. This is a great labor by Aleksandra Sergeievna."

"Our grandmother is actually the all-powerful master. You know, we fear her, but more truthfully, we love and honor her."

Grandmother became emotional, and began to cry a little. She is very sentimental with us.

"And now, dear guests, from the heart, I ask you to take bread and salt with us." Grandmother bowed to the guests according to the old custom. Nikolai Nikolaevich took the mistress on his arm and everyone went into the house.

The table was set on the veranda. Flowers were all around. On the festive table stood a vase filled with wild flowers. This bouquet had been arranged by our daughter, Lyudechka, with ripening rye, light-blue corn-flowers, ox-eye daisies, clusters of scarlet rowan, very fragrant wild roses, and cute bluebells. Nikolai Nikolaevich commented that it smelled like old Russia here. Everyone sat down at the table. On the table were arrayed with pickled herring with green onions, domestic white mushrooms, (The mushrooms had already been marinated.) salads, olive and vegetable salad, red caviar, chilled water, cognac, Georgian wine, and Cahetian wine.

"The first toast I drink to the health of the matriarch of our family, to dear Mama—Grandmother. May God give you long years

---

*   Neskuchniy Garden — literally "Not Boring Garden"

and strong health for our joy." We drank a glass and began eating. "I drink to the health of our dear guests. Hurrah!"

Nina Sergeievna drank to the bread-and-salt host and hostess. Nikolai Nikolaevich stood. "Dear friends, we have lived in the wide world for many years, and suddenly, we find wonderful people— Ludmilla Nikolaevna and Valeriy Vladimirovich. I Wish you good and peaceful lives. Be healthy. Hurrah!"

Sofia Grigorievna and Semyon Ilich also raised toasts for strong friendship and for frequent gatherings. The first course began to be served. This was sorrel soup with small eggs and sour cream. The soup made an impression.

Ludmilla Nikolaevna brought a word. "Dear ones! We are very glad to have you at our place today, and that we are together today. We often remember our mushroom hunt, and the snowstorm at New Years. I must kiss everyone."

After finishing at the table, at Nikolai Nikolaevich's request, I sang a little. To complete the wonderful day, we went for a short stroll. With that ended the day we had spent with wonderful and good natured people.

To the end of this report, I must add that Natasha, the daughter of Sofia Grigorevna and Semyon Ilich Makeiev, and Valeriy, our son, became husband and wife. The sponsor of Natasha was Nikolai Nikolaevich Voronov and the sponsor of Valeriy was Gyeorgy Konstantinovich Zhukov, Four Times Hero of the Soviet Union.

SEVENTEEN

Gyeorgy Konstantinovich Zhukov

THE HERO — VITYAZ

Vityaz was born in Kaluzhskiy Governance.
He grew and grew and grew up to be a giant.
An enemy fell upon the land of our birth.
Vityaz went out to battle to defend the land of our
birth.
For five years Vityaz fought
On the field of conflict.
Vityaz defeated the enemy.
The enemy fell.
The people gave honor to Vityaz,
Vityaz the hero!
Vityaz the strength!
Their rulers became afraid:
"He might defeat us suddenly,
And seat himself upon our throne."
In dark of night,
The rulers fell upon Vityaz,
And stripped away both honor and rank.
The rulers intimidated the people.

The people closed their eyes to truth.
"What is to be done?" thought Vityaz. "This is no
life."
"There remains just one thing—
To do away with my own life."
Vityaz raised the sword,
To annihilate himself.
Suddenly, Vityaz caught sight of his beloved wife,
And a small beloved daughter.
The hand shook.
The sword fell from the hand.
To live! Yes, to live!
Friends helped. Friends comforted.
They consoled, caressed, and tenderly cared.
The people matured and opened their eyes.
The people saw the real truth.
They valued the great service of Vityaz,
And in memory of Vityaz,
Raised up a memorial to him—Vityaz.
There he is, Vityaz on a bronze steed. Vityaz lived,
And he lives in our hearts, VITYAZ.

Faithful friends*

ACQUAINTANCE

I am going to tell about our family's friendship with Marshal of
the Soviet Union, Four Times Hero, Gyeorgy Konstantinovich

---

*   Comment:In order to appreciate this poem, the reader needs to know that
Marshal Gyeorgy Konstantinovich Zhukov (i.e. Vityaz) commanded the
the Russian Army during World War II, and was greatly honored for it.
Following the war, he was stripped of his position, and was only restored
to official public esteem after several years.

Zhukov and his wife, Galina Aleksandrovna. This friendship spanned many years. After Gyeorgy Konstantinovich was dismissed from all military duty, he became a ruined civilian. Furthermore, you will learn that Gyeorgy Konstantinovich was an amazing man, distinguished by the wonderful soulful quality of a noble man.

G. K. Zhukov

The wife of Gyeorgy Konstantinovich, Galina Aleksandrovna, was a beautiful, darling, kind, and very sympathetic woman. She was the one who saved Gyeorgy Konstantinovich from the deadly blow delivered by an unkind hand. It was she, Galina Aleksandrovna, who helped Gyeorgy Konstantinovich stay alive. It was she who at that moment gave Gyeorgy Konstantinovich her heart, her soul, and her love in order to help her husband tear himself out of what seemed to be an intollerable situation that had been created around the priceless life of the great marshal.

Our first acquaintance with the figure of Gyeorgy Konstantinovich began with his brilliant victory over the Japanese samurai at Khal-Khin-Gol [in Mongolia] in 1937. We became interested in the successes of Gyeorgy Konstantinovich. We clipped articles from newspapers and magazines, bought a special scrap-book, and glued into it all this material concerning the military action at Khal-Khin-Gol.

One of our good acquaintances, the sculptor, Genzhan, cut a bas-relief in leather of Zhukov. On the sculptor's table lay several photographs of Gyeorgy Konstantinovich. We asked him to give us one photo of rather large dimensions. At last, we had a portrait of Gyeorgy Konstantinovich Zhukov in our home, and it hangs in plain sight. Our little son, when no one was home, took down the photograph, and drew a star on Zhukov's chest. Later, the portrait was put in a frame behind glass. Still later, the fate of Gyeorgy Konstantinovich Zhukov was arranged so that this added star was required.

179

At that time, we lived on Shevchenko Embankment as a five-member family. The family of the noted journalist Vladimir Tsvetov lived neighbors to us. From time to time, musician acquaintances came to our place. We played music, sang, and carried on conversations. Our neighbors reminded us, rather delicately, that the music should be a little quieter. Several excesses had occurred with regard to noise. We had been getting ready to exchange the apartment and move out, but there was no appropriate swap proposal available.

One beautiful day, we were getting ready to travel to the dacha. We made our preparations, but they took a long time. It got to be too late to leave for the train. At first, we regretted having to wait for the next train, but it all turned out for the best. We decided to have a cup of tea for the road. We warmed up the teapot and sat at the table. Suddenly, the door-bell rang. I went to answer the door. I opened the door and looked out. A tall man—a military man—was standing there.

He said, "I am answering the advertisement regarding an apartment."

I escorted this lieutenant colonel into the room. After inspecting the apartment, he stated the following: "Tomorrow, at half past one in the afternoon, a high-ranking officer will personally inspect your premises. This means: tomorrow at half past one in the afternoon." And he went away.

We decided not to go to the dacha of course. The next day, all morning, we were cleaning up the apartment, and our neighbors began to help us. Volodya Tsvetov wrapped his head in a ladies' kerchief and, with a swab in his hands, scrubbed the doors of the cabinets. Yulya Tsvetova teased Volodya saying, "You should always help me clean your own room this way." We all were very nervous, and kept looking out the window.

"Is anyone coming?"

"No, no-one has come."

Suddenly, a big "ZIL" automobile approached and stopped

directly opposite our windows. The military officer we were familiar with got out of the car, and opened the car door. Out stepped a man of medium height, broad-shouldered, in a snow-white shirt, and with a suit-coat draped over his shoulder. He directed an attentive gaze at all the surroundings and went into the entry-way. At this time my wife, Ludmilla Nikolaevna had sent our son for milk. Our son had not yet left the entry-way and almost collided with the man coming toward him. By some miracle, our son recognized the marshal, turned 180 degrees, and ran back. At the elevator, the marshal caught up with him, and they entered it together. Then our son led the guest to the door of our quarters, and opened the door with a key. My wife was preparing to open the door when the door opened of itself.

Good Lord! Marshal Zhukov himself stood before her! Of course, she was taken aback. She didn't believe her eyes, and wanted so much to pinch the marshal in order to make sure this was not a ghost but the real, live Marshal Zhukov. Amazingly, from this moment and for long years after, fate itself brought us close to this great man.

"Greet the guest," said Gyeorgy Konstantinovich.

"Come in. Come in, please," replied Ludmilla Nikolaevna, coming to herself.

"Thank you. Show your living quarters." He went on into the room. Gyeorgy Konstantinovich immediately began to be interested in everything. "What is this you have? The corridor is a little narrow."

But my wife answered, "We have cabinets that are in the corridor. We will take them out."

"And what do they call you?"

"Me? Ludmilla Nikolaevna."

Zhukov looked at her and said, "Very pleased."

The spouses Tsvetov, Volodya and Yulya, laughed about how the marshal ran from one cupboard to another. The Marshal went over to the window and looked a long time at the wonderful panorama the opened before his gaze. There was a green public square, yellow benches, the Moscow River flowed below, a pretty bridge, in the distance the tallest of buildings, and all around was greenery and cleanliness. The marshal prepared to leave and asked my wife, "Did you recognize me?"

"Yes, Gyeorgy Konstantinovich. " I recognized you right away, but I was preoccupied with other business."

"Tomorrow, at ten o'clock in the morning, I will give you an answer," and the marshal went out.

We watched out the window.

The next day, exactly at ten o'clock, the marshal phoned us and said, "We will register the apartment exchange." On the following day, the marshal's wife came. She was pleased with the apartment.

One morning, Galina Aleksandrovna Zhukova phoned us and asked Ludmilla Nikolaevna if we would like to go to the French ballet at the Bolshoi Theater. Ludmilla Nikolaevna gladly agreed.

"Today, then, at seven o'clock at the main entrance. Good-bye. Greet Valeriy Vladimirovich."

At about four o'clock we began to get dressed. What kind of scarf to wear? How is the hair? Good Lord, which shoes? Which shoes to wear? But there was no panic. There was a long session seated in front of the mirror. At last we were ready. One last nod to the mirror, and we were on the street.

At half past six, we were approaching the theater. They were waiting for us. We greeted each other. Galina Aleksandrovna was looking very good, in the costume of an English countess, a snow-white jabot set off her dark complexion very well. Gyeorgy Konstantinovich was dressed in a light gray suit, and the dark blue silk necktie harmonized very well with the gray color. The suit was a surprisingly elegant fit. I was sure, that a frock coat would have fit the marshal just as wonderfully. Ludmilla Nikolaevna, as always, looked good. I was wearing a dark blue suit. After exchanging a few light comments, we entered the theater and went into the spectator hall with its gilded loges, and the storied Pompei-like chandelier. Our seats were in the fourth row. Instinctively, I looked at the orchestra, as they say, my home. (I should add, that at this time I was working in the Bolshoi Theater orchestra.) Several curious musicians caught sight of me and became interested in learning with whom I had come to our theater. Several of them recognized the marshal and began to lean out of the orchestra pit.

During intermission, we went to the buffet. I ordered a bottle of champagne and buttered bread with black caviar. This is the traditional buffet of the Bolshoi Theater. We liked the show. Gyeorgy Konstantinovich commented, "It's just that the men are very effeminate."

After the show, we decided to walk home. When we approached the Zhukov's home, (They lived on Gorky Street.) which would be ours in the future, Ludmilla Nikolaevna joked, "Valeriy and I have already arrived, and you are preparing to continue on farther"

To which Gyeorgy Konstantinovich remarked, "By the way, the process of our apartment exchange is progressing, and we will soon have a house-warming."

DACHA STATION

In these recollections, I want to tell about the glorious and unforgettable days our family spent with a great marshal and a great man, Gyeorgy Konstantinovich Zhukov, his wife Galina Aleksandrovna, and their daughter, Mashenka.

My wife, Ludmilla Nikolaevna, became very good friends with Galina Aleksandrovna and our little daughter, Lyudechka, was very attached to Mashenka. Such happy days were in our life's calendar—often one day was better than the one before. Gyeorgy Konstantinovich with his family often came to our dacha in Aprelevka at Dacha Station. He always drove over early, about ten in the morning, with his wife Galina Aleksandrovna and little daughter, Mashenka. The ladies became united in conversation. They always had something to talk about. Lyudechka and Mashenka would run to the children's nook where they had toys and dolls. We always greeted Gyeorgy Konstantinovich like family, and Gyeorgy Konstantinovich came to visit like a family member. At a greeting, we kissed and hugged each other. We always prepared thoroughly for the arrival of Gyeorgy Konstantinovich. The house was cleaned and set in order. Fresh flowers were put in the vases. The paths were swept and cleaned.

We especially reserved the strawberry bed for him. Gyeorgy Konstantinovich loved to eat strawberries right from the vine. He loved to crunch carrots and turnips. After eating, we would sit on a bench. I had specially made this bench in the Pushkin style. Gyeorgy Konstantinovich laughingly would say, "Let's go to Pushkin." Sitting with Gyeorgy Konstantinovich was always enjoyable. For example, he was interested in the affairs of the Bolshoi Theater. What kind of shows were they preparing to present? Were new and interesting lady singers appearing? Which shows were they working in? Were they good to listen to? How were Sergey Yakovlevich Lemeshev and Ivan Semyonovich Kozlovskiy doing? "I never once met them in the Kremlin at the governmental concerts. It would be very interesting to know what creative plans they have."

"Gyeorgy Konstantinovich, it's said Sergey Yakovlevich Lemeshev is preparing a concert program composed of romantic Russian songs. Ivan Semyonovich Kozlovskiy and I are rehearsing a composition by the modern English composer B. Britten. It has an interesting cast of performers: lyric tenor, French horn, and chamber orchestra."

Gyeorgy Konstantinovich said, "What a combination! A lyric

tenor and a wind instrument. You know, a horn could drown out a tenor. It's true, I have heard you in concerts, and you play very softly when it is required. There are moments when your instrument is like a cello. But all the same, for you to play with such a delicate, and I repeat, delicate tenor... Say, Valeriy, tell me how this composition came to you."

An interesting conversation developed. Gyeorgy Konstantinovich loved to hear interesting histories. I began the narration.

"The the Bolshoi Theater Ballet prepared to go beyond the border for the first time – to England."

"Excuse me, you know, the ballet had gone beyond the border earlier. I read it in a magazine, myself," Gyeorgy Konstantinovich interrupted me.

"Yes, small groups had gone. However, this time it was not just a small group going, but the full-bodied production, decorations, and staging section."

"Now, I understand."

"At last, it was the day of departure. We all were nervous. How would the English receive our production? Moreover, we were taking *Romeo and Juliet* to the homeland of W. Shakespeare."

"We have brave people. You know, that was a real gamble!" said Gyeorgy Konstantinovich.

"We loaded everything in an airplane and took off. When it was time to land, it was reported from London that we would be landing at the airfield on an American base. We landed at the base successfully. It turned out, that London was far away, and we would travel on buses."

Gyeorgy Konstantinovich observed, "How is it that the Americans were not afraid to permit a Russian landing party to come in?"

"Evidently, there was an agreement." (Of course, I was joking.) "The trip turned out to be unpleasant because the buses, minute by minute, were stopping and starting because of the traffic jams. Several people began to feel sick. We were concerned for Galina

Sergeievna Ulanova because she had to do a very important rehearsal the next morning. However, Galina Sergeievna was a fine lady. She withstood everything, and the next. day, rehearsed, as they say, at full speed. Our premiere began with the production of *Romeo and Juliet*. The participants in the production were G. Ulanova, Yu. Zhdanov, A. Ermolaev, S. Koren, N. Timofeieva, and others. The directors were Yu. F. Faier and Rozhdestvenskiy. The head ballet-master was L. Lavrovskiy. The production was a triumph, and the audience gave a standing ovation."

"I once was sitting in one of the first rows during a rehearsal of the ballet, Fountain of Bakhtchisaray by the composer, V. Asafiev. Yu. Faier was directing. Suddenly, Faier stopped the rehearsal, and looked in the spectator hall, and saw me. After turning to face the orchestra again, he made the following announcement, 'Gentlemen, I present to you the famous French horn musician, a soloist of the Bolshoi Theater Orchestra, Valeriy Polekh.' As a mark of greeting, the musicians of the orchestra tapped their bows on the music stands, and the wind instrument musicians clattered their valves. 'In addition to this,' said Yu. Faier, 'Valeriy Polekh is a deputy conductor of the Bolshoi Theater.' It must be said, that the horn musicians of the orchestra hardly believed that a good French horn musician was also a conductor of the Theater. They had never heard of such a thing. I have to say, that I had brought my instrument with me and played a bit on it. My presentation pleased the English horn players very much. They kept asking me to play more. The horn musicians were especially delighted with my presentation of the waltz by F. Chopin."

"Why did you impress your colleagues so much?" asked Gyeorgy Konstantinovich.

"The fact of the mater is, that F. Chopin wrote the waltz for the pianoforte. I transposed the waltz for the French horn. On the piano, this waltz is performed by skilled pianists, and a horn player can play this waltz but not with strength. From that moment we became friends with the London French horn musicians. As a memento of our meeting, they presented me with the score of *Serenade* by the composer, B. Britten. Upon returning to Moscow, I gave the composition to Director Gennadiy Rozhdestvenskiy. He, in his turn, gave the music to his mama, the famous singer, Natasha Rozhdestvenskiy. She has a good command of the English language, and made a Russian translation. After that, we showed the music to Ivan Semyonovich Kozlovskiy, who went into ecstasy over the composition. We decided to perform *Serenade* in the Great Hall of the Moscow Conservatory. The work began to heat up."

"Yes, this is an interesting story," said Zhukov. "But you are a sharp fellow. It is evident that you did not travel to England in vain. But all the same, a horn and a tenor.... But listen. Tell me, please, is there another similar composition?" asked Gyeorgy Konstantinovich with interest.

I said, "Yes, there is. The composer Franz Schubert wrote a very interesting duet for voice and French horn. I performed this composition with the singer, Nadezhda Kazantsevaya, a wonderful singer, in the Small Hall of the Moscow Conservatory. At that time, the audience received our performance very well."

As though to himself, Gyeorgy Konstantinovich said, "I love Schubert, and his famous *Evening Serenade*, *Barcarolle*, and *A Miller Conducts Life In Movement*. I heard *Forest King*, and *The Unfinished Symphony*."

I enjoyed talking with Gyeorgy Konstantinovich very much. As an intelligent person, he knew how to listen to a fellow conversationalist. I must say that Gyeorgy Konstantinovich made it a time of interesting conversation in the area of music and in the area of art in general. Later, evidently, he decided to change the subject.

"Well, now, show me what you have made as a wood-worker." (At that time I was making a small cabinet.) "You are a master craftsman," and Gyeorgy Konstantinovich ran his hands over the boards I had planed. "Well, now, give me the plane. In order to join the edges of the boards, it is necessary to plane them. Here, watch."

Gyeorgy Konstantinovich began to work. The boards soon were smoothed down, and began to fit together very solidly.

We worked for more than an hour until the ladies appeared. They invited us to have lunch. Ludmilla Nikolaevna said, "It's obvious you're starving, and need to rebuild your strength. Lunch is waiting for us on the veranda."

Our grandmother, Aleksandra Sergeievna, loved Gyeorgy Konstantinovich very much, and in Honor of his coming wanted to treat him to *kulebyaky.* At home, Gyeorgy Konstantinovich almost never drank wine, but at the dacha in pleasant company, he loved to allow himself a small glass, and to snack on lightly salted cucumbers and green onions also. He loved to crunch salted mushrooms, and enjoyed home-grown, home-made sauerkraut. Tender, lightly salted red fish was served, and there was also ham. The men drank vodka, and the women drank Georgian wine. Gyeorgy Konstantinovich raised the first toast. He stood, approached Aleksandra Sergeievna, and gave her a Christian kiss. Grandmother was deeply touched and wept of course. Lightly chilled kvass soup appeared on the table. Everyone liked the kvass soup. For the second course, Ludmilla Nikolaevna served cutlets, and revealed this was a family recipe. Everyone clapped their hands in honor of the mistress of the house, and Gyeorgy Konstantinovich immediately raised a toast to the charming chef, Ludmilla Nikolaevna. For the third course, strawberries with cream were served. After lunch, we decided to go

---

*   *kulebyaky* — patties with eggs and meat.

for a walk. "Valeriy Vladimirovich, my old acquaintance, Nikandr Sergeievich Khanaev, lives somewhere nearby. Let's drop in on him."

"With pleasure," I responded.

The weather was good. We were dressed lightly. We took the kids with us and went out. The ladies were under pretty umbrellas. The children ran ahead of us. We went slowly with pleasant conversation. Gyeorgy Konstantinovich looked over every blade of grass. He loved nature very much. He loved to listen to the birds' song. He asked us to stop and listen. He commented, "Well, the little cuckoo doesn't sing, but always just cuckoos sadly. It's a pleasant bird."

So, we arrived at the house of Nikandr Sergeievich. The gate was locked. We knocked, and a tenor voice rang out, "Who is there?" After opening the gate, Nikandr Sergeievich was taken aback, and could not believe his eyes. "My God! Fancy that!" When he saw the ladies, he took their hands. "Valeriy," Khanaev greeted me. "I don't believe my eyes. Please, come on in."

Ladies came out of the house. Gyeorgy Konstantinovich took their hands and presented them with a bouquet of flowers. We followed after the master and mistress of the house. They were completely perplexed, not knowing where to seat us or what to show us. However, Gyeorgy Konstantinovich took charge. "Nikandr Sergeievich, you know, we are old friends. I love you a lot. Don't fret yourself. We are at ease."

There was a multitude of flowers on the property. Gyeorgy Konstantinovich immediately became interested in the flowers. He loved flowers very much. He was knew many flowers. Zhukov called to my wife, "Ludmilla, come quick and look! What a lovely sight! What roses! What a charming rose. Such color! Just you look—a scarlet hue, and the scent is wonderful — an incomparable aroma. Look, a tea rose, Lord, but it's pink! Look! Asters, marigolds of various colors, pansies, and the stock gives off an enchanting scent—a divine aroma. Nikandr Sergeievich you are a magician, a wizard. This is a beautiful arrangement."

"I will reveal a secret to you," said Khanaev. "All these flowers were planted by a gardener. Just like you, Gyeorgy Konstantinovich, I love flowers"

While we were occupying ourselves with the flowers, Nikandr Sergeievich brought a tray with small glasses and decanters containing home-grown wine and fruit drinks. Everyone became interested and the tasting began.

Khanaev offered, "Here is a man's wine, and this is especially for the ladies. My women praise it highly."

"It's an amazing wine. Try it. It's a little tart, but tasty."

"And here, this fruit drink medicates many ailments."

"Give me some, and I will try the ladies'. Wonderful. In order to drink such a wine, I would agree to be a lady," said Gyeorgy Konstantinovich. "A marvelous drink." Then Gyeorgy Konstantinovich commented, "Listen. We have gotten ourselves so loaded, that we won't find our own home."

The hosts responded that in such a case we would drink tea. They cleared the table and spread an oil-cloth tablecloth.

"Look! Look! The tablecloth is all flowers!" exclaimed Zhukov.

The ladies took their places. They began to pass little bowls of jam, and very delicious home-made pastries that just melted in your mouth. The day was hot. We were sitting under a blooming fruit tree, having quiet conversation, and drinking aromatic tea. With delight, Gyeorgy Konstantinovich recalled how wonderfully Nikandr Sergeievich sang, and how enjoyable it had been to listen to his *Othello, Hermann*, and *Radomes*. In the Great Hall at the

Conservatory, he had performed wonderfully the romantic songs of Tchaikovsky and the romances *The Sun has Set*, an"Thank you for your wonderful artistry."

"I give heartfelt appreciation," said Khanaev, "for the warm words, and it was even so very much more pleasant for me to hear these words from you, dear Gyeorgy Konstantinovich."

Khanaev, Makeiev, Ludmilla Nikolaevna, and Zhuko v.

It began to get dark. Before we took our leave of these kind and dear hosts, Khanaev brought a rather large photograph of Zhukov. He asked that in honor of this present evening and as a sign of old friendship Zukov would write a few words in kind remembrance. Gyeorgy Konstantinovich took the photograph and wrote, "To a dear comrade and wonderful singer, Nikandr Sergeievich Khanaev. Gyeorgy Zhukov." Khanaev gave heartfelt thanks to Zhukov. The host and hostess saw us off.

A BIRTHDAY AND A VISIT TO THE GENERAL.

Today, in the month of July, the weather turned out to be wonderful. Both my wife, Ludmilla Nikolaevna, and I were born in this month. I was born of the fifth of July, and Ludmilla Nikolaevna on the twelfth. Because of this situation, we have always celebrated our birthdays together

As always, we were at our place awaiting the arrival of Gyeorgy Konstantinovich and his wife Galina Aleksandrovna. Other guests and relatives were coming. We had run our legs off getting ready for the celebration. At last, the familiar car arrived. The adjutant helped Gyeorgy Konstantinovich out of the car, and after that helped Galina Aleksandrovna out of the car. The Zhukovs' little daughter, Mashenka, steamed out of the car and fell into the embrace of her friend, our daughter, Lyudechka. In society, Gyeorgy Konstantinovich conducted himself modestly and very simply. He talked with everyone, joked, and laughed very infectiously—when something actually was humorous. With the ladies, he was a real chevalier— very protective and attentive. He loved to entertain the ladies with interesting stories. Here is an interesting story he told:

"I was a young cavalry man, and, rode my steed home on leave. The horse was hot and energetic. It was evening and getting dark. My heart was thumping, and at last I caught sight of my family's home, and our gates.  Above the gate, was placed the traditional cross-beam, as is found everywhere in the countryside. In my haste, I did not notice it, and flew into the cross-beam. I flew over the cross-beam, the horse went off to the side, and I, the young cavalry man, fell right on the table at which my parents were eating supper. They were startled. From where did their long-awaited, darling son come flying? They began to hug and kiss, saying, "God himself sent Igor the Victorious."

Everyone enjoyed this surprsing history. With men, Gyeorgy Konstantinovich comported himself simply, but in the simplicity, one sensed a sort of internal pride and strength. As they used to say in old Russia, "Know ourselves."

The evening continued. Everyone was scattered like still-life groupings on the various sofas and chairs. The ladies were chattering, and the affair resounded with happy laughter and gracious conversations. Gyeorgy Konstantinovich entertained the ladies. The men exchanged opinions and news. After all, they did not get together very often, and when they did get together, each one tried to talk himself out. At the festive table, toasts for the coming year rang out and conversations were happy and unconstrained.

After dining, we went for a walk. Gyeorgy Konstantinovich had been wanting to buy a dacha closer to us for a long time, and a situation had turned up. A general was selling a nice dacha not far from ours.

We reached it successfully, and the general was at home. The gate was locked, and we were asked to wait. Then, the general himself appeared—with a rather haughty expression. He was dressed rather extravagantly—without a shirt and in shorts. Gyeorgy Konstantinovich asked if we could come in. This general did not change his expression—so that we should know with whom we were dealing. However, when he caught sight of Gyeorgy Konstantinovich, in a word, the general turned to stone. Then, he quickly collected himself, and drew himself up to full height. He made a motion with his right hand, and started to raise his hand to salute, but then caught himself in time. He said, "Excuse me, Comrade Marshal. I just... I just... Come in, please. Come in."

We went in. Inside, the lady of the house met us and invited us to be seated, but at the same time, she was in a state of confusion. Gyeorgy Konstantinovich took command.

"Excuse us for dropping in on you without an invitation. For goodness sake, do not upset yourself. We came because of the advertisement. We would like very much to look around your dacha. Allow me to present my wife, Galina Aleksandrovna, Valeriy Vladimirovich Polekh, an artist at the Bolshoi Theater, and his wife, Ludmilla Nikolaevna. You know, I like the area here very much. It is known for its scenic views, as though this were the nature of a Shishkin or a Levitan. True, I live not far from here in Forest Village, but they have built a mass of stone structures there and of course spoiled the natural character."

Little by little, the hostess calmed down. She turned out to be a very nice. friendly woman. Gyeorgy Konstantinovich asked her about the dacha, about the gardens, and about the flowers. It turned out that everyone here loved flowers.

Then the general appeared. "Hello, Comrade Marshal."

"Hello," Gyeorgy Konstantinovich greeted the general. "I remember you; I met you on the Front Lines. What are you occupied with now, besides gardening. Are you writing memoirs, recollections?"

"You know, no, I'm not writing,' said the general. "I'm just thinking about beginning to write, Comrade Marshal. A great thanks to you for everything. It is not for nothing that your name stands in the rank of names of celebrated heroes of our fatherland."

Gyeorgy Konstantinovich thanked the general. We were siting in a room completely covered with bookshelves. All around were books and more books. Zhukov was surprised—so many books and such order.

"Tell me, do you have a system for indexing the books?"

"Yes, I do," replies the general. "There is a card catalog. There one can learn the contents of my books."

"That is stupendous! I congratulate you, General."

"Thank you, Comrade Marshal. Look out the window. Do you like this beauty?"

Gyeorgy Konstantinovich looked out the window. Before him opened a wondrous view: a rather large lawn was planted with every possible kind of flower. Gyeorgy Konstantinovich was enthralled. As they say, it was a wonder of wonders.

"General, you are again forcing me to be astonished."

Afterward, we inspected the whole property. Orderliness and cleanliness were everywhere. "Look, what exemplary orderliness, and so much work has been invested in this dacha," said Ludmilla Nikolaevna. "Excuse me. My question may seem to you to be indelicate, but how can you sell such beauty?"

"The fact of the mater is, I was ordered to go to one of the Western countries on a mission. I was all prepared to leave, but at the last moment the mission was canceled. You see, I was going to be gone for three years. I only have the one daughter, and she lives in England. I had no one to leave the property to, and therefore, I

decided to sell this beauty. However, praise God, my mission has been canceled, and I will again live with my beauty."

In parting, we thanked the hospitable host and hostess and bowed ourselves out. At the dacha, lunch was waiting for us. Lunch went noisily and happily. There were many toasts, jokes, and anecdotes. Toward evening, the guests began to leave.

Night was falling. The weather was wonderful. Only Gyeorgy Konstantinovich, Galina Aleksandrovna, General Semyon Ilich Makeiev, Sofia Grigorevna [Makeiev] and we remained at the house. Semyon Ilich proposed, "Let's go to our place. We'll sit a while and drink a some tea."

Everyone joyfully agreed. They had a large house and a beautiful property. The Zhukovs loved to visit them very much. The master and mistress loved and respected Gyeorgy Konstantinovich and Galina Aleksandrovna very much, and it must be said that their love was reciprocated. They always had something to talk about. They both had fought, and both had come from the countryside. I listened to their conversation with great delight and even pleasure.

Of course, a table was spread in the garden. We drank tea, talked, tried various drinks, and a very tasty home-brewed wine. Gyeorgy Konstantinovich loved to crack nuts, and Sofia Grigorievna always kept a supply for him.

So passed yet another bright and unforgettable day—a day of

association with the Great Marshal and Great Man, his wife Galina
Aleksandrovna, and their daughter Mashenka.

WE GO SWIMMING

One day at the beginning of August, when he happened to be
at our dacha, Gyeorgy Konstantinovich asked me, "Valeriy, do you
have a place to go swimming here? A nice stream or river or maybe
a lake?"

"Yes, there is a river with the mighty designation 'Desna.'"

"Well, you see, that means there is someplace to swim," rejoiced
Gyeorgy Konstantinovich.

"The river is there, but a bit too shallow for us. In short, it is a
shallow little river, although the name of the river is well-known.
It's true, we do have a medium-sized stream called the Generalskiy
Stream. In this water, swimming is possible."

"Dear Valeriy, well, that's beautiful. That means we'll go
swimming in the Generalskiy Stream." The weather was staying
nice, and the sun was scorching hot. We agreed upon tomorrow.

The next day, the Zhukovs drove up exactly at ten o'clock in the
morning. After they'd been at our place for a little while, we walked
to the stream, taking the kids with us. They were in ecstasy. The
ladies decided to accompany us.

There we were on the bank of the stream. We spread out a
blanket. The ladies decided to stroll a little. They had umbrellas, and
the sun was hot. Gyeorgy Konstantinovich and I went to find a pool
where we could swim. We found such a place. On one side was a
rather nice bush and on the other side the place was open. We
decided to establish our base right there. We brought over the blanket
and things and began to get ready for swimming. The ladies seated
themselves on the blanket. The children were already splashing in
the water not far from the bank. It turned out, Gyeorgy
Konstantinovich loved to swim very much, and swam very well.

Before entering the water, he did a few exercises and immediately threw himself into the water. It immediately became evident that he loved to swim. He swam stormily. Waves formed around him and the water sort of boiled under him. He tried to swim with various styles. His results were classical. He swam a long time and with a kind of delight. He did not like to get his head underwater. I was convinced; clearly, he loved the watery element. I swam and observed for myself how he was swimming. Gyeorgy Konstantinovich, after springing from the water, began jumping first on one foot and then on the other. Drying himself off with a terry-cloth towel, he noisily quacked with pleasure.

Gyeorgy Konstantinovich immediately began to bring himself back to order. He dressed, combed his hair, got a small field mirror, looked at himself, and corrected his hair somewhat.

I looked at Gyeorgy Konstantinovich. From him flowed some kind of great strength of soul and health. A sort of Herculean strength showed. I was enchanted with his strength of soul, health, and freshness.

We were silent. I did not dare to begin to speak with him, fearing to interrupt all my vision. Lordy, this was a man who was so powerful and at the same time gentle. The water had a healing effect on Gyeorgy Konstantinovich, as though it cleansed his soul of a burden and sorrow.

"Shall we play checkers?" said Gyeorgy Konstantinovich after a long silence. I got the checkers. I must say, he did not allow an element of unimportance to enter the process of the game. Gyeorgy Konstantinovich played with passion and loved to win.

He loved very much to play seriously. It was a little hard to play with him, but it was interesting. The ladies sat with the children on the blanket, ate fruit, and shaded themselves from the sun with umbrellas.

FOREST VILLAGE

Our whole family loved to be at Gyeorgy Konstantinovich Zhukov's dacha in Katuary, which is now called Forest Village. It was a wonderful time.

For this visit, we arrived early, and as was normal, Gyeorgy Konstantinovich and Galina Aleksandrovna met us at the train station. As we met, Ludmilla Nikolaevna presented Gyeorgy Konstantinovich with a basket of strawberries. He walked, ate berries, and entertained everyone. Mashenka ran there, and was waiting for our daughter, Lyudechka. They held hands and ran on ahead of us. It was not far to go, and we walked slowly in order to prolong the stroll. There the house was—such a comfortable, nice house. It was a timbered house. On the second floor was an open veranda – just like a dance pavilion. I joked, "Let's have a dance."

Gyeorgy Konstantinovich laughed and said, "We put on a dance once. You may imagine the local dacha denizens came to look at us."

"And what about music?" I asked.

"We had a famous disk-jockey, and danced to phonograph music."

The property was bright and green. Here grew many *rosa-rogoza* [rose of Sharon]. (This bush bears beautiful rose blossoms, and flowers from spring until fall itself.) There was a small kitchen-garden. Gyeorgy Konstantinovich tried his hand at agriculture. He fervently loved nature. He wanted to wash up out of doors.

He bought a little wash-stand and fastened it to a tree. Above it, he made a small awning of sheet-metal, but he didn't roll the edge over. He decided to try out the wash-stand. He poured in some water and rolled up his sleeves, but when he stooped over he hit his forehead on the edge of the sheet-metal and, of course, cut the skin on his forehead. "This scratch on my forehead is the fruit of my labors."

They called us to lunch. We went to wash our hands in the new wash-stand, but now all the edges of the metal had been turned under. We sat at the table. Everyone was in a good mood, and the weather was wonderful. We were situated on the veranda. The hostess, Galina Aleksandrovna, bustled about to serve everyone, and Ludmilla Nikolaevna helped her. They set out hors d'oeuvre— snacks that were simple and Russian: herring with green onions in vinegar that had been lightly sweetened, a hot boiled potato, and also our salted mushrooms. There was salmon and ham and, of course, bread—dark Borodinskiy. Gyeorgy Konstantinovich loved to break off a chunk of the crust and crunch it. He rubbed his hands together in anticipation. Then, we each took some. They served vodka in a crystal decanter. We did not talk a much, and paid more attention to the hors d'oeuvre. We were eating with an appetite. We praised the hostess, drank to her health, drank to the health of Ludmilla Nikolaevna, and drank to nature. Today, nature was simply wonderful. After hors d'oeuvre, sorel borscht with chopped eggs and sour cream was served. The borscht was praiseworthy; bravo to the hostess. We learned a surprise awaited us: a ruddy, well-done roast suckling pig with horse-radish. Galina Aleksandrovna raised a toast to a good stroll after lunch. Ludmilla Nikolaevna raised a toast to the health of Gyeorgy Konstantinovich. I raised a toast to the wonderful lunch which our hospitable hostess had prepared. Lunch ended, and we sat in the garden. Some drank coffee, some drank tea, and the children asked for ice cream. Gyeorgy Konstantinovich told an anecdote.

It was so relaxed, and so peaceful as we sat in the garden. Gyeorgy Konstantinovich was in a wonderful state of mind. He proposed a stroll, and we all agreed and began to get ready. The children jumped for joy and shouted, "Hurray!" We walked through meadows of rye and cornflowers. We went out in a large clearing. In the center of the clearing, a wonderful, fluffy linden tree was growing.

The children began to play with a ball, and the adults began to play with hoops. Here is how the game went. We played in pairs. You held in your hands two wooden canes resembling swords and very pretty-looking. One was bright red and the other bright yellow. It also used a wicker hoop with a diameter approximately that of a soccer ball. The play consisted of the following: You took a sword (which we called a cane) in the right hand and held the hoop in the left hand. Then you lowered the hoop over the end of the sword in the right hand, and pulled on the hoop with the other sword. When you felt the there was enough tension on the hoop, you slipped the sword out of the hoop. The hoop flew in the direction of the other participant. If the participant caught the hoop with a sword, he was awarded a point. If he did not catch the hoop, a point was awarded to the one who tossed the hoop. Everyone got really involved in the game, and the competition went on a long time. I must note, that the ladies were victorious. They played an elegant, athletic game.

Gyeorgy Konstantinovich proposed, "Let's do a singing ring dance around this delightful linden tree. Take one another by the hand, and let's go singing around the linden. The song-leader, of course, was Gyeorgy Konstantinovich. Everyone joined in. We went first in one direction and then in the other. We went gently and wonderfully well. We said farewell to the delightful linden tree and went home. Along the way, we gathered flowers. We returned home joyfully and with singing, aided by a famous songbook I had brought along.

Now we would have tea. Gyeorgy Konstantinovich decided to set up the samovar. Fortunately, we had brought fir pine cones from the forest. Gyeorgy Konstantinovich said that such pine cones would burn very well, give very good heat, and generate a very tasty fir aroma. Out of the house, he brought an old, small samovar, a Tulla, the genuine article. Gyeorgy Konstantinovich brought an old boot out of a shed, and said, "I'll use the boot to fan the flame, and we'll make the fire with these very cones." The samovar stovepipe was found. We shaved thin splinters, lit them, pushed them into the firebox of the little samovar, and the project was underway. The fire sort of flared up, but after a while began to go out. Then the boot proved to be useful. Gyeorgy Konstantinovich put the top of the boot on the firebox of the samovar and began to quickly, quickly pump air with the boot. The flames began to flare up, and burned brightly. We watched with interest as Gyeorgy Konstantinovich skillfully performed all this. I must say, the pine cones did their job. Galina Aleksandrovna boiled the tea with great understanding about the art of making tea. We drank tea with sugar lumps, and used little tongs for this of course. We drank tea with strawberry jam, and, for the aficionado, black currant jam. Home-made pastries also appeared, which Galina Aleksandrovna had baked.

We sat a long time, not wanting to disperse. The Little samovar had not cooled down. We drank yet another cup of strong, fragrant tea. It was a wonderful day, wonderful weather, and a warm beautiful evening. They escorted us to the station, and we said good-bye. It was already dark when we returned home. We laid our little daughter in bed, and we, ourselves, exchanged impressions for a long time about the wonderfully constructive way the day had gone. What amazing people Galina Aleksandrovna and Gyeorgy Konstantinovich were! We arranged the little bouquet Gyeorgy Konstantinovich had presented to Ludmilla Nikolaevna in a little vase.

In the middle of July, I was occupied with creating a textbook, and was so engrossed that I did not hear the horn of Gyeorgy Konstantinovich's car. Realizing what had happened, I quickly went out my gate and looked. There stood the familiar ZIS automobile. Aleksei Mironov, Gyeorgy Konstantinovich's adutant, was just opening the car door and getting out of the machine. We said, "Hello, How are you? How are you getting along?" and similar pleasantries.

Aleksei Mironov addressed me, "Valeriy Vladimirovich, I

have two matters for you. First, come here and see what I have brought you."

Good Lord! He pulled a big, beautiful keg out of the car.

"Accept this gift from the marshal."

"Enormous thanks. What a thoughtful person to not forget about me here!"

Mironov brought four kegs and carried each in turn in his arms. I said, "Put the keg on the ground and roll it on the ground.

"The Marshal ordered, 'Carry the kegs in your arms so they won't get dirty.' and later the Marshal ordered that they be delivered for him to Ludmilla Nikolaevnaat your dacha, and that I not forget to fetch you. Oh, the daughter, Mashenka, will be so very glad."

Then our Grandmother, Aleksandra, came out, and they greeted one another. They went on the veranda to drink tea, and we began to get ready for the drive. After a short while, Aleksei Mironov came out to us accompanied by Grandmother.

Claudia Evgenevna, Aleksandra Sergeievna, Masha, and Lyuda

"Well, a cup of tea immediately took away all fatigue," said Aleksei Mironov.

"Aleksei, please give my beloved Gyeorgy Konstantinovich a jar of currants. He loves them so. Give him my deep regards."

We drove to the Zhukovs' house, opened the gate, and entered the property. The host himself came to meet us. "Come in."

Galina Aleksandrovna came out to greet the guests. Mashenka ran up to us to say hello and immediately ran with our Lyudechka to play. The Marshal was dressed in a special workman's outfit.

"Lyudechka, come to me. I will give you a kiss," said Gyeorgy Konstantinovich.

"Come. Come here. Well, now."

"Where did such a monster come from?" I asked.

"You look. What a beauty of a stump!"

"This ia not a monster. This is something Gyeorgy Konstantinovich himself grubbed out," said Galina Aleksandrovna. "Just think. He has been working on it for several days."

"Well, this is a stump of a stump," I said. "What strength was needed to get it out!"

"Not just strength, but cunning also," said the Marshal. I made a plan of how to take it. You may be sure that here strength alone would not take it. As you can see, I carried out the plan. Yes, I got it."

"Gyeorgy Konstantinovich, why did you take it out?"

"Well, it was sitting almost on the road itself."

"Look! The stump looks like an octopus. Its roots are the tentacles and the base is the body."

Gyeorgy Konstantinovich approached the stump and began to look it over carefully. "I've thought it through. I'll even off the roots and stand the stump on its legs—just like an octopus. It would be good to stand the octopus over there. It will look very good there."

We all sat on the bench that Gyeorgy Konstantinovich and I had built together here in Forest Village.

"You know, I've not ridden the electric train for a long time. A steam locomotive, now, that's another matter. It's a beautiful machine. One sees it standing, and it's a beauty. It puffs. It hisses, and these iron arms begin to turn the powerful wheels. It's a pleasure to watch it."

The ladies came and sat beside us.

"As I look at this stump, I'm reminded of a story. I don't remember the author. This affair was in pre-revolutionary Russia, and maybe even in our governance. In this governance, lived a baron. The baron decided to build a new road to a large village. The baron loved to visit this village quite often because his sweet-heart lived there, but the road to the village was terrible," related Gyeorgy Konstantinovich.] "The baron summoned the steward and said, 'Here, I've drawn up a plan. I want to make a new, good road to the village.' The steward heard out the baron, and said only, 'We'll do it.' But first the baron decided to inspect the location where the future road would be. What did the baron see? Everything was good, except for one circumstance that interfered with the construction of the road. In the middle of the road lay an enormous rock. No one knew how this enormous rock came to be there. The baron rode away. At home he thought about it. What to do? He had a thought. He called for the steward and commanded him to remove the rock. The steward only said, 'We'll do it.' The next day, the steward called together the whole countryside. 'Guys, you all are such big people. It is obvious you are very strong. We will move the rock from the road.' 'We'll move it!' shouted the people. They came to the place, and began to push the rock. But it did not move from it's place. They pushed and shoved but they were not able to move it. With every last bit of strength they pushed, but it did not move from its place. The steward appeared before the baron. This way and that. They pushed the rock and shoved the rock, but were not able to move this accursed rock. Could we change the direction of the road?'

"'What!' shouted the baron. 'Should I change the route? Never! I don't want to even hear about it.' They rode to the rock. The baron ordered them to push. 'Move the rock, and I'll reward with a half-ruble for vodka.' The men got really hot — a half-ruble for vodka was no joke. They spit on their hands, and said, 'We'll move it.' They began to shove. The rock stirred but did not move from its place.

"Now, it so happened that some muzhiks* from a neighboring village were passing by. Seeing such a scene, they approached. The muzhiks asked, 'What? Can't you move the rock from its place?' These muzhiks from the neighboring village threw themselves at the baron's noble feet. 'What are you?' asked the baron. 'We, Father, are going to pray, but we have become so poor, we do not have enough to buy a candle to set before God.' 'What's your request?' said the baron. 'Allow us to remove the obstacle.' 'Are you in your right mind?' asked the baron. 'My servants could not move the obstacle

*   muzhiks = peasants

aside.' 'Give us the half-ruble, Baron, and we will take away the little rock.' The baron said, 'The half-ruble is yours if you take away the obstacle.' 'Father Baron, bring us six shovels and also six pry-bars.' There were six muzhiks. The baron ordered that what the muzhiks requested be brought. The baron rode off. He ordered, without fail, as soon as the muzhiks had dealt with the rock to send a courier at a gallop to the manor. The muzhiks spit on their hands, crossed themselves in all four directions, and began to dig. They dug for a long time. Food and drink were brought to the haggard-looking muzhiks. The muzhiks were really exhausted. Then the muzhiks stopped digging, and formed a sort of council about what to do next. The pit was deep. The rock stood on the very edge of this pit. Then the muzhiks took the pry-bars in hand, and pushed the rock toward the pit. Nothing doing. They took the shovels again, descended into the pit, and began to dig the dirt away from under the rock.

"When it became impossible and dangerous to dig under the rock, the muzhiks crawled out of the pit, and there they appealed to the local peasants standing there with a request that they nudge the rock into the pit. The whole community shoved and pushed the rock into the pit. Everyone took a deep breath, 'Glory to you, Lord. The rock is as though it has never been.' Someone drove off with horses to get the baron. 'Well, muzhiks! Well, wise ones, you will get the half-ruble from the baron.' The muzhiks from the neighboring village stood on their knees thanking God. The muzhiks set to work filling in the pit. At last, the rock disappeared. Then the baron clattered up in a light carriage. He asked, "Where is the rock?' ' There, Father. There, under the ground.' 'Well, muzhiks, you are wise ones. Really wise ones. Receive your half-ruble. You worked honorably, men. Thank you for your keen wit. For your keen Russian wit.' "

"I must tell you, I did not always use strength; I often used keen wit. That's the way things were."

Gyeorgy Konstantinovich's story made a very strong impression on us. It may be, that Gyeorgy Konstantinovich composed this narrative himself. You know, he was a wonderful story teller. We all thanked the author of the story from our hearts.

"Well, Valeriy, you promised to help me make a lattice like  you have at your dacha. It seems to me it's called a trellis lattice. Boards have been brought. Let's go take a look."

"Yes, the boards are excellent," I said. "We can start."

We went into the barn on the side of the property. There stood a wood-turning lathe. You could turn whatever you wanted on that.

"What a beauty," I observed. "And what is this beautiful, enormous, red-colored case?"

Gyeorgy Konstantinovich opened the lid of the case, and I saw a colossal collection of cabinet-maker's and machinist's tools.

"Where is this beauty from?"

"This, dear Valeriy, is a gift to me from Tulchan. Here, look at the monogram."

"With tools like this, we could start to work right away."

"No, Valeriy. Right now, we'll go to the table. Breakfast is waiting for us."

Galina Aleksandrovna, in a simple but rather elegant dress, together with Ludmilla Nikolaevna, began to serve breakfast. It was true that we had already succeeded in getting hungry. The light breakfast was similar to an English breakfast: oatmeal porridge, bacon with fried eggs, coffee with cream, and small meat patties. With good appetite, we gobbled it all up. Though Galina Aleksandrovna offered seconds, we said thanks, but we were completely satisfied. We spent the day beautifully. It was a wonderful time. All the same, we had to say good-bye. Our grandmother, Aleksandra Sergeievna, was waiting for us at home.

One summer day, it seems to me it was in the month of August,

I was a guest at Gyeorgy Konstantinovich's dacha. During our conversation, he asked me, "How should I do this? I have decided to remodel the dacha, replace the steel roof in some places, change the rain-gutters, and the down spouts. Also, there will be some carpentry work. You understand, I'll need craftsmen."

I told him I would give him good craftsmen. Artists! Real artists in their affairs.

"Well, Valeriy. Thank you," said Gyeorgy Konstantinovich. "Introduce me to your artists."

I began to list my craftsmen. One, Misha Solomko, was a metal worker. He'd made decorations at the Bolshoi Theater. Besides that, in our settlement, he'd made almost all the rain-gutters and pipes. roof ridges, and little gates. Everything was well-planned and solid. The other was Uncle Fedya – a wonderful carpenter. I had promised the Marshal I would bring the craftsmen as soon as possible. At my first meeting with the craftsmen, we came to an agreement, and I warned them that they would be working on the dacha of Marshal Zhukov. At first, they were fearful, because, in the past, they had served in the army, and understood very well who this Marshal Zhukov was. I had to reassure them that I would introduce them properly.

At last, I escorted my artists to Gyeorgy Konstantinovich. As we stood by the gate, my guys were gripped by fear. I had to pull them onto the property. Having heard the racket, Gyeorgy Konstantinovich came out. The craftsmen stood with their hands along the seams of their trousers.*

"Hello, friends," greeted Zhukov.

"Health to you, Comrade Marshal of the Soviet Union!" They spoke out loudly, as though on parade.

"I immediately see that you are army men. Where did you serve?"

---

*   As though standing at attention.

"From the very beginning of the war, and we went to Berlin, Comrade Marshal.

Gyeorgy Konstantinovich invited us to the veranda. A conversation began. After a while, I bowed out because I was on my way to work.

Some time later I met Solomko. "Well, how is the work going?" I asked.

"We are working. We are working," replied Solomko.

The first day possible, I traveled to Forest Village. I looked. I saw no eave troughs, no down pipes, and no roof-ridge trim. I wondered, "What have you been doing all this time? What did you do, forget why you came here? You are letting me down. Don't you have a conscience?"

Out came Gyeorgy Konstantinovich, and we greeted each other.

"Well, Valeriy, those are golden men you have sent me."

"But, excuse me," I said. "They have not done anything at all."

"They are doing it," said Gyeorgy Konstantinovich. "Here, you just listen. Well, the guys are giving us a priceless 'living newspaper' of the Front Line."

It turned out, the Marshal was listening to the "Living Newspaper" of the Front Line, and it pleased him very much. There were stories and fables.

"They have done this for me here at the dacha with real enthusiasm and have not forgotten anything. They repeated it several times for me."

Gyeorgy Konstantinovich said it was very pleasant to recall the heroic and terrible days and times. Gyeorgy Konstantinovich said that he listened to these great guys and relaxed and forgot for a time his own cares in connection with the colossal war effort. Then Gyeorgy Konstantinovich told us a lot about his war experiences. He related how he had been covered over with dirt, "And thanks be to the soldiers who dug me out."

At the end of the conversation, Gyeorgy Konstantinovich said, "The army amateur musicians, the soldier-artists – they were real heroes. In rare, free hours, they rehearsed their wonderful concert programs; not forgetting that after the concert they needed to go into battle."

"Gyeorgy Konstantinovich, you remember," said I, "in the 1920's the amateur musicians with the designation 'Dark Blues' were very much in fashion. We sang, 'We are union men. We are Dark Blues Men.' At that time, without fail Dark Blues performed after gatherings and meetings. This was an agitational performance, and propagandistic poems on the current theme were in the program. The Dark Blues musicians sang songs, igniting the whole auditorium, so that the entire audience was stirred by the singing; and there was also recitation to music. They sang such songs as *Our Train, We Sailed on a Ship, We are Blacksmiths, Bricklayers,* and finished with singing *The Internationale.* At the end of the performance, they demonstrated a variety of gymnastic exercises."

"Yes, Valeriy, Now, I remember these presentations. Actually, Dark Blues was very much beloved by the military audiences. They performed in the regiments and on the Front Lines of the Civil War."

Gyeorgy Konstantinovich asked me, "Well, how do you like my artists?"

"You know, I like them very much. I simply simply did not expect this from my familiar craftsmen. Well, guys, you're good men! Yes, by God! Good guys."

A few days later, I again dropped in on Gyeorgy Konstantinovich, but did not find him at home. The Craftsmen were already finishing all the work, and they had done everything excellently. When they saw me, they took a break. We talked a long time, and then Gyeorgy Konstantinovich drove up. He praised the work of the craftsmen.

"You're doing great, guys. Good-bye, guys, until tomorrow. Let's go drink some tea. I 'm a little tired from the road." Gyeorgy Konstantinovich and I talked til late in the evening. As he was parting with me, he said, "Tomorrow I'm going on a fishing trip. I'll have to bring you some perch."

WE GO FOR MUSHROOMS.

One day at the dacha in Forest Village, we were sitting on the veranda and drinking tea. Galina Aleksandrovna had baked a nicely browned apple pie. A bowl of strawberry preserves, "Crimean Assortment" cookies, and candy were on the table. A samovar was puffing on the table, and on the upper cooking ring of the samovar sat a teapot with the brew. Gyeorgy Konstantinovich was telling us about something very interesting, and we were listening with enjoyment. He only interrupted his exposition to remind everyone about the tea, and we began to drink the hot, excellently-brewed tea. The tea had been very skillfully brewed by Galina Aleksandrovna, a remarkable hostess. The pie also turned out gloriously – it just melted in your mouth. As an aside, Gyeorgy Konstantinovich remarked that it would not hurt anything for us to go mushroom hunting. This proposition met with everyone's approval. We all began to relate stories of hunting mushrooms.

Gyeorgy Konstantinovich proposed, "Tomorrow evening, Valeriy, you and Ludmilla come to our place in Forest Village, spend the night, and the next day, early in the morning, we'll drive out to the forest." Gyeorgy Konstantinovich had decided to visit one of the military farms.

In the evening the next day, we were at Forest Village. We arrived in time for evening tea. Gyeorgy Konstantinovich showed us to the room where we'd spend the night. After tea, we went out into the garden. The weather was excellent. Somewhere, frogs were croaking, and sometimes, in the distance, cicadas chirped. We were silent, enchanted by the charming evening.

In the morning, Gyeorgy Konstantinovich woke us up. "Hey, layabouts. Get up! The time is six o'clock."

We quickly brought ourselves to order, and went to the dining room to drink tea. After tea, I began to help Gyeorgy Konstantinovich get big baskets for the mushrooms and small ones for berries. They said that on the farm, where we were planning to go, there was a lot of wild strawberries and mushrooms. Gyeorgy Konstantinovich asked me to go up to the second floor and bring a folding knife. Quickly, I went up to the second floor, and looked for it in the office. I opened a drawer of the desk, and was thunder-struck. In the drawer lay the four gold stars of a Hero. I was even afraid, but I took the knife and quickly went down.

When I ran up to Gyeorgy Konstantinovich, he asked, "Why are you so out of breath?"

"Lord! What I saw in you drawer!"

"What was it?"

"I opened the drawer of your desk, and your four gold stars were lying in the drawer."

"Dear friend, you have gotten upset for nothing. These gold stars are not the real ones. They are duplicates. The real stars are lying in a safe, and these I wear on a uniform."

"Well, praise the Lord! I thought they were real."

When everyone was ready, we got in the car, and we were off. It was a good drive. We exchanged jokes, and talked a lot about our impressions of the road. At last, we arrived at the farm. An elderly man, all surrounded by a thick beard, came to meet us. He was dressed in an old army uniform, and even his trousers were decorated with red stripes down the leg. When he caught sight of Gyeorgy Konstantinovich, he brightened up completely.

"Lord! Who's this I see? It's Marshal Zhukov himself! Respected. So respected. Evidently, fate itself has decided to make me happy. Here, they call me Uncle Forest. That's what I am called."

Gyeorgy Konstantinovich extended a hand. "Hello. Hello, kind fellow. How are you getting along here? Is this your dwelling?"

"Yes, Comrade Marshal. I live here. I'm used to it. The surroundings are heavenly, and I live in the embrace of nature itself. It's good to me. I'm like the miller in Pushkin's *Rusalka*. I invite you to my hut. Are you seeking mushrooms? Yes, we have mushrooms here. Comrade Marshal, I will show you a place where mushrooms and berries are found."

Meanwhile, the ladies were looking around at the beautiful blossoms in the huntsman's garden.

A dense forest opened before us with ages-old trees, and tall pine trees embracing trees standing nearby with their branches. Fir trees were sort of interlaced with birches. It was a little dark in the forest. Only an occasional ray of light pierced the through the mighty trees. In spite of the sunny weather, it was cool in the forest and, at times, even a little damp. This was it – Forest. One could go into it, rebuild health, breathe with the full chest, and delight in the aromas of Forest—aromas of resin, and the elixir of leafy birch. It seemed that one inhaled and did not exhale. This was it – Forest. We were going into it, going to hear the melody of the trees, and the melody of singing birds. Good Lord! How wonderful it was to be in the forest!

We all were lightly dressed. Gyeorgy Konstantinovich was wearing a light shirt with long sleeves, trousers, and rubber shoes. The ladies were dressed in beautiful floral-print dresses, and wore light jackets over them. In place of light shoes, they wore rubber half-boots. I wore a Scottish, checked shirt and rubber boots.

We spread out in various directions, giving halloo's to each other. We spent more than an hour this way. By some coincidence, we all gathered together.

"Let's brag, who has gathered what?" said Gyeorgy Konstantinovich.

His basket was covered with several ferns. He began to show his "catch" – ten whites, eight Boletus versipellus, and one rough-stemmed boletus.* Galina Aleksandrovna showed eight whites, seven Boletus versipellus, and two rough-stemmed boletus. Ludmilla Nikolaevna showed off six whites, but made up for it with four rather large Boletus Versipellus, and three rough-stemmed boletus. I gathered eleven whites, six Boletus versipellus, and three rough-stemmed boletus.

---

*   Boletus scaber

Gyeorgy Konstantinovich congratulated everyone on the catch. "Let's go farther into the depths of the forest," he advised. "Over there, beyond a clearing, I saw a stream. Let's go that way." We moved in the direction of the stream. Good Lord! We saw a fairy-tale wandering stream all covered with pond scum. Thick forest rushes covered almost half the stream.

"Quiet. Quiet. Listen. The frogs are croaking," said Gyeorgy Konstantinovich. "They are giving us a concert. They are greeting us." We listened; truly, it was a frog choir. It seemed to us that they croaked in various voices. We caught sight of these singers, who were sitting on a fallen pine tree that was almost rotted away, and evidently, had fallen many years before. As soon as we made a move in the direction of the frogs, as though at a command, they leaped into the water and dived, and poked their heads out and began to look at us. Evidently, they were wondering to themselves, "Who has come to visit us?"

"I think," said Gyeorgy Konstantinovich, "at one time this stream was clean, and people came here to swim, catch fish, and, evidently, swans swam here on the stream. Look, over there in the distance, some sort of ruin is visible. Evidently, it was a nobleman's estate, and Onegins, Dbrovskiys, and Troekurovs lived there. Let's go there and have a little picnic." We reached the ruins, and saw that only the foundation and part of a wall remained of the manor. "This is very fortunate. The foundation can serve us as a table."

Galina Aleksandrovna pulled a tablecloth out of her basket, spread it on the foundation, and placed buttered bread on it. From his basket. Gyeorgy Konstantinovich got out a rather large thermos of strong tea. We ate the buttered bread and drank their strong, aromatic tea with much pleasure. Strengthened, we decided to continue our outing.

The voices of birds rang in the forest. Suddenly, There began to be the voices of Lemeshev, Kozlovskiy, and somewhere the voice of Utesov. I was beginning to imitate the famous singers to amuse our women.

After a while, we gathered together again. It began to be obvious that our baskets had filled significantly. Gyeorgy Konstantinovich made a little gift for our children. He cut two grass stalks and threaded strawberries on them. Pretty, tasty beads resulted. Gyeorgy Konstantinovich looked at a watch and decided it was time to go home. "The strawberries we all gathered will be jam, and we'll drink tea. The jam will be wonderful."

We began walking past familiar places. There was the ruin, and here was the fairytale stream. We approached the cabin of the huntsman.

He was already waiting for us in order to escort Gyeorgy Konstantinovich. In his hand, he held a birch-bark basket of his own, full of ripe raspberries. "Take them. Don't be bashful." He extended the basket to the marshal. Gyeorgy Konstantinovich was overjoyed. He hugged the old man and kissed him.

The car was waiting for us. In an hour and a half, we were again in Forest Village. The ladies went to put themselves in order, and Gyeorgy Konstantinovich and I sat quietly in wicker arm-chairs and rested. They set out hors d'oeuvre, and "Russian Gorka" vodka appeared on the table. In honor of the "harvest," we decided to drink a small glassful. The cold kvass soup went down well, and everyone was in delighted. (This was the creation of Galina Aleksandrovna.) At the table, we joked and laughed.

I told a few anecdotes:

Two fleas came out of a tavern. "What should we do? " one said. "Shall we walk or wait for a dog?"

"Comrade policeman, tell me. Is it dangerous to go on this street?"

"If it were dangerous, I would not be standing here!"

Everyone laughed heartily. After lunch, Gyeorgy Konstantinovich went to take a nap. We sat a while longer, and talked with Galina Aleksandrovna. We thanked her for a wonderful outing. The ladies kissed each other.

I almost forgot. When we arrived back from the outing, the

kids were already waiting for us. They received the strawberry beads. Gyeorgy Konstantinovich told the children how we gathered the mushrooms, and how the frog chorus entertained us. He told of the old man we got acquainted with, and called him Uncle Forest, and how he gave us a basket of raspberries. Mashenka and Lyudechka sat side-by-side with Gyeorgy Konstantinovich and listened to him.

THE NEW YEAR

On December 31st, at eleven o'clock in the evening, guests began to arrive at Gyeorgy Konstantinovich's dacha – the one in Rublevo. The automobiles were arriving one after the other. These were friends of Gyeorgy Konstantinovich Zhukov who were coming to greet the New Year. One hour remained until the New Year. The entryway was filling up with all the new guests. Gyeorgy Konstantinovich loved promptness. If he said at eleven, that meant at eleven. There was pleasant noise and the charming conversation of the ladies. The men were helping the ladies out of their wraps. The women were greeting one another. A festive atmosphere was everywhere. Floods of French perfume were wafting in the air. The light sound of classical music was coming from the drawing room. The host and hostess of the evening, Gyeorgy Konstantinovich and Galina Aleksandrovna, were welcoming the guests.

Everyone was making his way to the sitting room. After getting out of their wraps, the ladies joined Galina Aleksandrovna Zhukova in the boudoir. In small clusters or in groups, the men were sharing the latest news with one another. Everyone felt young. Everyone was jolly. At half-past eleven, Gyeorgy Konstantinovich invited everyone to the table. The doors opened, and to the music of F. Chopin's *Polonaise*, everyone hurried to the dining room.

However, there was a New Year holiday surprise present awaiting us – a Christmas tree. Good Lord! Yes, it was simply a wonder. It was a tall, smartly decorated fir tree. Everyone was delighted. The guests paused and admired the tree for a long time; it was so fine. However, time was flying. All the guests seated themselves at the table in order to observe the passing of the old year.

Gyeorgy Konstantinovich rose with a goblet in his hand and called for attention. "Friends! The old year is passing! It is annoying that this good year has passed so quickly. We remember the way we have gathered with you and joyfully passed the time. Today is the last meeting with you dear friends in the old year. I am very glad we have gathered again, and I see once more my charming, dear, and trustworthy friends. Hurrah! We will drink to the old, good year! Hurrah!"

The chiming of goblets was heard. After a few moments, the clock chimed twelve times. Everyone stood and shouted out, "Hurrah! Hurrah! Hurrah! To the New Year!" Corks flew from champagne bottles. Everyone turned their attention to the  wine and hors d'oeuvre. There were toasts, jokes, and songs sung in chorus. After a fairly extended time at the table, during which everyone felt young and happy, by general agreement, a break was announced.

The guests dispersed throughout the dacha. After a short time, Gyeorgy Konstantinovich appeared and said, "Attention! Attention!" In his hands, he was holding a large bottle. He asked the guests to stand in a circle. Gyeorgy Konstantinovich placed the bottle in the center of the circle.

"Attention! I will now begin to spin the bottle. The bottle is spinning, and now it is beginning to stop. When the bottle stops, whoever the top is pointing at has to relate an anecdote or some sort of interesting story."

Gyeorgy Konstantinovich gave the bottle a spin, and it came to a stop. The top of the bottle pointed at General Semyon Ilich Makeiev. Everyone laughed happily.

The General began, "Because I am a military man, I will tell you a military anecdote. Well, now! In a stadium, a reporter with a tape recorder was conducting interviews with soccer fans. The reporter approached a young man. 'What is your favorite team?' 'Spartak, of course,' the young man answered. The reporter approached a group of girls. 'Girls, what is your favorite team?' 'Dynamo, of course!' The reporter approached a general. 'Comrade General, what is you favorite team?' 'My favorite team,' replied the general, 'is 'Stand at attention!'"*

Everyone enjoyed the anecdote. My turn came. I told a musical anecdote.

"A fireman was taking a test at a music school. They asked him, 'What is the difference between a violin and a grand piano?' The fireman answered, 'A grand piano burns longer.'"

Galina Aleksandrovna: "A fellow, who had burns on his ears, was brought into the emergency room. 'What happened?' they asked. 'I was ironing my slacks, and suddenly the telephone rang. Instead of the receiver, I put the iron up to my ear.' 'But, why is your other ear burned?' 'I called for an ambulance.'

Everyone was delighted with that anecdote.

Ludmilla Nikolaevna told this one. " 'Doctor, is it true, that those who eat carrots have good vision?' 'Of course! Really, have you ever seen a rabbit with glasses?'"

Sofia Grigorievna Panova, an artist at the Bolshoi Theater, told this one: "A wife came to work with a bruise under one eye. 'Who hit you?' they asked. 'My husband.' 'But we thought he was on a business trip.' "I thought so too.'"

That anecdote was pleasing. Gyeorgy Konstantinovich told his favorite anecdote.

---

*   This joke is a play on words. In Russian the word for sports team and military order are the same — kommanda.

"A raven was sitting on a tree branch, and saw a cow climbing the tree. 'Cow, why are you climbing the tree?' asked the crow. 'I want to eat apples,' answered the cow. 'You know, this is a birch tree.' The cow replied, 'I brought the apples with me.'"

Friendly applause resounded. Galina Aleksandrovna asked us to come have something hot to eat. It was too bad we had just dispersed, but something hot was extremely tempting. I had to go to the dining room. After eating, Gyeorgy Konstantinovich suddenly made the suggestion that we all go out on the street for a breath of fresh air. The proposal was accepted with delight.

We went outside and started playing in the snow. Someone took off on skis. Gyeorgy Konstantinovich appeared with several large pans in his hands. He turned his steps to an icy hill, and was the first to climb it. The hill was quite high. He sat on a pan, pushed off with his feet, and rushed down the hill. The pan simply did not fly straight. No, it was spinning around and taking the rider with it. It swirled its way to the very bottom. Gyeorgy Konstantinovich very briskly sprang to his feet and ran. He ran up to me and said, "Climb the hill," and handed me the pan. I quickly climbed the hill, sat on the pan, and stayed in one place. Gyeorgy Konstantinovich shouted up to me from the bottom of the hill, "Sit cross-legged. Sit cross-legged." I tucked in my feet, pushed off, and went rushing and turning and beginning to spin. I cannot remember how I came to be at the bottom. I was not able to spring up quickly as Gyeorgy Konstantinovich had. I tumbled out of the pan into the snow, and only after that rose to my feet. Someone tumbled out of the pan in the middle of the hill, and someone else slid down the hill without a pan – sliding right down on his coat. Even two brave ladies expressed a desire to go sliding, and they slid down rather successfully. There was laughter, hilarity, and everyone was getting ruddy faced.

We looked and saw that Gyeorgy Konstantinovich had brought out something else. He was carrying a small board, and climbed to the top of the hill with it. He put one foot on the board, pushed off with the other foot, and only just succeeded in standing on the board when he darted down, balancing with his arms in order to not fall and not loose equilibrium. I must say, Gyeorgy Konstantinovich made the descent very successfully. He quickly jumped from the board and ran a little. We all watched this flight with frozen hearts. We rewarded Gyeorgy Konstantinovich with friendly, warm applause.

Gyeorgy Konstantinovich, always and everywhere, was first in leadership. The whole evening, all the enjoyment was supported by him. Frozen, happy, and exhausted guests returned to the dacha where they warmed themselves with wonderful hot punch. Til five o'clock in the morning we enjoyed ourselves, and drank tea. In the sixth hour, they all drove off to their homes. There remained just myself, Ludmilla Nikolaevna Polekh, and our relatives— General Semyon Ilich Makeiev, and Sofia Grigorievna Makeieva. We were staying the night with Gyeorgy Konstantinovich. They had designated suites for us. We wished Galina Aleksandrovna and Gyeorgy Konstantinovich a good night and went upstairs to our rooms.

We lingered in the small sitting room and began to share impressions of the New Year gathering that had just ended. Really, the gathering had proceeded brilliantly, thanks to Gyeorgy Konstantinovich. What a remarkable holiday he had constructed for us. What an amazing fellow. It seemed that he had held the whole evening in his hands, but at the same time, everyone had felt freely, wonderfully, and truly festive.

Ludmilla Nikolaevna and me

I am reminded, now, of an incident that happened that New Years night. Earlier, when we were still at home, getting ready for the New Year gathering, I put a New Year's mask in the pocket of my sport coat. It was a big Georgian nose with a black

219

mustache on glasses.* Now I decided to put on the mask with the nose, and showed such a funny face to the relatives and my wife. Lord! How they laughed! We asked General Semyon Ilich to put on the Georgian nose. At first he refused—he is so serious—but then he finally agreed. Oh, my! We practically fell over from laughing. We all laughed so loudly and exuberantly that Gyeorgy Konstantinovich came running in. "Tell me about it, please! What happened? What are you laughing so hard about?"

We asked Semyon Ilich to put on the mask again. My Lord! How it affected Gyeorgy Konstantinovich! He caught himself by the stomach and ran about the room and laughed and laughed. When he got himself under control and began to quiet down. Gyeorgy Konstantinovich laughed and said, "Where is sleep, now? Come on. We will drink to the health of Semyon Ilich."

So ended that wondrous New Years party.

ATTENDING THEATERS AND CONCERTS

During the first visit of the Bolshoi Theater to the French Ballet, we compared impressions of operas, dramatic productions, and concerts. I came to the conclusion that Gyeorgy Konstantinovich was a real aficionado of the theater. Ludmilla Nikolaevna and I decided to give a gift to Gyeorgy Konstantinovich on the day of Gyeorgy Victorious,** and get tickets tickets to the production, *Konarmiya*, at the Bakhtangov Theater. It turned out to be very difficult to get the tickets. My wife appealed to the administrator of the theater, Spektor.

The administrator welcomed Ludmilla Nikolaevna into his office. His wife, Yuliya Borisova, a well known actress in the Bakhtangov Theater, was with him in the office. My wife made a

---

* Like Groucho Marx
** Saint Georges Day — Some Russians celebrate their saint's "name day" just like a birthday.

request to put together tickets for the production of Konarmiya for Marshal Gyeorgy Konstantinovich Zhukov.

Spektor immediately became animated. "What's this? What's this? I met the Marshal on the Front!" He handed Ludmilla Nikolaevna four tickets for the second row of the box seats.

Yuliya Borisova entered the conversation, and a very interesting conference developed. Yuliya asked my wife, "Who are you to Gyeorgy Konstantinovich?"

She answered, "Now, only the most true friends surround Marshal Zhukov, and I am one of them." On that note, they parted. Spektor promised to meet the Marshal.

That evening, Yuliya and Spektor greeted us. Gyeorgy Konstantinovich introduced his wife, Galina Aleksandrovna. They accompanied us to the buffet, we engaged in conversation. "Wait. Wait. Your face is very familiar to me," the Marshal said, turning to Spektor. "It seems to me we met somewhere on the Front. It's clear. You have not lost your military bearing."

"Comrade Marshal, I will remind you where we saw each other. You came to us in the hospital. When everybody learned that Marshal Zhukov was coming to us, we all somehow pulled ourselves together. You came to us in the ward and greeted everyone like a father. You went to each wounded man and asked where he had been fighting, and where he was wounded. You came over to me too, very tenderly talked with me a little, asked about the wound, and in parting, shook my hand."

"Yes," said the Marshal. "I remember this incident. You were good fellows. With such, one can battle and battle."

"Imagine, Comrade Marshal, I never thought I would meet you in my theater! Excuse me, Comrade Marshal, the third bell has rung. It is time to go into the the spectator hall."

After the performance, the whole troupe warmly applauded, greeting the honored marshal. In his turn, Gyeorgy Konstantinovich greeted the famous artists. We liked the performance very much.

Evidently, the Marshal remembered his service in the Civil War,[28]*
and how he galloped on his good steed. On the road home, we long
excitedly discussed the wonderful production.

Once, in a conversation with Gyeorgy Konstantinovich, I learned
that he had always been excited by the theme of the Decembrist
Uprising. He had read a lot about this uprising of the Tsarist military.
I asked if he would like to hear the opera *The Decembrists*, by the
composer, Shaporin. The opera was being presented in the Bolshoi
Theater. "Really?" Gyeorgy Konstantinovich could not imagine how
such an heroic theme could be presented in an opera. However he
became very interested in this production, and, in truth, I wanted
very much to show Gyeorgy Konstantinovich the opera, *Decembrists*.
I set myself the goal of inviting him as an honored guest, and seating
the honored Marshal in the Director's loge. To this end, I turned to
the Director of the Theater, Mikhail Ivanovich Chulakin.

"How about us inviting the Four Times Hero of the Soviet
Union Gyeorgy Konstantinovich Zhukov to the theater to attend the
opera *Decembrists*? It would be good if you met him as an honored
guest, and could seat the Marshal with his wife in your loge."

Even the director's bald spot became wet.

"Excuse me," said the director, "You know, the Marshal has
been repressed."

"Well, you see," I said, "you yourself called Zhukov a marshal.
It means, he was a marshal, and so he remains — Marshal and Four
Times Hero of the Soviet Union. You, probably, have not forgotten
who saved us from the Fascists."

"But aren't you," said the director to me, "afraid to take such
responsibility on yourself?"

On that, I replied to the director, "I am not afraid! Even if I am
called to answer for it, and they fire me from the theater."

"Very well," said the director. "You may invite Marshal Zhukov

---

*   The Civil War is known as the Russian Revolution in the West.

with all honors. I will not be in the theater at that time, and you will take all the responsibility on yourself."

I did not fear to invite the honored Marshal to the Bolshoi Theater, and we would sit in the Director's loge.

We arrived at the theater a little early, and were met with respect. Everyone just said, "Hello, Comrade Zhukov. This way, please, Comrade Marshal." We were showered with attention, and conducted to the Director's loge.

Gyeorgy Konstantinovich loved to arrive at the theater early, get situated, and breathe the theatrical atmosphere. "I love the theater," said Gyeorgy Konstantinovich. "Galina Aleksandrovna and I always feel elated and festive. It would be interesting to know; how each spectator perceives the theater," said Gyeorgy Konstantinovich. "For some, it is an exciting event in their lives—like a joyful holiday of art, and they are always dressed festively. Others come to look at the rich surroundings of the theater: its glittering loges and the legendary, incomparable chandelier. All this, of course, prepares the spectator, but the most important thing is the expectation of the miracle that must soon come to pass. As soon as they open the curtain, you forget all your cares, service affairs, and, perhaps, some sort of misfortune. You will be under the power of the activity that is occurring on the stage. Well, did I get a carried away with what I was saying?" Gyeorgy Konstantinovich looked at us and saw approval in our eyes.

As the loge attendant handed Gyeorgy Konstantinovich his program of the performance, she said, " Gyeorgy Konstantinovich, we are pleased to see you in our theater."

After receiving the program, Gyeorgy Konstantinovich began a solemn ceremony: he smiled, put on glasses, and sort of gently, lovingly held the program in his hands. He did not start to read it yet, but simply looked it over. He felt the program gave off some sort of typographical aroma. At last, the program was opened. Gyeorgy Konstantinovich immersed himself in reading, and it was better not to disturb or distract him. Rather quickly, he devoured the

223

contents, not just once or twice did he repeat the reading of it. After this he held, as the musicians say, a general pause. Now, he wanted to talk about what he'd read. Gyeorgy Konstantinovich was interested in who would sing the part of Nikolas I. "Aha! Here. See, A. Ognivitsev." Who was Pestel? Who was Ryleiev? And for all of them he had to give a short characterization. Who is the director? A. Sh. Melik-Pashaev.

At this point, Galina Aleksandrovna interrupted the conversation. " Gyeorgy, do you remember the opera, *Carmen*? Melik-Pashaev directed it also. How beautifully he led the orchestra! How wonderfully the singers performed! I believe it was because of the guidance of the director."

Then the lights went down, and Aleksandr Shamlevich Pashaev strode to the director's podium. He greeted the musicians, and applause resounded in the audience. The conductor turned his face to the audience and bowed. His hands were raised, and music poured out. During intermission, we went out to the foyer, and many recognised Gyeorgy Konstantinovich. The four gold stars of a Hero glittered on his chest.* Many from the audience greeted the Marshal, offering him marks of attention and respect. In the theater, Gyeorgy Konstantinovich asked me if there were any other operas by the composer, Shaporin. I answered, that I did not know. But it was known, for example, that Shaporin worked on this opera for twenty-five years. Also, I knew that in the beginning, the collective at the Bolshoi Theater did not accept it, and only after significant corrections was the opera accepted. Gyeorgy Konstantinovich listened very attentively to the production. Gyeorgy Konstantinovich kept silent. He was impressed.

He broke the silence. "You, probably, are waiting for an analysis. No, there will be no analysis. I must think, and ponder and possibly

---

*   In Russia, it is customary to wear awarded medals on civilian suites for
      special ocassions.

listen to the production again. Would you be able to sing one or another melody from this production, that is, this opera?"

I answered that I could. "I'll sing the *leit-motif* of *The Decembrists* for you — the famous lines by A. S. Pushikin. " I sang, "*Comrade, believe! It is dawning—the daybreak of captivating happiness. Russia awakens from slumber, and on the wreckage of autocracy, your name will be written.*"

"Yes, I remember; that's the very melody. Bravo, Valeriy! It seems you really have an ear! Bravo!"

All the same, we listened to the opera, *The Decembrists*, again. This time, Gyeorgy Konstantinovich preferred to sit in the audience. Gyeorgy Konstantinovich liked the opera. During this time, Gyeorgy Konstantinovich partially sang a little of the familiar *motief*, and only wished the generals would reduce their stomachs; "The generals are very fat."

Over the years of our acquaintance and friendship, we attended theaters, dramas, and operas quite often. We also attended concerts. Gycorgy Konstantinovich loved the Maliy Theater* very much, and he liked the Red Army Theater. The wonderful actress, Ludmilla Kasatkina played there. Gyeorgy Konstantinovich liked the Stanislavsky Theater very much, and Nemirovich-Danchenko; there, one could hear opera and operetta and see ballet. These variety actors had a special place with Gyeorgy Konstantinovich: A. Raikin, K. Shulzhenko, Ya. Utesov, Izabella Yureva, M, Magamaiev and others. A concert by S. Ya. Lemeshev in the Great Hall of the Conservatory stuck in his memory. Gyeorgy Konstantinovich was simply delighted with the artistry of S. Ya. Lemeshev's singing. He presented Russian romantic songs. After the concert, we went backstage. When he saw me with my wife, Sergei Yakovlevich Lemeshev called out, "My 'April' friends have come!" After catching sight of Gyeorgy Konstantinovich, he smiled broadly. "Good Lord! Such is fate!

---

* The Maliy Theater translates as "Small" theater as opposed Bolshoi Theater which means "Big" theater.

Usually, we met you in the Kremlin at the governmental concerts. Great thanks for coming to my concert."

"Allow me to introduce my wife, Galina Aleksandrovna." Sergei Yakovlevich took the hand of Galina Aleksandrovna and the hand of Ludmilla Nikolaevna. "Wonderful! Wonderful! You have charmed us! Thank you, Sergei Yakovlevich."

I invited Gyeorgy Konstantinovich and Galina Aleksandrovna to a concert of modern music in the Great Hall of the Conservatory. Works by the English composer, B. Britten. were in the program Among other compositions that would be performed was *Serenade for Stringed Orchestra and Two Soloists* by tenor, Ivan Semyonovich Kozlovskiy, and Hornist -- your humble servant.

Gyeorgy Konstantinovich sat with Galina Aleksandorvna in the fourth row of the audience,. My wife, of course, was nervous as always. Noticing her agitation, Gyeorgy Konstantinovich moved to calm her. He said, "You know, this is not the first of Valeriy Vladimirovich's concerts that we have attended. He is a fine fellow. He handles himself well on stage, and his playing is a delight to listen to."

All of artistic Moscow was present in the audience. The master of ceremonies announced us. Ivan Semyonovich Kozlovskiy went out. Applause resounded. The lights in the hall went down. Everything became quiet. As planned by the composer, I began to play off-stage. The audience listened to the enchanting music of the prologue. When the notes had died away, the lights went up in the hall, and I went out on the stage. Applause resounded, and I bowed. The conductor motioned with his hands, and the orchestra began playing. The music flowed out. The contest between voice and horn began. We were featured in this wonderful composition — Ivan Semyonovich and I. It seemed we gave everything we had. The audience rewarded us with tumultuous applause. Artists and musicians came backstage to greet and congratulate us on our success. Gyeorgy Konstantinovich with Galina Aleksandrovna came backstage, and, of course, my life's happy fellow-traveler, my wife. This was a real musical holiday.

226

SEVENTIETH YEAR CELEBRATION

In the evening of the second of December, 1966, at the dacha of Gyeorgy Konstantinovich Zhukov in Rublevo, automobiles began to arrive. The first to arrive were General Antipenko and his spouse. Then Gyeorgy Konstantinovich's daughters, Ehra and Ella, arrived with their husbands. Then, a car with friends of Galina Aleksandrovna Zhukova arrived. I saw the car of Accademican Tarnovskiy. a cousin of Gyeorgy Konstantinovich, arrived with his wife and daughter, Margarita Pilikhina. She was a noted cinema director, having done the film, *Tchaikovsky*. Then, Ivan Kozhedub, Thrice Hero of the Soviet Union, drove up with his wife. Next was the car of the famous surgeon, Vishnevskiy. After a short while, General Makeiev drove up with his spouse, the famous singer of the Bolshoi Theater, Sofia Grigorievna Panova. The last guests to arrive were Marshal Bagramyan with his wife.

Everyone was looking beautiful, and everyone was in a festive mood. The evening's host and hostess, Gyeorgy Konstantinovich and Galina Aleksandrovna were cordially greeting their dear guests. The guests came forward to congratulate Gyeorgy Konstantinovich on his birthday. The men kissed the hand of Galina Aleksandrovna. She was radiant on that day. She was gazing at her dear husband with tenderness and love. Outside, it was frosty and cold, but in the dacha it was warm and comfortable. From out of the drawing-room, wafted pleasant, symphonic music. Everyone was present; there were no late-comers. Gyeorgy Konstantinovich loved promptness. Light conversations flowed. Some stood, and some arranged themselves on the comfortable chairs and divans. The host and hostess bustled about with preparations, and the guests were occupied with conversations. The host showed guests his trophies. "Here, look at the chandelier. Soldiers took it down from Hitler's office and presented it to me." He showed gifts received from Stalin personally.

The time came to sit at the table. Two small friends—these were Mashenka, the daughter of Gyeorgy Konstantinovich and Galina

Aleksandrovna, and Lyudechka, our daughter—came from the children's room holding in their hands small bells making a chiming sound. This was the signal: everyone to the table.

The doors to the dining room were opened, and the first pair, Gyeorgy Konstantinovich and Galina Aleksandrovna entered to the music of Chopin's *Polonaise*. (I, usually, made all the arrangements for background music.) Then, the guests entered in pairs. The result was quite effective. The large, festive table was decorated with live flowers. Near each place-setting stood a little card with the name of the guest. Everyone seated himself at his designated place. A pleasant festive hubbub combined with the delicate music.

At last, a solemn silence fell. Gyeorgy Konstantinovich rose, and announced that General Antipenko would be in charge of the evening. The General said, "It has been given to me to have the great honor of being the master of ceremonies during an evening to honor a remarkable military leader and the noblest of men. All honorable people love and deeply respect you, dear Gyeorgy Konstantinovich. We would want to see you have many years looking as we see you today. Health and love to you! Hurrah!"

Among other guests, Ivan Kzhedub, Thrice hero of the Soviet Union, brought a word. "Dear Gyeorgy Konstantinovich, today, you have shown us these trophies. Only you know how you obtained these trophies, but today, Gyeorgy Konstantinovich, I am giving you this.

It is the aircraft on which I flew and destroyed many enemy aircraft. I love you, dear marshal. I bow before you, and present to you this souvenir. I wish you health. I drink to you. I drink to life."

I asked to give a word, and read a message from faithful friends.

VITYAZ

Vityaz was born in Kaluzhskiy Governance.
He grew and grew and grew up to be a giant.

An enemy fell upon the land of our birth.
Vityaz went out to battle to defend the land of our
birth.
For five years Vityaz fought
On the field of conflict.
Vityaz defeated the enemy.
The enemy fell.
The people gave honor to Vityaz,
Vityaz the hero!
Vityaz the strength!
Their rulers became afraid:
"He might defeat us suddenly,
And seat himself upon our throne."
In dark of night,
The rulers fell upon Vityaz,
And stripped away both honor and rank.
The rulers intimidated the people.
The people closed their eyes to truth.
"What is to be done?" thought Vityaz. "This is no
life."
"There remains just one thing—
To do away with my own life."
Vityaz raised the sword,
To annihilate himself.
Suddenly, Vityaz caught sight of his beloved wife,
And a small beloved daughter.
The hand shook.
The sword fell from the hand.
To live! Yes, to live!
Friends helped. Friends comforted.
They consoled, caressed, and tenderly cared.
The people matured and opened their eyes.
The people saw the real truth.
They valued the great service of Vityaz,

And in memory of Vityaz,
Raised up a memorial to him—Vityaz.
There he is, Vityaz on a bronze steed. Vityaz lived,
And he lives in our hearts, VITYAZ.

There were other presentations. In closing, Gyeorgy Konstantinovich gave a word. "Dear friends, Thank you. It is true, as you said in your message, Valeriy, friends warmed my soul, and supported me in a difficult moment. I am alive. I am with you. I am always glad to see you, dear ones. Once more, great thanks for love and affection."

After the formal time at the table, some went to the billiard room, and some watched a movie in the theater.

After a while, little bells rang again—this time as a tambourine sounds. They were more joyful and beckoning. Our children were summoning us to participate in a spontaneous activity. All the guests directed themselves to the sitting room. A concert began. Gyeorgy Konstantinovich sang in duet with Sofia Grigorievna, an artist of the Bolshoi Theater. They sang folk songs very well and soulfully. They were applauded in a friendly fashion. For a second number, Sofia Grigorievna sang an aria from an opera. Her singing made a colossal impression. She had a dramatic soprano voice. (This is a very rare voice.)

Academician Tarnovskiy read poetry of A. S. Pushkin with great feeling. Ivan Kozhedub read the story *Cinema Drama* by Zoshchenko. It was interesting to see how Gyeorgy Konstantinovich reacted to the various activities. When Kozhedub went to read the story, I was watching Gyeorgy Konstantinovich. He was all attention—don't interrupt him. His eyes were a little narrowed, and his mouth was in a half-smile. He was awaiting the activity. Kozhedub began. Gyeorgy Konstantinovich seemed to begin to live together with the exposition and in concert with the author. He reacted phenomenally. When Kozhedub said, "Well, I think they took them from the sleeves or pulled them out of the trousers," it was the culmination. Earlier,

Gyeorgy Konstantinovich could have laughed loudly but restrained himself. At this point, he began to laugh so hard that he cried. He had to pull out a handkerchief. Everyone began to laugh.

For the most part, everyone was laughing about Gyeorgy Konstantinovich's reaction. He was really quite a sensitive soul, and was really very receptive. Suddenly, Gyeorgy Konstantinovich began to try to catch the eye of Ludmilla Nikolaevna, and when he did, he loudly said, "Ludmilla. Ludmilla, give us *The Baroness. The Baroness.*" He sang, *"The baroness has gone bonkers. She has eaten too much sugar."* My wife began to play *The Baroness* as Gyeorgy Konstantinovich asked, and he, himself, went into a dance. At first, slowly, decorously leading his wife by the hand, and then he went faster and faster. Then, by himself, at full speed, he began to cut such capers and finished the dance in a spin. The guests did not hold back, and also went to dancing. Tired and flushed, everyone turned to the prepared, chilled drinks.

After a little while, Gyeorgy Konstantinovich said, "Let's sing together. Ludmilla, begin." She began to play the well-known revolutionary song, *Tormented by Heavy Slavery.* This was a favorite song of Gyeorgy Konstantinovich. I brought a song book with me, and it helped us remember the words of the songs. We all sang. We sang songs from the lyrics of the Civil War, and of course *Katyusha* and *Moscow Nights.* Gyeorgy Konstantinovich sang all the songs with great enthusiasm, and he sang very musically. After singing, we decided to wet our throats, and went to drink tea.

When everyone was sitting at the table, I appeared in the costume of a wizard. I was wearing a black cloak, a black mask, and of course, a conical hat with sliver stars, and in my hand was the traditional wizard's wand. I made magical gestures with the wand. The dining-room door opened, and two men carried in a large box and placed it on the table. Again, the wizard made magical gestures with the wand, and pronounced the Eastern incantation, "Khalai-Makhalai!" With the wand, he struck the box and the box opened. Everyone gasped. It was a big cake map. We could see the dacha property with grass and flowers. In the middle stood a little house. It was not a simple one, but it was a sugar house with little windows and a door. The roof was conical and made of chocolate. On one side of the roof was written, "How many summers have you?" On the other side was written, "The same number as winters."* The guests could not restrain themselves from expressing their praise for the wonderful culinary artistry. The guests long expressed their delight.

PORTRAIT

You know, we bought a croquet set, but in order to play croquet, it is necessary to have a very even court. Well, we took on the project. We located a likely area, and it's true it had grass all over—tall grass. We sharpened shovels until they were sharp and began to trim the grass. This turned out to be no easy task. We worked a while, and not being used to it, became worn out. We put off the work for a while. The next day, we got up a little earlier. Suddenly, we heard a familiar automobile horn. Of course, it was Gyeorgy Konstantinovich. He loved to make impromptu visits to our dacha. He would get the impulse and come, just like now. An arrival of Gyeorgy Konstantinovich like this was always like a holiday for us.

"What are you digging here?" he asked.

"Yes, well, we are making a playing field. We bought a croquet set."

"Well. Good idea. That means we will play croquet. I am including myself in the work. Give me a shovel."

We worked well, but only got a little done.

"Don't be concerned," said Gyeorgy Konstantinovich. "The work is perking along in a friendly fashion."

I remember, he came more than once and helped us clean up

---

*   This is a play on words. The Russian question "How old are you?" is literally "How many summers do you have?" At a birthday celebration, like this, age is a natural topic.

the playing field. At last, everything was ready, and we could play croquet. We waited for Gyeorgy Konstantinovich to drive over in order to inaugurate the season—the croquet season. One fine day, Gyeorgy Konstantinovich appeared. The mood was wonderful, the playing field was shining, the pegs were in place, the hoops were in place, the balls and mallets were waiting for action. One pair was yellow, and the other was bright red. We cast lots, and as a result, Gyeorgy Konstantinovich was paired with Ludmilla Nikolaevna. They had the red color. Galina Aleksandrovna and I were paired up, and we had the yellow mallets and balls. The play began. The first round Galina Aleksandrovna and I lost, but the second round we won. We liked playing croquet, and would have liked to continue playing, but just then our Grandmother, Aleksandra Sergeievna called us to drink tea.

After that time, Gyeorgy Konstantinovich and Galina Aleksandrovna began to come to our place often to play croquet. Once, when Gyeorgy Konstantinovich came, and we went to our veranda. Ludmilla Nikolaevna brought out a rather large photographic portrait of Gyeorgy Konstantinovich and showed it to him. Gyeorgy Konstantinovich liked the portrait very much. Then, she asked him to write something on it as a remembrance.

"What should I write?"

Ludmilla Nikolaevna answered, "Write what you have on your heart."

Gyeorgy Konstantinovich wrote, "To dear friends, Ludmilla Nikolaevna and Valeriy Vladimirovich Polekh. 29 July, 1962."

That is how a portrait of the Great Marshal and man appeared at our place. Now, the portrait hangs in our house in a most visible location.

VALERIY POLEKH, (BORN) JULY 5, 1918, MOSCOW

1933—Began professional studies at the October Revolution Music Technical College in the class of V. N. Soloduev, a soloist of the Bolshoi Theater Orchestra.

1936—Began professional activities in the Kamerniy Theater Orchestra under the direction of T. Tairov.

1937—Student at Moscow Conservatory, class of Professor F. F. Ehkkert.

1938—Soloist of the Radio Orchestra under the direction of N. S. Golovanov.

Soloist of the Bolshoi Theater Orchestra.

March, 1941—Moscow, All-Union Contest. First Premium.

1941-1945—On the Front of the Great Fatherland War (WWII) on the staff of the Ensemble under the direction of A. V. Aleksandrov.

1946—Return to the Bolshoi Theater Orchestra after demobilization from the army.

1949—International Competition in Buda Pest. First Premium.

May, 1951—Premiere of R. Gliere's *Concerto for French Horn* in the Great Hall of the Leningrad Philharmonic.

1952—Phonograph recording of Gliere's Concerto with the Bolshoi Theater Orchestra directed by the author.

1955—Began teaching activity at the Music College attached to the Moscow Conservatory.

1959—First performance in Russia of the composer B. Britten's *Serenade* for tenor, French horn, and stringed orchestra in the Great Hall of the Moscow Conservatory with soloists I. Kozlovskiy and V. Polekh conducted by I. Gusman. Phonograph recording of B. Britten's *Serenade* with the All-Union Radio Orchestra directed by G. Rozhdestvenskiy.

1963—Recording of the V. Mozart concertos, with the Bolshoi Theater Orchestra directed by B. Khaikin.

1976-1981—Teacher at the Moscow Conservatory.

1970's—Creation of an instructional repertoire for music schools and colleges. Edited the V. Mozart concertos and the Concerto Rondo with the subsequent publication of them.

1979—Participation in the symposium of the International Union of French Horn Musicians in Los Angeles.

1984—Publication of *Schools of Playing the French Horn.* Participation in the jury of the International Contests (Prague), and International Festival of Music (Luxemburg). Tour as a member of the Bolshoi Theater Orchestra in Italy, Canada, Japan, Poland, and Germany.

2002—Became an honorary member of the International Union of French Horn Musicians.

Honored Artist of Russia.

Holder of the Medal "Mark of Honor."

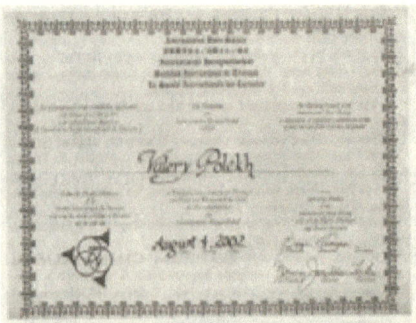

Photocopy: Certificate designating Valeriy Polekh an honorary member of the the International Horn Society.

Pacific Book Review

helping authors succeed'

Title: Valeriy Polekh: French Hornist Laureate of All Russia
Author: David Gladen
Publisher: Workbook Press
ISBN: 9781960752208
Language: English
Pages: 246
Genre: Biographical Translation
Reviewed by: David Allen

Pacific Book Review

David Gladen's favor to his father-in-law, a noted horn player and personal friend of horn player Valeriy Polekh, is a gift to all readers as well. French horn player Polenkh's autobiography is a timely and lovely reminder of the Russian spirit in days gone by: a world of music; a world of intellectuals and passionate souls variously in love, variously fevered, or otherwise consumed by the melodies of life. Think onion domes and minarets. Think country dachas, ice sleds and dray horses.

Polekh's narrative is pithy, direct, conversational. So is Gladen's translation. In skillfully crafted *glissando* prose, we learn of Polekh's childhood, his early leanings, his time in music school. Polekh's time with his estimable music Professor Ferdinand Ferdinandovich Ehkkert is likewise indelibly scored. The character sketches of important people on his journey are equally memorable and crafted with love, honor, humor, and respect.

Check out this description of the father of Polekh's friend: Mikhail Nikolaevich Buyanovskiy (Vitaliy's father) was a French horn musician, teacher, Honored Artist, and the son of a flutist of the Court Orchestra. He graduated from the Petersburg Conservatory and was awarded the Gold Medal and Diploma of a Free Artist. As a result, his name was engraved on the marble plaque listing the graduates of the Leningrad Conservatory.

And this very upbeat decidedly *continental* description of a seminar at the academy: *For the occasion of the end of the seminar, Tanechka baked a wonderful pie. A small company assembled - about ten people. A horn player from the Republic of Georgia brought an excellent wine, a couple from the Asian republics obtained a basket of fruit. There also appeared strong wines, an olive salad, and various snacks.*

The intellectual and musical tradition which Polekh celebrates - a tradition of excellence, high art, and cosmopolitanism - wails for recognition. Polekh's book delivers just that. This is the world originally brought to us by Pushkin, Gogol, Turgenev, Rimsky-Korsakov: a world of tears, laughter, music.

Best fit: Listen to Rachmaninoff while reading this book. It is filled with memory and harmony, a 'dance to the music of time' colored by nostalgia, affection, and deep triumph for reading and listening audiences everywhere.